≣ NAGAS IN THE 21ST CENTURY

Edited by
Jelle J P Wouters and Michael Heneise

≣ THE
HIGHLANDER
BOOKS

KOHIMA + EDINBURGH + THIMPHU

THE
HIGHLANDER
BOOKS

http://www.highlanderbooks.org

Highlander Books – Kohima
The Kohima Institute
Kohima, Nagaland 797003

Highlander Books – Thimphu
Royal Thimphu College
PO Box 1122, Ngabiphu, Bhutan

Highlander Books – Edinburgh
C/o Arkotong Longkumer
New College, Mound Place, Edinburgh
United Kingdom EH1 2LX

ISBN: 978-0-692-98335-5
Library of Congress Control Number: 2017961425

Cover image by Edward Moon-Little
Design and layout by Alina Ronghangpi

CONTENTS

ILLUSTRATIONS

ILLUSTRATIONS

CONTRIBUTORS

Iliyana Angelova is a Postdoctoral Fellow (Excellence Initiative) at the Department of Social and Cultural Anthropology, University of Tübingen (Germany) and a Postdoctoral Associate at the Institute of Social and Cultural Anthropology, University of Oxford. Iliyana received her doctorate in Anthropology from the University of Oxford where she studied the intersection between Christianity, identity formation and cultural heritage in the Indo-Burma borderlands, with an ethnographic focus on the Sumi Naga from the State of Nagaland. Her research generally focuses on the study of non-Western Christianity, urban anthropology and borderland regions.

Francis Cheerangal is a native of Kerala and a long-time resident of Nagaland. A Catholic Priest, educator, and scholar, he holds degrees in Education, Theology, Religious Philosophy, Sociology and English, and received his doctorate from Nagaland University for his thesis 'Governing system of the Yimchunger Nagas'. He has worked in eastern Nagaland for many years, including pioneering two schools in the border areas with Myanmar. He is fluent in several Naga languages, and is presently Principal of St. Xavier College in Jalukie, Nagaland.

Michael Heneise is Director of the Kohima Institute, and Publisher of Highlander Books. He has carried out fieldwork in upland South America and South Asia, most recently among the Naga in Northeast India, where he explored the relationship between dreams, personhood, and agency. His research generally focuses on the intersection between indigenous knowledge, sacred ecology and modernity. In addition to his work with the Highlander, he is editor-in-chief of the South Asianist, an academic journal published by the University of Edinburgh where he received his PhD.

Asojiini Rachel Kashena is a research associate at the North Eastern Social Research Centre (NESRC), Guwahati, and has been working and writing on forgiveness and reconciliation in the Northeast Indian states of Manipur and Nagaland. Her current research focuses on post conflict reconstruction of trust and space in Western Assam, Manipur and Nagaland and on women's role in peace building in the North East. She is the author of *Enduring Loss: Stories from the Kuki-Naga Conflict in Manipur* (NESRC, 2017).

Arkotong Longkumer is an anthropologist at the University of Edinburgh, Scotland, UK. He is the author of *Reform, identity and narratives of belonging: The Heraka movement of Northeast India* (Continuum, 2010) and has published in journals such as Himalaya, Contributions to Indian Sociology, South Asia: Journal of South Asian Studies and HAU: Journal of Ethnographic Theory. He is currently a British Academy Mid-Career Fellow and is writing a book on Hindu nationalism in Northeast India and Hindu nationalists' engagement with indigenous peoples.

Shonreiphy Longvah is a guest faculty in the department of Peace and Conflict Studies and Management, Sikkim Central University. Her research focuses on Peace, Conflict, and Conflict Resolution Processes, particularly in relation to the protracted Indo-Naga conundrum and the post 1997 Naga peace process. She is the author of: 'Security aspect in the Naga peace process' (in: Paswan ed., 2017), 'India's soft power image: a Naga perspective' (*International Journal of Linguistics and Literature*, 2016), and 'Territorial dimension in the Naga Peace Process' (*International Research Journal of Social Sciences*, 2014).

Somingam Mawon is an independent researcher and currently a project fellow at Firebird Foundation for Anthropological Research. Mawon received his doctorate in Folkloristics from North-Eastern Hill University with a thesis titled: 'Traditional Tangkhul Naga festivals: A study of the use of music and musical instruments.' His research revolves around folklore, gender, and ethnicity.

Edward Moon-Little is a PhD candidate in Social Anthropology at Cambridge University, having previously completed an MSc in Visual, Museum, and Material Anthropology at Oxford University, where he was an Arts and Humanities Research Scholar at Trinity College. He has conducted fieldwork in Jharkhand, Meghalaya, Nagaland, and Assam. Alongside writing about Northeast India, Edward has contributed images of the region to the Horniman Museum, the Museum of Archaeology and Anthropology in Cambridge, the Glasgow Museum, Hau Journal, the South Asianist, and the Berlin Ethnological Museum.

Venusa Tinyi is Assistant Professor in the Department of Philosophy, University of Hyderabad. His areas of specialisation include logic, philosophy of religion, and moral philosophy, and he holds long-term interests in Christian studies and Naga culture and identity. Tinyi jointly authored (with Paul Pimono and Eyingbeni) the book *Nagas: Essays for Responsible Change* (2012). His monograph *Politics of Naga Nationalism: State and the Politicians* (International Centre for Research, Interfaith Relations and Reconciliation), was published in 2014.

Matthew Wilkinson conducts research focused on the intersection of governance and informality in South Asia, and in particular Northeast India and Bangladesh, exploring how governance at the local level functions in contexts of, is influenced by, and influences conflict and violent politics. He is currently a PhD scholar and research officer at the University of New South Wales, Sydney, Australia. His PhD research considers the ways violent political competition shape corruption and community in the Indian state of Nagaland. Matt's previous research considered peacebuilding and local politics in the Chittagong Hill Tracts of Bangladesh, where contentious power-sharing arrangements have encouraged ethnic fracturing and continuing communal conflict.

Jelle J P Wouters studied Anthropology in Amsterdam, Oxford, and Shillong, and is currently a senior lecturer at Royal Thimphu College. Previously he taught at Sikkim Central University and Eberhard Karls University. His publications include: 'The making of tribes: the Chang and Chakhesang Nagas in India's Northeast' (*Contributions to Indian Sociology*, 2017), 'Sovereignty, integration or bifurcation? Troubles histories, contentious territories and the political horizons of the long lingering Naga Movement' (*Studies in History*, 2016), and 'Polythetic democracy: Tribal elections, bogus votes, and political imagination in the Naga uplands of Northeast India' (*Hau: Journal of Ethnographic Theory*, 2015).

01

NAGAS IN THE 21ˢᵀ CENTURY

Jelle J P Wouters and Michael Heneise

The title of this book; 'Nagas in the 21ˢᵗ Century', is both an adaptation and a (modest) self-proclaimed sequel to Verrier Elwin's (1969) iconic *Nagas in the Nineteenth Century*. In this anthology, Elwin introduces and brings together a collection of administrative reports, tour diaries, and ethnographic descriptions on Naga tribes, all written in the 19ᵗʰ century. The book was first published in 1969, five years after Elwin's demise, and was made possible through the efforts of N.K. Rustomji (later author of *Enchanted Frontiers* 1971) who had been closely associated with Verrier Elwin and gladly accepted 'Mrs. Elwin's and the Oxford University Press' request to tie up the loose ends of the manuscript' and prepare it for publication (Rustomji 1969: vi). Elwin's anthology soon turned into an important reference on Naga colonial history and society, and this status it has retained since.

Both during and after his life, Verrier Elwin had a prominent presence in debates about India's 'tribal question', and he has been variously celebrated and criticized for his writings, philosophy of NEFA (Elwin 1957), and lifestyle (Cf. Guha 1999). Subba and Som (2005: 1) write thus: 'The presence of Verrier Elwin in various academic fora, writings on tribes of India, and the writings on Northeast India in particular is heavy even about forty years after this death.' Much of what has been written about him, they continue, 'either eulogized him or was acrimoniously critical of him as a person and writer.' While Elwin did not have a formal degree in anthropology, his long and intimate knowledge of a number of tribes, both in

Central and Northeast India, 'gave him the identity of an anthropologist that even his most staunch critic, Ghurye, did not contest' (Subba and Wouters 2013: 199).

But while this edited volume takes Elwin's book as its point of departure, its contributors and contributions are not about Verrier Elwin. Rather, they are about the peoples that appeared in Elwin's anthology, and about some of the changes, continuities, and 'changing continuities' (Schulte-Nordholt 2005) that have taken place in Naga society since these early writings on Naga communities, cultures, and customs. That said, we nevertheless start with a few caveats Elwin (1969: 1) himself emphasized about the contents of the Naga colonial archive. 'This record', Elwin (1969: 1) wrote in his introduction, 'is not presented as a correct picture, but to illustrate how outsiders looked at the Nagas at the time. There are certainly many mistakes of fact, misunderstanding of custom and institutions; almost everything is very different now.' The 114 reports and accounts that appeared in the volume were also clearly written for European audiences and fellow administrators. They were never meant to be read in the light of post-colonialism or by Nagas themselves (Wouters 2012: 119). Elwin's volume was about Nagas, but with few, if any, Naga voices finding a place in it. Nagas have now long returned the gaze on these colonial writings, as well as on the people who wrote them (Thong 2012ab).

Elwin (1969: 2) further cautioned that 'none of the writers represented here were professional anthropologists', although he judged that 'some of them wrote better anthropology than many of the supposedly [anthropologically] "trained" young men of the present.' The ethnographic detail of early colonial writings was despite, Elwin stressed, the fact that most of them were written during trying circumstances, often under 'military escort' and amidst hostilities. Skirmishes along the way also meant that 'precious notes and documents were lost' (ibid.: 2), making Elwin insist that 'far from criticizing the nineteenth century men for their defects we should be astonished that, under the circumstances, they collected so much information and wrote as well as they did' (ibid.).

To be sure, this special book does not offer a re-evaluation of the Naga colonial archive. Many have already done so (Subba and Wouters 2013; Thong 2012ab; Misra 2012; Rivzi 2012; Wouters 2012; Lotha 2007). Most contributors take Elwin's anthology, or other colonial sources, as a point of reference, and then link these texts to their own areas of research, offering critiques, comparisons, and contrasts as they proceed. Taken together, the chapters aim to offer a set of insights and new departures into the study of contemporary Naga society.

A CRADLE OF BRITISH SOCIAL ANTHROPOLOGY

As the colonial government expanded its sway across the Subcontinent, few communities drew as wide attention and scholarship as Nagas. While administrated 'lightly', Naga culture and customs were subjected to intense ethnological study and speculation, mostly by so-called 'administrator-anthropologists.' Nagas became an ethnological hotbed, arguably even a cradle of British Social Anthropology. British military and civil officers like Butler, David, Godden, Reid, Woodthorpe, Mills, and Hutton regularly addressed gathering of the Royal Anthropological Institute of Great Britain and Ireland, and amongst whose audiences their ethnographic material incited lively, if at times fantastical, discussions. After retiring from the colonial Indian Civil Service Hutton and Mills were, based on their ethnological studies of Nagas, appointed as university professors at Cambridge University and the London School for Oriental and African Studies respectively.

Till date, most reputed university libraries, in places across the world, flaunt a shelf of Naga monographs, most of them bound in characteristic dark blue colour, and carrying such titles as *The Angami Nagas* (Hutton 1921a), *the Sema Nagas* (Hutton 1921b), *The Lhota* [later respelled as Lotha] *Nagas* (Mills 1922), *The Ao Nagas* (Smith 1925), another *The Ao Nagas* (Mills 1926), *The Rengma Nagas* (Mills 1937), *The Naked Nagas* (Fürer-Haimendorf 1939), *The Naga tribes of Manipur* (Hodson 1911), *Manipur and the Naga Hills* (Johnstone 1896) and *Naga Path* (Bower 1950). Ethnographic museums – be they in Oxford, Basel, or Berlin – too continue to showcase Naga skulls, spears, headgear, and a host of other artefacts. Reportedly, there are 'over 12000 Naga artefacts in Britain alone' (MacFarlane and Turin 2009: 370), all of which were variously confiscated, gifted, and procured by colonial administrators, missionaries, and curators, today spurring, besides a continuing popular interest in Naga history and culture, complicated debates on authenticity and ownership, including calls to have these artefacts returned to their places of origin.

In the heydays of colonial rule, administrators, missionaries, travellers, curators, and later also trained anthropologists, most notably Christoph von Fürer-Haimendorf, flocked to the Naga uplands and from where they returned with often rich accounts of Naga culture and lifeworlds. Back then, writings on Nagas were varied and colourful, including detailed narrations of religious beliefs and rituals, origin and migration stories, headhunting, megalithic culture, *khel* (village ward) and clan set-ups, political structures and sentiments, ornaments and dress, architecture, tigermen, and feasts of merit. Of these, 'Naga headhunting', as Venusa Tinyi in this book illustrates, became seen as a defining Naga trait in popular discourse. In anthropological annals, it was the Naga feast of merit – a traditional complex combining redistribution, a prestige economy, and social stratification – that perhaps became most widely known, and referred to. The Naga feast of merit, alas, was amongst the first sacrifices mostly American and Welsh missionaries demanded from new Naga converts, interpreting them as an ostentatious wastage of wealth and its free-flowing rice-beer as inducing immoralities (Wouters 2015a).

While colonial writings were certainly rich, not all early writers were, as noted by Elwin, equally careful in their gathering and interpretation of data. Most colonial writers themselves made confessional statements about the limitations of their research. They detailed the great difficulties they faced in obtaining information – often in their limited spare time – and they usually did not claim to offer definite conclusions. Paradoxically, perhaps, it was only during the post-colonial reading of these accounts that they became ascribed with a more authoritative and definite character. This has led to a nascent trend of 'corrective anthropology' embarked upon by many Naga PhD students and scholars who now aim to 'set the record straight' by pointing towards inaccuracies and misrepresentations in colonial texts. But while such works offer important insights, this is perhaps not the most productive, or intellectually enriching, way to engage colonial writings, or to bridge the gap between those early publications and present-day Naga society, and the social changes that occurred along the way.

For one, colonial writings were guided by a now defunct ideological framework. British colonialists, after all, entered the hills with then dominant theories of evolution, utilitarianism, and race, taught to them in established universities in the United Kingdom. With evolutionary anthropologists as Tylor, Spencer, Morgan, and Frazer dominating much anthropological thought, it was inevitable that colonial writings reflected their evolutionary paradigms. With the advantage of hindsight, we may now argue that the views advanced by colonial writers on Naga society were the product of British hegemony and suffered from multiple biases (cf. Asad 1973; Said 1978). However, this reflectivity, cannot be reasonably expected from the colonial authors themselves, who, after all, were products of their time. For another, the chapterisation and contents of these monographs were largely pre-set by the colonial government, which institutionalized the collection of ethnological data as part of an administrator's call to duty (Subba and Wouters 2013: 198). It was Bampfylde Fuller, then Chief Commissioner of Assam, who proposed that a series of monographs be prepared on the important castes and tribes the British governed in the region. About this series Balfour remarked:

> It is of the utmost importance not only to the Science of Man, but also to responsible officialdom, since a just and enlightened administration of native affairs cannot be established and pursued without an intimate knowledge of and sympathetic interest in the natives themselves, their customs and their point of view (Balfour in Hutton 1921b: xv).

The collection of ethnological data, thence, was as much an exercise of 'applied anthropology', to effectuate administration, than it was a purely academic undertaking (Wouters 2012). To streamline research and publications the colonial government offered guidelines about the topics and chapters administrators were expected to cover. These invariably included 'compulsory' sections on domestic life, laws and customs, political organization, and folklore – irrespective of the community being studied. Any restudy of such texts to the letter today therefore risk confinement to those areas then considered relevant, in the upshot precluding a fine-grained ethnographic engagement with topic, trends, and themes central to present-day Naga society.

The ethnographic richness produced during the colonial era, despite their obvious shortcomings, now exists in stark contrast with the scanty ethnographic material generated during the post-colonial period. This is to the extent that, in tracing social change, contemporary scholars on Naga society grapple with a decades-wide ethnographic void. This is largely an immediate side-effect of the protracted Indo-Naga conflict which created hurdles for Naga scholars to carry out research and long made it virtually impossible for foreign scholars to enter the Naga uplands. The few efforts to enter and conduct fieldwork during this time, however, merit some mention, and the following is a summary of these, as well as mention of important publications based on secondary sources that also emerged in this period. To be sure, what follows is not an exhaustive overview on postcolonial Naga studies, but serves to point to some important contributions and nascent themes and trends. In discussing these, we focus especially, though not exclusively, on those writings that have been informed by ethnographic research.

20TH CENTURY POST-COLONIAL RESEARCH

From the time of British withdrawal in 1947 until the early '60s, little known fieldwork took place in the Naga areas. One notable exception is the work of Calcutta-based journalist Ashim Roy and his foray into Konyak country in 1949 (see Heneise 2013). Based on this fieldwork, and several later trips, Roy published the surprisingly rich *The Konyak Nagas: a socio-cultural profile* (2004). This early post-colonial period also saw a few Naga scholars producing the first locally published and disseminated studies, including Tajenyuba's *Ao Naga Customary Laws* (1957) and *A History of Anglo-Naga Affairs* (1958), and later M. Alemchiba's *A Brief Historical Account of Nagaland* (1970). Haimendorf's continued interest in the region merits mention as well. After a twenty-six year 'pause', he obtains a permit to enter Nagaland in 1962, and then again in 1970 for brief visits to the Konyak area he knew well (Stockhausen 2013). This culminated in his *The Konyak Nagas* (1969), essentially an augmented reprint of his successful 1939 book *The Naked Nagas*, followed, in 1976, by *Return to the Naked Nagas: An Anthropologist's view of Nagaland 1936-1970*. In addition, Haimendorf produced one of the few full-length ethnographic films on the Naga, namely *The Men Who Hunted Heads* (1970). Worth mentioning, too, is the 1963 visit of Czech ethnologist Milada Ganguli (an Indian citizen through marriage), who upon gaining entry is 'escorted' by a company of 120 Indian military trucks traveling from Imphal to Kohima. Based on her week-long first visit, and several more extended visits over the course of twenty years (and considerable secondary research), Ganguli publishes the widely-read *Pilgrimage to the Nagas* (1984), which is prefaced by Haimendorf. Though lacking in ethnographic depth, it is encyclopaedic in nature, and remains an important link across an otherwise considerable chasm in fieldwork-based literature in the region in that period.

During the latter part of the 1960s, N.K. Das, of the Anthropological Survey of India (ASI), enters the Naga uplands and in 1980 carries out a total of eight months of fieldwork in the southern Angami village of Viswema. While his subsequent write-up is originally conceived as an ASI report titled 'social organisation of a Naga tribe', Das later revises and submits it as a PhD thesis to Gauhati University where he is advised and later examined by Haimendorf, who remains closely attached to Naga society until long after his retirement from SOAS in 1976. Das eventually publishes *Kinship, Politics, and Law in Naga Society* (1993), a work clearly influenced by the structuralist tradition of Claude Lévi-Strauss (see also Das 1980, 1982a, 1982b, 1984, 1989a, 1989b, and 1994). The 1980s and 1990s is also the period Vibha Joshi begins fieldwork in Nagaland, mostly on the Angami Nagas, and dealing, among others, with material culture, Christian conversion, and traditional forms and practices of healing (Joshi 2007, 2012, 2013). It is also during this period that the Cambridge anthropologists Alan Macfarlane (Haimendorf's last student) begins compiling thousands of texts and images from colonial archives and collections across Britain, and which eventually culminate in the *Naga Videodisc* project, which has become a valuable resource for researchers. Drawing on this material, Julian Jacobs, with contributions from Macfarlane, Sarah Harrison and Anita Herle, published *The Nagas: Hill Peoples of Northeast India* (1990).

Important to mention, too, is the work of, then *New York Times* reporter, Sanjoy Hazarika. His *Strangers of the Mist: Tales of War and Peace from India's Northeast* (1995), while not ethnographic, is based on in-depth investigative research and interviews with both over- and underground leaders across India's Northeast, including Nagas. Similar studies were conducted by Sanjib Baruah (1999, 2007), and which, while not exclusively dealing with Naga society, offer a set of fresh political insights. This period also sees the publication of Charles Chasie's *Naga Imbroglio: A Personal Perspective* (1999) and Kaka Iralu's deeply provocative *Nagaland and India: The Blood and the Tears* (1999; then republished 2000, 2009). Though self-published and locally printed, Iralu's research is widely cited in contemporary Naga studies of the Indo-Naga conflict. Finally, we like to mention a few authors who researched the Indo-Naga conflict and wrote accounts based on secondary research or personal experiences. These are Horam (1988, 1975), Gundevia (1975), Haskar and Luithui (1984), Yonuo (1974), Maxwell (1980), Nibedon (1978), Anand (1980), Vashum (2000), Singh (2004, 2008), Shimray (2005), Nuh (1986, 2002), Misra (2000), Aosenba (2001), Ao (2002), Zhimomi (2004).

Fortunately, the Indo-Naga ceasefire in 1997 ushered in a new era of ethnographic and empirical research, and which was boosted further by the partial withdrawal of the Inner-Line in 2011. We now turn to a brief discussion on emergent topics and themes in contemporary studies on Naga society.

THE 21ST CENTURY: IDENTITY CONSCIOUSNESS AND REINVIGORATED ARCHIVE

The gradual opening of the Naga areas from the 1997 ceasefire onward was accompanied by a concerted attempt by state planners to promote tourism in Nagaland.

At the centre of this effort was the 2000 launch of the Hornbill festival – a weeklong potpourri of traditional Naga ritual re-enactments, dances, handicrafts, and food traditions, and which inspired critical scholarship (e.g. Kikon 2005; Longkumer 2016; and Lotha 2016). This trend coincided with a wave of new discourses in museum studies, centred on the ethics of colonial acquisition (Thomas 1991), the politics of repatriation (especially of sacred objects), the contemporary relevance of 'curiosity box' curatorial practices, and perhaps more presciently, the cultural and historical relevance of indigenous material culture amid a worldwide re-genesis of indigenous cultural and identity politics (Arnold-de Simine 2013; Barrett 2011; and Bennet 2004). As colonial collections re-emerge, curators and scholars wrangle over correctly portraying continuities and discontinuities, but also, in a sense, seeking to educate visitors (and readers of associated write-ups) about the fraught history of orientalist portrayals (West 2011, 1999). The first significant impetus in terms of Naga collections is the already mentioned Digital Himalaya project developed by Alan Macfarlane and Mark Turin at Cambridge University.

Not surprisingly, European collections of Naga visual and material culture also see a resurgence. In 2009, for example, an exhibition titled 'Material Culture, Oral Traditions and Identity Among the Nagas' organised by Michael Oppitz and a team of researchers at the Ethnographic Museum of Zurich - which toured cities in Switzerland, Germany, and Austria - featured objects sourced by collectors Adolf Bastian, Lucian Scherman, and Hans-Eberhard Kauffman (Oppitz et al 2008). In its contemporary reification, these were accompanied by recent images and studies based on short visits to Naga areas, and subsequently published in the 2008 volume *Naga Identities: Changing Local Cultures in the Northeast of India* (Ibid). Explaining the rationale behind the project, one of the editors stated it was intended 'to project today's Nagas, which shall include the disillusioning or even the deconstruction of current exotic photograph books' (Stockhausen in Oppitz 2008: 127). Chapters in Oppitz' book include several prominent Naga scholars (e.g. Arkotong Longkumer and Dolly Kikon), and titles highlight the blatant omissions in much hitherto published 'orientalising' books on the Nagas. Two of these chapters are 'Religion Today' and 'Fashion Trends in Contemporary Nagaland', which include images of modern Naga fashion design, and Christian church buildings standing dominant in village and urban settings.

Whether such efforts succeed in steering the European imagination away from exoticising the Naga 'Other' is questionable. Especially in view of the ballooning of Naga 'coffee-table' books featuring the colourful portrayals of Nagas, their culture, dresses, and festivals, in the past decade. Here we might especially highlight the collaborative work of Vibha Joshi with Richard Kunz (2008), and with Aditya Arya (2004). Also worth mentioning is the collaborative work of photographer Peter van Ham and Aglaja Stirn (2003), and with Jamie Saul (2008). Describing the new genre of pictorial works (and echoing the above-mentioned re-invigoration of European interest in the Nagas), Joshi (2012: 260) writes:

> While these coffee-table books do not purport to scholarly analysis, their pursuit of the exotic give us some idea of the continuity of some traditions and thus counter the pessimistically styled writings of some Western scholars who consider that Christianity has led to the destruction of a people's culture and a feeling of shame about past cultural practices. These books capture a resurgence of interest among the Europeans.

NAGA STUDIES TODAY AND 'NATIVE ANTHROPOLOGY'

Recent years also witnessed a new 'ethnographic turn' in research on Nagas, one that is facilitated by the ceasefire and freer access to the Naga uplands. Naga studies today encompass new areas of research such as Christianity, nationalism, gender, territorial politics, modernisation, oral and new literature. This is not to suggest a departure from colonial themes and categories, as much of this new scholarship begins with a critique of British administrator-ethnography. This is sure to continue for a while, as the colonial archive (which, as discussed already, is massive) simply towers over the few in-depth contemporary studies currently available to scholars. This is further exacerbated by the cumbersome pricing and distribution tactics of western academic publishers, juxtaposed with the freely accessible, and searchable online colonial archive (the Digital Himalaya project is a case in point)[1]. As ethnographic methodologies in local higher education institutions in India improve, a shift will certainly be felt. However, much more difficult is the task of correcting the seemingly intractable 'orientalism' and 'home-grown orientalism' (Poddar and Subba 1992) continually articulated in western writing on the Nagas and increasingly from those belonging to India's caste Hindu societies (Subba and Wouters 2013). Moreover, 'colonial nostalgia' remains as much the brand language of local tour operators as with most former European colonies, and is also a residue that haunts Naga studies.

Long term anthropological engagement, although still limited, has now increased, and a few prominent themes, as touched on already, have emerged

---

[1]See http://www.digitalhimalaya.com/

in the available published texts and articles, including: Christianity (especially Angelova 2014; Joshi 2013; Longkumer 2011, 2015, 2016; and Thomas 2016); and Christianity in relation to Naga nationalism, with Abraham Lotha (2014), and John Thomas (2016). We also have the rise of the 'Naga voice', or what is sometimes called 'native anthropology', most prominently Dolly Kikon (2005; 2015) and Arkotong Longkumer and his monograph on the Heraka Movement (2010), in addition to a host of articles (e.g. Longkumer 2016ab, 2015).

Other fields and trends include interest in territory, boundaries, and customary laws, as well as overlap with development studies in areas such as changes in agricultural patterns such as shifting cultivation, material, visual, and museum anthropology (especially Elliott 2014; Heneise and Moon-Little 2014; Stockhausen 2014; Wettstein 2014; and West 2011), Naga identity (especially Longkumer 2011, 2015; and Oppitz 2008); cosmology, dreams, and sentient landscapes (Heneise 2016, and this issue); governmentality, militarisation and political and gender violence (Kikon 2009, 2002); and democracy, elections, territorial politics, and tribal social formations (Wouters 2017, 2016, 2015ab, 2014).

Finally, there is also an important and growing corpus of published articles and books (and hundreds of unpublished masters and doctoral dissertations in local college and university libraries) by upcoming (and established) Naga scholars (e.g. Jimo 2008; Kashena this issue; Kuotsu 2013; Mawon 2016 and this issue; Assumi 2009, Nshoga 2009; Ngully 2015; Pongener 2011, Ezung 2012, Ovung 2012, Yeptho 2011, Khiamniungan 2014, Chophy 2015; Khamrang 2015, Venuh 2005, Tunyi 2016; among others). Regular workshops and conferences organised by the newly established Kohima Institute (2013); the Naga Scholars Association at Jawaharlal Nehru University; the Centre for Northeast Studies at Jamia Milia University; the Centre for Community Knowledge (CCK), and North East Forum (NEF) at Ambedkar University; the North East Social Research Centre (NESRC) in Guwahati; and the Department of Sociology at Japfü Christian College in Nagaland, among others, have energised a new generation of social scientists able to gain access to publications and archival materials now readily available online, and to engage in research activities that remain difficult for many foreign scholars. The growing capacity of young local scholars to publish, debate, and critique research on the Nagas in conjunction with scholars based in foreign institutions, has begun to re-assert Naga studies as an important anthropological focus area, perhaps in a sense also ensuring the further relevance and longevity of the old archive that began in the 1830s.

THE CHAPTERS

In the next chapter, Wouters engages historically and ethnographically the form and substance of the prototypical Naga 'village republic'. Even as the popular imagination of Naga villages as 'republics' has clear origins in early colonial writing, he illustrates the historical manifestation and remarkable resilience of the 'Naga village' as a political, partisan, self-protective, and affective unit. In discussing 'who is a Naga village?', he shows how a Naga village encompasses a moral community characterized by its temporal and spatial rootedness, and how its inhabitants orient their social relations through the conduit of historical memory – a nexus locally between history, locality, ancestral genealogy, and identity.

Chapter three, by Moon-Little, examines a somewhat obscure Zeme Naga 'fame taboo' drawing on ethnographic work among Zeme communities in Assam, Manipur and Nagaland, and archival work on early observations by Ursula Graham Bower. Moon-Little sheds light on the interesting ways in which fame was a significant Zeme preoccupation - both an aspiration, but also potentially threatening. Indeed, individuals would go to great lengths to ameliorate the potential harms or evils that followed fame and fortune, including animal sacrifice. One way a person could measure his susceptibility to harm was by listening to dreams. Symbols, especially of radically different 'others' - guns, trains, tigers – indicated an accumulation of dangerous fame. Particularly salient is Moon-Little's demonstration of how the *hamui-hera* taboo elucidates Zeme concerns with powers beyond their control – powerful neighbours, but especially British colonialism.

In the following chapter, Angelova explores the substance of the contemporary Sumi identity by focusing on the continuities and discontinuities in terms of sociocultural customs. She concentrates on the legacies of missionaries and the social impact of Christian conversions, and argues how Christianity should not, or no longer, be viewed as a major agent of social change but as an intrinsic part of a new Sumi identity and tradition reinventing and reasserting itself, one which is 'creatively embedding Christianity within a solid substratum of cultural reproduction.'

Next, Longkumer invites us to the annual Hornbill festival celebrated in Nagaland where he introduces us to the various activities and actors involved in the festival. Nagaland state capitalizes on 'exotic' images of Naga tribes, traditional culture, and pristine landscape to market Nagaland as a compelling tourist destination. Behind such aspirations, however, Longkumer illustrates, linger several issues, such as ideas of Naga sovereignty, the militarization of the landscape, the local tension between cultural revival and Christianity, and the contested ethno-territorial contours of the Naga nation, as well as wider debates around staging traditions and culture for external consumption.

Kashena's chapter offers an ethnography of victims of the Kuki-Naga conflict in the 1990s. Through the use of personal narratives, she illustrates vividly how Christian theology and prayer offers some comfort for victims of ethnic violence to cope with personal trauma and loss. This helped them to rationalize tragic events, and to pursue often painful and complex processes of forgiveness and reconciliation.

Tinyi, in chapter seven, offers a reinterpretation of Naga headhunting by locating its practice within the normative structures of Naga society, rather than seeing it, as most colonial writers did, as symptomatic of a then flourishing 'culture of lawlessness'. In an attempt to read past headhunting from a modern liberal perspective, he relates its practice to core Naga traditional values and beliefs of equality, freedom, and justice.

Longvah's chapter contributes to our understanding of the complex linkages between Christianity, the rise of Naga nationalism, and Naga nationalist politics. She contrasts traditional Naga religion, which did not give rise to a larger Naga political consciousness, to Naga Christianity, which offered Nagas with a common denominator and so fostered Nagas self-awareness as a political community with a shared identity and political destiny.

Chapter 9, by Wilkinson, explores modern constructions of masculinity in Nagaland. While he shows how contemporary ideas of Naga manhood and masculinity operate at multiple levels, and are therefore fluid and dynamic, popular images of the stereotypical 'Naga man' remain nevertheless shaped by 'externally informed' images of a 'pre-modern, warrior savage', an image that is variously reproduced and re-appropriated by the tourist industry and Indian mass media.

In chapter 10, Mawon examines the impact of modernity on community life among the Hao (Tangkhul) Nagas of Manipur, through an ethnographic study of Hao festivals. Examining the Luira festival, the seed sowing festival, and considered the most important annual Hao festival, Mawon examines the ways in which Christianity, and the advent of education, created a disjuncture in community consciousness regarding the location of livelihood responsibility. Whereas pre-Christian practices predicated spirit-mediated community provision; Christianity and education placed the community on an altogether different path: one of progress centred on human-initiative.

Cheerangal, in chapter 11, explores the form and functioning of traditional governance among the still little researched Yimchunger Nagas. He discusses the main traditional offices, and then shows how the roles and responsibilities associated with these offices changed over time as the result of the colonial experience and post-statehood policies.

Finally, Heneise examines both what can be learned from the ethnographic study of dreams, and the kinds of cultural insights one gleans in comparing contemporary dream accounts in a community, with accounts collected a century earlier by British administrator-ethnographers, in this case J.H. Hutton, in the same community. Whereas Hutton raises questions about the relationship between seemingly quite different experiences, namely of ordinary dreams, and the dream-mediated practices of healers, sorcerers, and lycanthropes, Heneise finds ways of articulating a continuum.

■ ■■ ■■

02

WHO IS A NAGA VILLAGE? THE NAGA 'VILLAGE REPUBLIC' THROUGH THE AGES

Jelle J P Wouters

'Nothing much happens these days. We are just fulfilling our duty being here', Chuba, a village defence guard in the Chang Naga hilltop village of Noksen, says while brewing 'pica', or black tea, to taste on a smouldering fire. Firewood is stacked close by. Lunch is to be prepared next. The place is Noksen's village defence post, a makeshift fortification, erected a few steps above the village's towering, newly built, neatly whitewashed Baptist church, but nonetheless complete with an underground escape route, a weapon and ammunition storage stocked with rifles and ammunition, and gun emplacements all around.

Once upon a time this part of present-day Nagaland was not known as Tuensang District, as it is called today, but as 'the land of the free Nagas', or 'Freeland', in reference to its location outside the immediate pale of colonial offices and officers. Of the Chang Naga specifically, Hutton (1987[1929]: iii) wrote, in the 1920s, that they are 'one of those Naga tribes which occupy the hinterland, as it were, of the Naga Hills District stretching back to the high range, which divides Assam from Burma... the bulk of the tribe being situated in the area of loose political control...' But despite being called 'Freeland' during the colonial era, many of its inhabitants did not consider themselves 'free' by the mid-1950s and joined the A.Z. Phizo-

▪ Who is a Naga village? The Naga 'village republic' through the ages

14

led Naga National Council (NNC) in its armed struggle for Naga Independence. Amongst them were several Noksen villagers.

Besides Chuba, four other men are on duty in the defence post, sitting clustered around the fire-place and wrapped into shawls to keep out the January cold. Their assigned duty: to 'protect' the village against Naga undergrounds of rivalling factions and with whose cadres, called 'national workers', the Noksen villagers share complex and fluctuating relationships of kinship and resentment, sympathy and dislike, love and hate. Over the past decades, the political theory of the long running Naga Movement fragmented into a kaleidoscope of underground groups identified by often near identical initials – NSCN-IM, NSCN-K, NSCN-KK, NSCN-U, NSCN-R, NNC-NA, NNC-A, GPRN, FGN-NA, FGN-A – and which, to the eyes of villagers, seem to be endlessly engaged in warring over historical legitimacy, ideological differences, territorial domination, and the collection of taxes and donations (on Naga nationalism and factionalism see Longvah, this volume). In Noksen, it comes to Chuba and his men to protect the villagers from the occasional lawlessness unleashed by one, or multiple, underground factions.

While thus a militia of sorts, Noksen's village guards wear sandals, casual sweaters and simple pants rather than sturdy army boots and neatly ironed uniforms embroidered with insignias and medals, and instead of busying themselves with daily patrols, routine roll-calls, and regimented training exercises, they spend most of their time playing Carrom board, cooking meals, and chewing betel-nut. But then, the salaries paid to them by the government were low; 'next to nothing', as Chuba complains. However, with duties few (only a handful of 12-hour shifts a month) and with agriculture the prime mainstay, any cash at the end of the month is always welcomed.

The necessity of guarding one's village against invaders and foes has long been intrinsic to Nagas' political history, and in days now bygone Noksen villagers variously assumed the role of perpetuator and recipient of raids and retaliations. Before British pacification (a colonial euphemism for the slaying and subduing of recalcitrant populations), it was customarily for each Naga village to guard its village gates against intrusions, ever looming. In Noksen, it was traditionally and ritually the Houngang clan that was associated with the manufacture and maintenance of elaborate village defence walls, even as the task of actually guarding and protecting the village befell on every able-bodied man.

Noksen was hardly exceptional in barricading its surroundings. When Mofatt-Mills toured the Angami Hills in 1854, he found most villages enclosed by 'stiff stockades, deep ditches, bristling with panjies, and massive stone walls' (Mofatt-Mills in Elwin 1969: 229). In times of war, Mofatt-Mills explained:

> The hill sides are scraped and thickly studded with panjies. These panjies vary in length from 6 inches to 3 or 4 feet, and give very nasty wounds. Deep pit-falls, artfully concealed by a light layer of earth and leaves, line the path by which the

Who is a Naga village? The Naga 'village republic' through the ages ▪

15

enemy is expected. The entrances to the villagers are through long narrow tortuous lanes, with high banks of stone and earth on either side... admitting only of the passage of one man at a time. These lanes lead up to gates, or rather doorways closed by strong, thick, and heavy wooden doors made out of one piece of wood... When an attack is imminent the roads are often planted thickly with tall strong pegs, which are easily threaded when walking quietly, but are an effectual protection against a sudden rush (ibid: 229-230).

While such elaborate defence works already impeded the entrance of unwelcome guests, in Noksen, akin to most Naga villages, the additional act of 'watching' over the village was a duty vested in morungs, or bachelor sleeping-houses, and of which each of Noksen's four khels (also known as village wards or sectors) had one. 'To guard the whole village was one of the most important duties of the members of the morung', Mar Pongener (2011: 24) explains. Its members

Figure 1. Old village gate in *Phugwumi*.(Photo courtesy Zhoto Tunyi.)

Figure 2. Old village gate in *Phugwumi*.(Photo courtesy Zhoto Tunyi.)

were deployed as 'sentries at the village gates' where they 'kept vigil in turn throughout the day and night' and 'signal the possible intrusion of an enemy.' But if such village and morung-wise defence strategies would frame Noksen's current village guards in a continuous past, in their present form its concrete origins trace back to the late 1950s and to a controversial counter-insurgency strategy adopted by Indian military and paramilitary troops to counteract the then surging sway of the NNC. The NNC's Naga Army relied on villages for food, shelter, monies, intelligence, and, of course, recruits, and it was in a classic attempt to separate 'insurgents' from 'civilians' that Indian Army officers sought to establish village militias. To persuade Naga villages into accepting this military scheme, special development packages were offered to consenting villages and monthly salaries, weaponry, and basic military training to those villagers who enlisted themselves as guards. A former Indian Army general recounted thus: 'We supplied them [village defence guards] with smooth bore muskets and established camps to train them in musketry and simple field-craft. This force proved effective because I gave them the task of guarding only their own village' (Thorat 1986: 83-4). Though most Naga villages swore fidelity to the NNC and could not be won over by the Indian Army, some villages heeded and accepted the enactment of a village defence post on its soil. In its effects, this policy was divisive, pitching certain Naga villages against the Naga Army. The NNC, on its part, labelled any village agreeing to a defence post as 'pro-Indian' and 'reactionary', and promised them a revenge that was lethal.

For long, much longer compared to several neighbouring and nearby villages, Noksen withstood army pressures and resisted the enactment of a village defence post. 'Some of our own boys were part of the Naga Army', Chuba explains. 'They were our fathers, husbands, brothers, and sons. How could we possibly accept weapons and training from the Indian Army to shoot at them?' It was only after the gradual decline of the NNC from the mid-1970s onward, the rise of the NSCN in the 1980s, its subsequent split into warring factions, and when earlier forms of annual 'house-tax' and 'army-ration tax' to the Naga Movement increasingly appeared like 'extortion' that Noksen gave in. A village defence post was built, paid for by the Indian Army, while a couple of dozen villagers were trained as guards. 'Still then', Chuba continues:

> We had an understanding with the Naga undergrounds. We told them that we would not attack them if they come to our village, but that they should inform us ahead of their coming. Although there is a lot of division in the underground, they are our own people struggling for our future. We are not against them. Even taxes they can come and collect. We are ready to contribute. But no force and no extortion. That we told them clearly. We also told them that we would not allow factionalism on our soil. And that if such would happen our guns would not stay quiet.

The guns owned by Chuba and his men indeed did not stay silent when, in 1997, cadres of two rivalling underground groups clashed head-on at the edge of the village, leaving one morung charred and bullet-holes in several houses. 'We chased them away that day', Chuba recalls. 'We emptied our guns at both the factions. We did not care who was who. We had warned them.'

This (rather lengthy) opening vignette introduces us not just to a controversial chapter in Nagaland's perverse theatre of insurgency and counter-insurgency, but it is also illustrative of the remarkable salience of the prototypical 'Naga village' as a political, partisan, and self-protective unit in Naga society. It is this, the telos and temporalities of the Naga 'village republic', that I wish to trace and place both historically and ethnographically in this essay.

In a way, devoting a chapter to the 'Naga village' runs the risk of descending into clichés, as the idea of Naga villages as 'republics', somewhat akin to Greek city states (Singh 2004: 13), is an old one, and one endlessly invoked in both scholarly and popular writings of Naga histories and lifeworlds. Its rhetoric also figures prominently in the political discourses circulated by Naga underground groups.

Figure 3. *Noksen* village.(Photo by Jelle J. P. Wouters.)

Who is a Naga village? The Naga 'village republic' through the ages ■

19

The NSCN manifesto tells thus:

> From time immemorial, Nagas maintained in their villages a type of self-government which could be called a little republic or a city state... This self-governing system worked excellently and people enjoyed peace and justice... the basis of the Naga system is the village organization.

So pervasive is the image of the Naga village as a self-governing unit that villagers themselves speak about their village as a republic. 'Our village is an independent republic', a villager told me as I started my fieldwork. 'We have our own customary laws and court, and nobody has the right to interfere with our village matters, not the government, not the police.'

Highlighting that Naga society is strongly oriented around the affective unit of 'the village', thence, is nothing new, and in itself amounts to no scholarly contribution. What makes me nevertheless write this essay is that this ubiquity of the Naga 'village republic', both in writing and popular imagination, usually remains devoid of ethnographic explorations that seek to establish its contemporary form, substance, and continuing analytical relevance. As elsewhere, much has changed among Nagas in the past 150 years or so – changes that can be captured along a number of axes; from a non-state to a state society, 'animism' to Christianity, tradition to modernity and 'developmentalism', from powerful chiefs and village elders to participatory democracy, or from a social landscape inhabited by disparate clans, villages, and tribes to a political projection of a Naga nation. It is amidst these changes that I explore the resilience of the prototypical Naga village as a foundational, affective, and structuring device of Naga society. I will do so ethnographically by discussing the role of 'the village' in relation to (1) identity and identification, (2) local governance, particularly Nagaland's policy of communitisation, and (3) democracy and elections.

The next section, however, first takes a step back to discuss the Naga 'village republic' as it was encountered and written about by colonial administrators and early anthropologists.

THE NAGA VILLAGE REPUBLIC IN COLONIAL TIMES

While colonial offices and officers, in their administrative and ethnological structuring and restructuring of the Naga uplands, sought to establish 'the tribe' as the pillar of Naga society (Wouters 2017), British administrators were nevertheless acutely aware that it was in the village, not the tribe, that the locus and ethos of everyday life was vested. In a version of Evans-Pritchard's (1940) classic segmentary lineage system, levels of tribal consciousness, cohesion, and cooperation always came second to the immediacies of the kinship and social bonds of clan and village. For the Sema, now Sumi, Naga, 'the tribe', Hutton (1921b: 121) wrote, 'is not an organized community at all', rather 'the basis of Sema society is the village, or part of a village.' For the Lotha Naga, Mills (1922: 96) similarly observed: 'Every village is an independent unit in the tribe. Leagues of villages were formed for the purposes of war, and in these cases the advice of the most powerful village would naturally carry much weight... But except for war, no village ever acknowledged the authority of any other village.' For the neighbouring Ao Nagas, the missionary Smith (1925: 1) noted how 'theoretically the village acts as a unit in all things.' Mills (1926: 176), in his monograph The Ao Nagas, could only agree: 'As with all Nagas, the real political unit of the tribe is the village.' As a definite and characterizing concept, the Naga village republic was born.

While the Naga village republic is variously accounted for in folktales, ritual arrangements, and origin and migration stories, its historical centrality – as a conduit of social life, a political actor, and a moral community – was also the cumulative outcome of two landscapes. First, a geography that was rugged and difficult to traverse and which long impeded communication and regular relations between villages. Secondly, a human landscape stained by frequent inter-village rivalries, raids, and retaliations that nourished an air, an atmosphere, that bristled with mutual suspicion, distrusts, and danger. Hutton (1965: 32) wrote thus:

> At the time of the British acquaintance with them, many villages were still isolated from their neighbours by thickly forested hills and by rivers unfordable for several months in the year, and they tended to be on terms of head-hunting warfare with their nearest neighbours, or at best of an armed and ever suspect truce, almost every village being an independent political entity.

The act of 'head-hunting warfare', long held to be a Naga trait of sorts, itself was informed by parochial convictions directed towards 'ritually fertilizing' the village, or so Elwin (1961: 11) postulated (on Naga headhunting see Tinyi, this volume):

> The practice of headhunting is probably based on a belief in a soul-matter or vital essence of great power which resides in the human head. By taking a head from another village, therefore, it was believed that a new injection of vital and creative energy would come to the aggressor's village when he brought the head home. This was valuable for human and animal fertility.

Distinct village identities were further reproduced by linguistic fragmentation, and this linguistic diversity did not usually align with wider tribal boundaries. In fact, for most Nagas the idea that a tribe should speak a single language is a strange idea indeed. This can be read in the following pun Hutton (1921b: 266-7) found in

Who is a Naga village? The Naga 'village republic' through the ages •

21

vogue among the Sema Naga.

> Seven men of different villages happened to meet by the road
> one evening. They asked one another what they had with
> them to eat with their rice. Each mentioned a different thing
> – atusheh, gwomishi, mngishi, amusa, akelho, etc. including,
> as some understood it, dried fish, meat, and various kinds of
> vegetables. They agreed to pool their good things and share
> alike and sat down prepared for a feast, each one thinking how
> he had scored by agreeing to share with his neighbours. When
> they opened their loads, they all produced chillies.

The Naga village also manifested itself as a ritual unit. Among the Angami
Naga, for instance, the Tevo, or village priest, who operated as 'the mediator
between the [village] community as a whole and the supernatural world' (Fürer-
Haimendorf 1976: 13) was to be kept 'safe' from the polluting touch of other
villages. Fürer-Haimendorf wrote: 'During the first three and a half years of his
office he [the Tevo] may not visit any other village, and even later on he may never
partake a meal in a strange village but must always carry his food with him' (ibid.:
13). Consider the following instance:

> A woman from a neighbouring village came to see the Tevo's
> wife, and during a friendly chat obliged her by picking a few
> lice out of her hair. Later it became known that the treacherous
> friend had abstracted one hair from the head of the Tevo's wife
> and taken it back to her own village. The Tevo and his wife
> were immediately deprived of their dignity and exiled, for a
> part of one of them, and therefore a part of the 'virtue' of the
> whole [village] community, had been carried off to a foreign
> village (ibid.: 14).

'Virtue', clearly, had geographical boundaries and these broadly aligned with
the village gates. Summarizing it all, Elwin (1961: 9) wrote how 'the basic interest of
every Naga is in his family, the clan, the khel, the village. This is what he regards as
his culture which must not be interfered with.'

Much, of course, changed since these colonial portrayals of the prototypical
Naga 'village republic.' And while the Naga village was probably never fully self-
enclosed, sealed, and self-sufficient (more on this below) its gates have been (forced)
open more widely in recent decades. Many also have passed through these gates to
more or less permanently settle in urban centres both inside and outside Nagaland,
while many more currently growing up in the village aspire to study and pursue
careers outside of it. Amidst this changing context, the sections that follow draw
on ethnography to show how the Naga village nevertheless remains situated at the
very heart of Naga social imagination and society.

A DANGEROUS VILLAGE?

Can a village, akin to an individual, have an identity, a behavioural profile and temperament characteristic only of itself, and which its inhabitants are expected to exhibit both individually and collectively? Are inhabitants of each Naga village conditioned socially to act and think differently from neighbouring villages, even if they may broadly share the same language and cultural practices? Do the collective experiences of village ancestors and forefathers down to the present-day generation impel particularistic attitudes, ideas, and values, even nourish a distinct habitus? The timely demise of national character studies notwithstanding (Mead 1946; Gorer 1949), in the animated world of social perceptions Naga villages are more than geographical places containing peoples, more than the background décor on which lives are lived, but they are also seen in the vernacular – and herein lies this section's main argument – as social personas with distinctive traits, attitudes, and outlooks.

A Naga village is seen to encompass a moral community characterized by its temporal and spatial rootedness, and whose inhabitants define themselves through the conduit of historical memory – a nexus, then, between history, locality, ancestral genealogy, and identity – and which orients their relations with neighbouring and nearby villages and villagers. Of course, identities, both of persons and places, are always as much ascribed as avowed, and during my fieldwork I heard my Naga friends and interlocutors variously typify certain villages as 'aggressive', 'greedy', 'weak', 'boisterous', 'aloof', 'drunkards', 'well-built', and so on, in the process collating territory and peoples in terms of character and behaviour. These, of course, are stereotypes, which, anthropologists know, are usually constitutive of social reality as much as they are a reflection thereof. Yet, such stereotypes nevertheless work to orient the social landscape, and, in the upshot, produce a social imagination across the Naga uplands in which an individual's genealogical tracing to a particular village is held to be indicative of his or her temperament and ways of 'thinking.' I will illustrate this for a Chakhesang Naga village I shall call Phugwumi.

'In the past Phugwumi behaved very aggressively to its neighbours', a Chakhesang government officer told me in his Kohima office. 'My own village often partnered with Phugwumi, and when a village attacked us Phugwumi warriors would come to our rescue. Also, my forefathers sometimes joined them in their raids on other villages.' Such levels of mutual cooperation and understanding were rare, however. The officer narrated:

> In the past, Phugwumi villagers were boisterous and proud.
> Many villages they attacked. In fact, it was because of their
> pride that Christianity and education took a long time to come
> to that village. Christianity preached peace, but Phugwumi
> villagers did not want to hear about peace. Being peace-loving
> was simply not in their blood. Even in Chakhesang villages

Who is a Naga village? The Naga 'village republic' through the ages •

23

much more remote than Phugwumi Christianity arrived decades earlier. That tells you something about the character of Phugwumi.

'Phugwumi is a very peculiar village', I was told on another occasion, also in Kohima. 'Forget about them attacking other villages. When they fought amongst themselves they would bite off their opponent's nose and earlobes. It is a dangerous village.' Such and similar remarks were made to me with some regularity when I spoke about my fieldwork to people outside the village. Important here is that my friends' views of Phugwumi were usually not based on any first-hand knowledge of the Phugwumi villagers but was based on the stories that circulated about them. In broad terms, albeit in strikingly different ways, the one-thousand odd villages dotted across Nagaland are similarly constructed by descriptions and depictions produced and reproduced about them.

But even as depictions of Phugwumi as dangerous were no doubt simplistic and stereotypical, the village's reputation had not emerged out of thin air, but was informed by a history that stretches back far beyond British colonialism. In those days, Phugwumi was a monopolistic protection racket, an overwhelming powerhouse known and feared from afar, and which levied widespread tribute. The biting of noses and ears, too, was more than just a 'saying' or a 'metaphor' but invoked a fighting technique remembered – and now joked about – by Phugwumi elders who spoke of this 'custom' as unique to the Phugwumi of not so long ago. They, however, did not see it as reflective of their hot-headed, aggressive nature the way people outside the village spoke about it. Phugwumi elders reasoned that 'biting' was a sign of restraint reserved for fights and scuffles with fellow-villagers, as, while certainly painful and disfiguring in its effects, it was nevertheless non-lethal. This was contrary to fights with non-villagers when the intention, in the past, was often to kill. At the time of my fieldwork, two Phugwumi elders particularly remembered the force teeth can have as both had a portion of an earlobe missing. Bitten off, indeed, in a dispute several decades ago.

It was long before British officers first climbed the Naga uplands that Phugwumi established itself as a powerful 'warrior village', uncompromising in its raids and unforgiving towards any village, or anyone, who tried to undermine its local status, standing, and sway. Among other factors, Phugwumi's location, perched high on a difficult to access hilltop, contributed to its ascend to local supremacy as enemies could be spotted from afar while the steep, rocky slope made for a natural defence wall. When British-led forced first surveyed the Naga uplands they recognized Phugwumi's might and repute, and an administrative report, published midway the 19th century, estimated the village to consist of '1000 houses' inhabited by no less than '5000 villagers.' The same report detailed that Phugwumi villagers 'were dreaded by all around as a bloodthirsty people, who think nothing of murder for the sake of plunder. They boasted of having a man in their village who had killed seventy men' (Butler 1855: 208).

■ Who is a Naga village? The Naga 'village republic' through the ages

24

Figure 4. *Phugwumi* village.(Photo courtesy Zhoto Tunyi.)

Phugwumi's supremacy received a blow in 1851 when it was attacked, and subdued, by a British-led force, although only after Phugwumi villagers had openly challenged them to a fight, not once, but twice (cf. Wouters 2015). Many died, and those who survived were made to swear allegiance to colonial rule. But even as Phugwumi never fought the British again, many of its villagers did not think twice about defying colonial orders. Note the following fragment of an administrative report written in 1880:

> On the 5th December the detachment marched to [Phugwumi], a powerful village. The march was a very difficult one... Next morning the village showed contumacy by not furnishing the coolies required. A few rockets and a shell were accordingly fired by Lieutenant Mansel, at the request of the political officer, over, and a little below, the village. This had the desired effect, and the coolies were speedily produced... During the march the [Phugwumi] coolies, though previously warned, threw down their loads and bolted. Some fifty actually got away, and the remainder were only stopped by being fired on.[1]

[1]See: 'Detailed report on the Naga Hills Expedition of 1878-80' accessed via Naga Video-disc. Url: http://himalaya.socanth.cam.ac.uk/collections/naga/record/r87665.html

Till today, narratives of past battles, including the clash with the British-led forces, heroic deeds, fearless warriors, and the subduing of other villages remain an essential and proud part of Phugwumi's repertoire of oral history, even though village pastors and church leaders now argue that this part of the village's history is best forgotten.

Whilst the British pacification of the Naga inhabited hills meant the discontinuation of inter-village raids and retaliations (or at least stopped their most violent expressions), inter-village antagonisms and rivalries occasionally continued, and Phugwumi's recent history, too, remains peppered with instances in which the village assembled in a protective and punitive force, determined to protect the village's honour or to exert revenge in the name of a Phugwumi villager wronged at the hands of a non-villager.

Amongst the many incidents that were narrated to me, there was the episode, recalled with gusto by those who participated in it, in which *dao* (broadsword) wielding villagers broke into a police station in the nearby administrative town to try and take a revenge of their own on a person incarcerated there for assaulting a Phugwumi villager. Fortunately, for the accused, he had been transferred to the state capital earlier that day. In another incident, a group of villagers invaded a wrestling tournament in Kohima and trashed, in public view, one of its contestants. They had recognized him as having manhandled a Phugwumi villager in Phek town, the administrative headquarters of the district Phugwumi is part of. For weeks, the villagers had stopped every bus and vehicle that had passed along the Phek-Kohima road, which bypasses Phugwumi, to search for the assaulter, but to no avail. Now seeing him participating in a wrestling tournament, they did not lose time in taking the revenge they had been waiting for. More recently, during the 2013 state elections, Phugwumi's youth was instructed to prevent supporters of a particular (non-village) candidate from campaigning inside the village, exerting force if needed. And when, after the closing of the polls, rumour spread that a few Phugwumi youths residing in a nearby administrative hub had been attacked with stones, village youth – transcending party lines – acted promptly, organized vehicles, and set off in large numbers to provide protection and exert revenge.

Phugwumi's youth today seem to have internalized the particularistic reputation 'earned' by their forefathers, and some may use this to their advantage. 'When I tell people I am from Phugwumi, no-one dares to do or say anything bad to me', as one college-going youth remarked. Another narrated the following incident: 'Once I found myself in a fight in Kohima. It was two of us against five of them. They stood around us in a half-circle, ready to attack. Then we dared them, saying: 'We are from Phugwumi. Come and beat us. We are not afraid of you.' They could have easily beaten us that night, but in the end they did nothing. They knew about our village. They knew that if they would hit us, our villagers would come and search for them.'

Several points emerge from this section. First, among Nagas, a village is more than a physical place as villagers are socially imagined to either 'inherit' or be 'conditioned' to parade behavioural traits, attitudes, and outlooks deemed characteristic of that village. As such, one's genealogical tracing to a particular village operates as a core component of both identity and identification locally. Secondly, a Naga village community is defined by its temporal and spatial rootedness to a place with its identity being framed through historical memory. Thirdly, this historical memory socially orients villagers' perception and relations vis-à-vis neighbouring and nearby villages, as well as shape the ways others perceive and engage with the village and its inhabitants.

THE KINSHIP OF COMMUNITISATION

Besides a continuing marker of identity and identification, in the postcolonial, post-statehood era the 'Naga village' also remapped itself as both the centre and channel of governance. Through Nagaland's 'Village Council Act, 1978' and Village Development Boards extraordinary executive and judicial powers were delegated to village levels. As a general principle, moreover, Naga customary institutions and laws supersede India's codes and courts through a special Amendment (Article 371A) to the Constitution specifically designed for Nagaland. Such levels of village autonomy became expanded further with the passing of Nagaland's unique 'Communitisation of Public Institutions and Services Act, 2001', which sanctioned the transfer of selected government functions and assets – among them fields of education, health, electricity, and water supply – down to village-level committees in an attempt to improve the delivery of public utilities.

This section illustrates, first, how the idea of the Naga 'village republic', as an enduring political and moral community, inspired Nagaland's communitisation policy. I then proceed by showing ethnographically how, in actual practice, communitisation may fail to achieve its set objectives. It fails not because modern phenomena of, say, exaggerated individualism, greed and capitalism, and electoral democracy have rendered obsolete the moral commensality, social cohesion, and corporate character of the Naga village, but communitisation fails, I argue, precisely because of the cross-cutting kinship relations and strong social bonds at village levels. For Phugwumi, I will show how the maintenance and nurturing of social bonds within the village community readily assume precedence over the stringent, detached, and rational monitoring village committees are expected to perform as part of the communitisation policy. I will illustrate this in the context of Phugwumi's health centre. But first I trace the genesis of Nagaland's communitisation policy. I do so through the writings and reflections of its maker, R.S. Pandey, who, for inventing communitisation in Nagaland, was bequeathed both national and internal awards, including the UN Public Service Award in 2008.

It did not take R.S. Pandey (2010: 1) long, after his deputation to Nagaland to serve as its chief secretary, to recognize how 'a sense of despondency in the society and the governance system was clearly evident.' He observed thus:

Nothing can happen here'; 'things will never improve' were some of the general feelings amongst the people. Although the feeling was most intensely associated with the common people, it was not exclusive to them. Even the civil society leadership and the government officers were in its grip. A deep sense of cynicism was evident. The option was to drift along with the current or to think of a change [of] process (ibid.: 2).

The problem was a pervasive malfunctioning of the government, whose record of delivering public service, Pandey wrote, was 'pitiful' and 'abysmally poor' (ibid.: 3). Things had to change, and drastically at that. While ruling out complete privatization of government institutions – given that 'profit motive would take precedence over social service' (ibid.: 12) – what Pandey proposed was the delegation of government services and assets down to village levels, a paradigmatic shift with the 'user community [Naga villagers], the real stakeholders, taking charge of the institutions and services set up by the Government and turning them around' (ibid.: ix).

In practice, communitisation meant that each Nagaland village was to constitute a number of committees staffed by villagers. Each community would subsequently adjudicate over a set of government services, i.e. village health and education. This delegation of duties also included the control over the payment of salaries for teachers, nurses, electricians, and the like, and in a drive against absenteeism village committees were empowered to deduct percentages of the salary of any employee found guilty of unauthorized leaves or other forms of misconduct. As Naga villages would certainly benefit from government employees carrying out their duties regularly and sincerely, and with village committees now empowered to enforce this, the problem of rampant absenteeism, as diagnosed by Pandey, was expected to reduce.

In proposing communitisation as particularly suitable to Nagaland, Pandey drew heavily on the concept of the Naga 'village republic.' 'The state of Nagaland', he wrote, 'is blessed with admirable community bonds reflecting dense and rich social capital, available in amazing abundance in the villages' (2010: 22). Traditionally, these villages functioned 'like a republic in themselves', were typically 'self-contained', and while 'inter-village clashes were common', 'intra-village ones', according to Pandey, took place 'rarely so.' He continued:

> The cohesion, or, in other words, the rich density of the social capital, within the villages is of ancient vintage, continuing through generations. Connections and bonds among the people belong to a tribe which covers several villages also exist, but the cohesiveness is stronger in a village then in a tribe as a whole... The manner in which the village community conducts its affairs in times of sorrow or mirth, adversity or merriment, is reflective of its genius and to an observer from the outside is

remarkably fascinating.

It was this density of social capital, the cohesiveness, and the overall social genius of the Naga village that Pandey envisaged as an organic solution to Nagaland's crisis of governance. The remainder of this section discusses an example of this communitisation policy in practice.

Phugwumi's health centre is housed in a spacious and neatly plastered building situated a little off the main village. In its vicinity, a handful of quarters were built for doctors and nurses to reside during their tenures in Phugwumi. At the time of my fieldwork, however, all quarters were locked with sturdy padlocks, its walls overgrown with moulds and shrubs, its wood decaying, and most of the windows broken. None of them, I learned, had ever been occupied. In the case of the nurses this was because nearly all of them hailed from Phugwumi itself. While most of them had initially been posted to other parts of the state, through various means – including the pulling of 'political strings' – they had over time managed to secure a transfer to Phugwumi, whose comforts and close social bonds they preferred over postings away. In the village, they had their own ancestral houses to live in, or had joined the extended families of their husbands as social norms prescribed.

Despite the nurses' close proximity to the health centre, both in terms of the minimal distance they had to travel, and in terms of social bonds as their patients were simultaneously family, clan, and village members, most nurses were irregular in attending to their duties. Many days no nurses were to be found around the clinic, while those who did report for duty usually stayed in the clinic only briefly. Villagers knew this, and anticipated on the nurses' absence by calling, in cases of sickness or injury, not on the clinic but on the private residence of one of the nurses (who, it must be said, were ever ready to diagnose and treat patients in their homes). Most nurses kept a small stock of medicines at home, as well as basic instruments to diagnose a patient. When a villager nevertheless needed to visit the clinic, for instance to have him or herself examined more thoroughly or to receive an injection, the patient would make sure to first call around to find out if any of the nurses meant to attend that day. Going to the clinic unannounced was seen as foolhardy.

Some villagers voiced their disappointment with the post-communitisation absenteeism in the health centre, and were critical about the health committee for not taking action against it. They, after all, now had the authority to enforce regular office hours, reducing the salaries of absentee nurses if they must. Most in Phugwumi, however, offered a more nuanced understanding of this predicament. 'The problem with communitisation is that most government employees are also our fellow villagers', Vezo explained.[2]

---

[2]Vezo, as well as other names that figure in this essay, is a pseudonym

Who is a Naga village? The Naga 'village republic' through the ages •

29

They have many other duties besides their jobs. They need
to tend to their fields, or do household chores. Most of our
nurses are also mothers, and need to look after their children.
They are our own family and clan-members; how can we tell
them to forsake their duties as wives, mothers, and daughters-
in-law, and be regular in the clinic? That would be quite wrong
on our part.

This cross-cutting of kinship bonds and loyalties not only complicated the
functioning of Phugwumi's health centre, it also prevented the village's education
committee from 'punishing' absentee teachers, most of whom were also fellow
villagers. 'The government tells us to deduct salary from those teachers who are
irregular', a member of the village education committee told me. 'But how can we
deduct salary from a neighbour, a clan-member or fellow-villager? That would be
shameful on our part to do. We can ask them indirectly to be serious in their work.
But nothing more than that.'[3] At times such cross-cutting of social bonds assumed
more complex forms. Vezo explained:

Look, the members of the village health committee too have
families and relatives, and some of them work in government
departments. Now, if the health committee decides to deduct
the salary of a nurse, surely the nurse's family but also her
relatives and clan members will feed bad. Then, if they know
that a relative of a health committee member works in a
local government office, they will take revenge by forcing the
concerned committee to deduct his or her salary. In this way,
communitisation, if we enforce it, will only cause conflict
and resentment. In the end, we are all related in the village.
The Government can't expect us to control and punish one
another.

For Phugwumi villagers the maintenance and nurturing of social bonds clearly
superseded the imperative of 'good governance', as communitisation was meant to
foster. What this section illustrated is that while social capital and close affective
bonds are indeed characteristic of the prototypical Naga village, this – rather
than an 'indigenous solution' to mal-governance, the way envisaged by Pandey –
provided village-level government employees with the social leverage to *not* attend

---

[3]In parts because of absenteeism among teachers, many in Phugwumi preferred to
send their children to the village's private school, which had earned a better reputation
in terms of the quality of education offered in comparison to the school funded by the
government.

their offices dutifully. It also prevented village committees from taking punitive action against absentee employees, given that doing so would upset social relations and invite divisions and disagreements into the village community. Analysed thus, it is precisely the social cohesion and cooperation – or the 'rich density of the social capital' (Pandey 2010: 22) – within Naga villages that complicated communitisation.

A VILLAGE BASED DEMOCRACY

From identity and governance, this third ethnographic section turns to the frenzied world of electoral politics, and the role of the Naga village therein.

At a political rally in the constituency's small administrative town – not far from Phugwumi – in the wake of the 2013 Nagaland state elections, party workers busied themselves in distributing party-manifestos, printed on colourful, glossy paper, to all and sundry. In a systematic and specific manner, the manifesto spelled out the party's political position on a host of state issues as well as offered details on the policies and projects it wished to implement if elected into political office. All there was to know about the party's vision, in short, was there in the booklet. Those who attended the rally indeed gladly received these party manifestos but then used them to sit on in order to prevent their clothes from dirtying, to wrap betel-nut or snacks in, or to hold it above their face as a protective screen against the sun. No sooner had the rally ended and most booklets were discarded, leaving the area littered with hundreds of party manifestos. The reason why but few bothered to read the booklet was not because Naga voters are mostly illiterate – which they are not – but because party manifestos, ideologies, or this or that political vision was not the core 'political stuff' of Nagaland elections.

'Nagaland's elections are fought in its villages. It is based on village politics', a former Nagaland politician explained me in an interview. He continued:

> To attract voters a politician must first find out about the history and contemporary issues of the individual villages in his constituency. A politician needs to know about each village's relations with its neighbours, and whether there are any land disputes or other outstanding issues. He also needs to understand the clan-relations inside the village. And to know who the clan and village leaders are, and what can be done to win those over. In the end, each village needs its own electoral strategy and campaign.

To capture a constituency, then, a political party required more than a state-wide political manifesto and the public articulation of its vision. It required multiple and detailed electoral strategies tailored at the village-level.

Phugwumi's constituency was made up of nine villages and an administrative hub, and in the run-up to the 2013 elections party-workers indeed articulated their political strategies, analyses, and predictions separately for each village. Comments and remarks, for instance, were: 'In this village the political wave favours us'; 'if we get 250 votes from this village, we must get no less than 400 from that one'; 'those villagers don't want to support a candidate from Phugwumi'; 'leaders of that village are against us', and so on. After the counting of the votes (whose tallies were declared village-wise) the political leaning of each village transformed from an area of speculation to that of fact, and thenceforward each village was talked about as, for instance, an 'NPF [Naga People's Front] village', a 'Congress village', or an 'Independent [candidate] village', as a 'ruling' or an 'opposition' village, and this tag became part of the village's political identity and standing, at least until the next election could reshuffle the cards.

For Phugwumi itself the 2013 election proved to be of a different kind. It was for the first time that two villagers decided to contest the same election, causing a village predicament whose inner-logic and intricacies I have sought to explain elsewhere (Wouters 2015). What I want to reiterate here was the common and colloquial distinction that was made in the run up to Polling Day between 'home' and 'away votes.' With constituencies in Nagaland comparatively small – miniscule compared to most parts of the country – it was widely held that without solid 'home-votes', or the number of votes a politician accrued from his natal village, it was difficult, if not impossible, to win the constituency. 'If you can't get the majority support of your own village, how can you expect other villages to favour you', as it was explained to me. 'Escape votes', in contrast, referred to those votes villagers polled for a non-village candidate when a fellow-villager also contested the election. While 'escape votes' were not unusual – and often the outcome of strained relations between a voter and a candidate, or perhaps vis-à-vis the clan he belonged to – they nevertheless carried a dubious moral quality as the act of 'giving away' one's vote to a politician of another village was seen as undermining the ideal of inter-village cohesion and cooperation (Wouters 2015: 136).

Moreover, for a village to 'produce' a Member of the Legislative Assembly (MLA) meant an immediate increase in its overall status and standing in the area. But village status was not the only reason explaining the distinction between 'home' and 'away votes.' There also existed a more instrumental hinge to this logic, but which I will invoke only briefly here. In the wake of Polling Day, a Phugwumi villager publicly criticized the gifts and monies fellow-villagers expected from the two village candidates in return for their electoral support. His criticism, however, was not founded on the ideal of 'clean elections' but was geared towards securing the long-term material benefits Phugwumi as a whole would accrue if a fellow-villager was elected as MLA. His reasoning went thus:

> We, as a village, should not demand money from a candidate

who himself belongs to our village. Instead, we should give him money, rice, and meat, as much as he needs, so he can use that in convincing voters in other villages to support him on Polling Day. Then, once he gets elected, he should serve our village, bringing more development funds and appointing our youth into government service.

Across Nagaland, any politician, once elected into office, was expected to privilege his clan and natal village in the allocation of government jobs, development resources, and other state benefits. This moral expectation, of an elected politician, rather than basing his decisions on detached, impersonal and rational-legal reasoning, to privilege his natal village in the allocation of state resources also runs through the following statement by a Phugwumi elder. 'I don't care about this or that political party, this or that candidate', he responded as I inquired about his political leanings. 'I just want a candidate from our village to become MLA. Then our village can really come up.' That the political parochialism of the village prevailed over broader notions of Naga citizenship is also evident from the following evaluation a Phugwumi villager made about his recent visit to the village of the (then) Chief Minister:

All houses are made of concrete and there is plenty of development. After he became Chief Minister he has made not less than twenty-five of his villagers first-class contractors, putting them in charge of big contracts. The others he provided government jobs. And not just small jobs, but with the rank of officer. He has really been a good politician for his villagers.

For obvious reasons, none of the above colloquial expressions, moral expectations, and village-centred politicking found its way into the party manifesto distributed during the rally. However, it is in these domains, the ways people talk and think about politics and elections and evaluate their politicians – and not in the pages of political manifestos – that we find clues towards better understanding the inner-logic and intricacies of Nagaland's democracy, and the crucial role of 'the

AN ANTITHESIS

village' in it.

Lest I be blamed for reproducing colonial views, or of perpetuating stereotypes, isolationist perspectives, and romanticized images, this section discusses some features and observations that work to eviscerate essentialist interpretations of the prototypical Naga village as an independent, necessarily cohesive, and self-enclosed republic.

To start with, it would be rather mistaken to portray any Naga village as historically self-enclosed and sealed. Among other things, this would fail to account for the historical relations (fluctuating between trade, tribute, and raids) certain Naga villages, or village clusters, cultivated with dynasties and peoples in the adjacent Brahmaputra, Barak, and Imphal Valleys (Devi 1968; Wouters 2011). It would also underestimate the frequent inter-village struggles over local standing and dominance fought out between villages, the tributary relations that thence emerged, and the rise of local hegemony of especially powerful villages, as the historical case of Phugwumi also illustrated.

Excessive focus on the locus of 'the political', as vested in the village, would also conceal the diversity of political structures and sentiments that existed, and in different forms persist, *within* the 'Naga village republic', none of which is quite like another. In fact, any approximation of the politico-historical form and substance of the prototypical Naga village must first acknowledge its heterogeneity. When reading colonial accounts, we find descriptions of Naga chiefs and democrats (Jacobs et al. 1990), nobles and commoners (Fürer-Haimendorf 1973), authoritative village councillors (Mills 1926), powerful clan elders (Mills 1922), sacrosanct chiefs and aristocrats (Fürer-Haimendorf 1939; Hutton 1921b), as well as the conspicuous absence of any permanent positions of leadership (Hutton 1921a). Naga village polities, thence, represented a continuum with hereditary autocracy, if not near dictatorship, and radical democracy at its opposite ends, with (a section of) Konyak Nagas associated with the former and Angami and Chakhesang Nagas perhaps best representative of the latter (Wouters 2014).

In addition to the fallacy of seeing the Naga village in isolation and as politically operative in broadly similar ways, it also remains problematic to characterize its social life primarily in terms of cohesion and cooperation, which, while certainly cherished ideals, often failed to materialize in practice. 'The Naga Hills was peaceful', an administrative report in 1890 reads, 'except for one serious riot at the Angami [now Chakhesang] village of [Phugwumi], in which one man was killed and several wounded.'[4] Such 'riots' could be the result of interpersonal disagreements, but often manifested themselves along the lines of clan and/or khel. During a visit to Tuensang village in the 1920s, Hutton (1929: 49), for instance, observed that:

> between the Bilaeshi and the Chongpho khels there is a deep
> ditch digged, formerly filled with 'panjis' most of which were
> pulled by Ongli Ngaku's [a Dobashi] orders last time he came
> here, when he tried to settle the long stranding feuding between

---

[4]Assam Administrative Report. Naga Videodisc. See The Naga Database, accessed September 9, 2015. http://himalaya.socanth.cam.ac.uk/collections/naga/record/r88456.html. It must be qualified here that before the making of the Chakhesang tribe in 1946, Phugwumi was classified as an Angami Naga village (Wouters 2017).

the Chongpho and Bilaeshi khels. For the present it is abated, but I saw in Chongpho khel a long row of hide shields set out as they are put when trouble with the Bilaeshi is toward.'

Among the Angami Nagas inter-clan struggles were also frequent: 'Although the village may be regarded as the unit of the political and religious sides of Angami life', Hutton wrote (1921a: 109), 'the real unit of the social side is the clan... the rivalry or antagonism of clan with clan within the village has coloured the whole of Angami life.' Hutton explained further:

> In war, even though the village were united, the jealousy and suspicion of one clan for another would inevitably be a source of weakness; in peace the village would from time to time break out into riot, while it is incessantly troubled by internal bickering. In almost every dispute between two men of different clans the clansmen on each side appear as partisans and foment the discord.

Such intra-village conflicts and contestations, while certainly less violent today, have not evaporated, however. The new domain of state-led development, for instance, injected new fault-lines, divisions, and desires in the village community and caused villagers to compete over access and control of state resources in unprecedented ways. This is to the extent that a large number of court cases in Nagaland today are being fought over competing claims to village development boards and village council membership. Community development, as purported by the idea of village development boards, if anything, has often seemed to end up dividing Naga village communities rather than developing them in unison.

Democracy and elections, too, regularly result in the (temporary) break-down of village communities. Phugwumi, for one, had earned itself a peculiar reputation in 'doing elections' as during two previous elections electronic voting machines in the village had been destroyed by angry party-workers, leading to re-polling. Partly because such antecedents, and partly because of the rivalries that emerged as the result of two villagers contesting the election fray, the Nagaland Government, in the wake of the 2013 elections, declared Phugwumi as 'hypersensitive', resulting in the presence of large numbers of soldiers to oversee the peaceful conduct of polling.

But while such historical and contemporary insights complicate the thesis of the Naga village republic, as outlined in this essay, it does not negate it, as 'some [I would say 'all'] Naga communities are recognized very strongly around the principle of the village as a unit' (Jacobs et al. 1990: 71), and from this it remains that 'the village rather than a group of villages or a tribe is the natural unit of organization and hence the correct basis of investigation' (Horam 1992: 60).

Who is a Naga village? The Naga 'village republic' through the ages ∎

35

CONCLUDING REMARKS

Barely a few decades ago the Dimapur plains were abhorred by upland villagers as a dangerous place stricken by heat, malaria, and malevolent spirits. At the most, it served as hunting grounds or as a doorway for occasional visits of Naga villagers to the Assam plains for reasons of trade. It was not considered a place worth living in. Today, Dimapur is a sprawling and bustling urban settlement where opportunities for business, employment, and education attract more and more Nagas away from their hilltop villages. The state capital of Kohima, in turn, has reportedly already exceeded its carrying capacity in terms of buildings, infrastructure, and available water supply. Akin to trends across the Subcontinent, Nagaland is urbanizing. What this will mean for the future of the Naga 'village republic' is hard to predict. As it stands, however, urbanization, while coming at cultural costs, does not obliterate the significance and character of the prototypical Naga village. Those who have left the village often remain deeply connected to it; they make sure to have their ancestral homes to return to, may lease out their land rather than selling it, return to the village to celebrate Christmas and traditional festivals, retain their local church memberships, and always respond with the name of their ancestral village when asked 'who they are' (even if they were not born there).

In reviewing the condition of South Asian Anthropology in the 1980s, Fuller and Spencer (1990: 86) diagnosed the demise of the once coveted 'village studies', plainly because anthropologists got 'bored' with them. A decade on, Gupta (2005) announced the withering of the traditional diacritics of Indian village life. Anthropologists, it was suggested, would better move away from villages and study mobility, migration, and urban spaces. Mines and Yazgi (2010: 13) recently offered a much-needed corrective to this conception, arguing how, despite rapid urbanization, villages persist as 'ontological existents, key aspects of experience, reservoirs of discourse or projections, units for collective actions, elements of consciousness of self or otherness.' This certainly applies to most Nagas, for whom – as I have variously sought to illustrate – the village remains firmly etched at the centre of social consciousness. Or as it was once explained to me:

> Those who leave their villages to settle in Kohima or Dimapur are often those with a salaried job. They therefore do not need to sell their land in the village. Nagas always want to keep some land in the village, even if they hardly come there and don't cultivate it. Without land it is difficult to claim that you belong to a village. And without belonging to a village, it is difficult to claim that you are a Naga.

∎ ∎∎ ∎∎

03

A FORGOTTEN FAME TABOO: DREAMS AND HIERARCHY AMONGST THE ZEME NAGAS

Edward Moon-Little

The unusually well-known or famous or anyone liable to be talked about is apt to become weighed down or weakened by being mentioned by so many people; he gets low fever, and suffers from weakness, coughs, colds, malaise and disorders generally. To cure this, a special ceremony is carried out, with a deer's foot, a cock, or a dog as a sacrifice. Anyone having performed the ceremony with say, a dog, cannot perform it again with anything less, as a cock, but must sacrifice at least a dog. Naga dobashis and other public persons perform the ceremony frequently to avoid any evil consequences of being well-known.

— Ursula Graham-Bower (1940a)

It is perhaps fitting for a taboo around fame to be forgotten; its efficiency strong enough to constrain a society and then be lost in the anthropological archive. This chapter was inspired by Ursula Graham-Bower's fieldwork amongst the Zeme Nagas and the archive she left behind. My own trips to the same Zeme communities in 2014 and 2016 allowed me to engage and reflect on Graham-Bower's archive.

When visiting a small Paupaise (animist) community near the village of Laisong in Assam in 2016 I observed *hgangi*, the Zeme winter solstice festival. I was particularly intrigued by two traditions. The first involved every man and boy in the village forming a procession and gathering outside each house of the village in turn. At each house, they chanted and beat drums in order to extract a feast from the richest man of the village. The second ritual was more unusual. The *mpe-kap-pe-ngi* (the wood-striking-ritual) of *hgangi* was once common amongst other Naga groups, particularly the Rengma, Lothas and Western Angami. It has now become exceedingly rare. In the ritual larger-than-life human figures are carved from a pure piece of wood, then marked by taboos, garlanded, and destroyed. The two rituals struck me as variations on the same theme, one virtual, and one actual. In both rituals, the men of the village made common cause to treat and then confront some other who had been raised above them, usually a famous figure, or an abstracted representation of fame. The more I read about Zeme ethnography, the more I found variations on this same theme. This pattern was so deep that have an excess of fame was subject to a taboo: *hamui-hera*.

A taboo against fame seems almost antithetical to Naga ethnography. One reason Northeast India has experienced so much anthropological interest is the vast amount of Naga material culture; material culture very often linked to celebrating the greatness and status of village aristocrats. Such artefacts have been the subject of so many publications that it is almost a sub-discipline in its own right (for an overview see: Barbier and Ferrazzini 1984; Kunz and Joshi 2008; Oppitz et al. 2008; Von Stockhausen 2014; and West 2011). *Hamui-hera*, literally the sin of fame, bridges ethnographic theory on dreams, name taboos, and exchange. The creation and management of fame was central to Zeme social life which makes a fame taboo something of paradox. Why was fame viewed as potentially lethal when nearly all aspects of Zeme life where measured through fame? As Graham-Bower wonderfully put it: 'the Zemi have more methods of getting cash in exchange for "honour" than anyone else I know' (Graham-Bower 1952: 49). I approach *hamui-hera* through a sort of anthropological diagnostic: first I address the symptoms, the dream and its immanence; secondly I explore the cause of the dangerous excess, the creation of fame in Zeme society; and lastly turn to the cure, the sacrifice and renewed commensality. When concluding, I link *hamui-hera* with Marcel Mauss' *The Gift* to ask: how do we confront each other better.

DREAMING AND NAMES IN NAGA ETHNOGRAPHY

Between 1939-46 Graham-Bower meticulously recorded Zeme village life in all its theatricality and suffering, focusing particularly on village histories and migration cycles. She also recorded a large amount of material related to dreaming. This line of enquiry was possibly influenced by British administrator-ethnographer J.H. Hutton and his research on the Angami Nagas[1], or possibly Graham-Bower's

---

[1] When Hutton wrote his ethnography of the Angami Nagas - also a Tenyimia com-

own interests in clairvoyance (personal communication, Khan 2017). Dreaming was perhaps the most highly valued form of second sight for the Zeme - as it was for many other Naga communities. That said, dreams needed the right social and temporal condition. Dreams needed elders to act as analysts, and when the seasons changed dreams were said to less reliable as form of second sight.

The role of the Zeme dream analyst - most often the kith and kin of the sufferer - was to consult an unwritten taxonomy of signs and to vocalise what awful or wonderful event was about to befall the dreamer. To dream of fish meant bumper crops; to dream of a snake foretold some future injury (Graham-Bower c.1940b). If we compare this to the Freudian tradition of dream analysis, and its focus on the repressions and distortions of unfulfilled wishes, the distinctiveness of the dream related to *hamui-hera* becomes clearer. The comparison also highlights the role of the Zeme dream analysts. For Freud dreams represented some unfulfilled desire - usually sexual - and it was the analyst's job to discern the cause of this lack, and to help the sufferer remedy the situation. Although Freud said that the possibility dreams predict the future was 'quite out of the question' (1997 [1889]: 452), what is prognosis but an educated form of future divination?[2] For the Zeme dream analyst what the dream revealed about the future was *the* question. Their role was to determine if the dream foretold good or bad events, or in the case of *hamui-hera*, to highlight the origin of the dream in order to cure it. Importantly for *hamui-hera*, the cause of the dream is societal as opposed being rooted in the individual's unconscious. Dreams are simultaneously collective and individual which is true in this case too.

In the Zeme oneiric catalogue of signs, the appearance of a European, tiger, gun or train, were linked to an excess of fame. Once diagnosed the sufferer was required to perform a sacrifice to neutralise the dangers of being talked about too much. The question then emerges: why would anyone admit they dreamed badly? Why not just lie and avoid paying for the sacrifice? This is the mystery at the heart of *hamui-hera*, and a clear example of how dreams shaped Zeme eventuation. One might suggest that the majority of dreams were ignored and what was recorded is a case of hearing the signal and not silence. But consider the evidence to the contrary. Graham-Bower repeatedly witnessed her closest Zeme companions perform the sacrifice of *hamui-hera*, which is all-the-more remarkable as each time the ritual was conducted an increasingly expensive animal sacrifice was required, a cock, then a dog, then a pig, and so forth. The sacrifice was not to pay for the divination of the dream -that was revealed through the signs- rather the sacrifice was a sort of cosmological license or realignment for habouring excess fame.

---

munity related to the Zeme - he stated that: 'of all forms of second sight, dreaming is the favourite and the best. The Angamis have almost a science of dreaming' (Hutton 1921: 246 as quoted in Heneise this volume).

[2]Personal communication with Sean Dowdy 2017

I argue that the dream of *hamui-hera* presents an intriguing example of an oneiric confrontation, one that mirrors the fear of encountering dangerous 'others' in forests. Specifically, I believe many elements of *hamui-hera* can usefully be explored through perspectivism, an interpretation inspired by Eduardo Viveiros de Castro's writings on Amerindians and supernatural encounters (2015: 289-91). His argument goes something like this: there is a fear common amongst forest communities of meeting some 'other' person - be it spirit, animal, or human - in the forest when travelling alone, and being transformed by this encounter. The perspectival transformation occurs due to a radical change in subjectivity. An example would be as follows. A hunter enters a forest in search of game and meets a malevolent spirit, the spirit sees the hunter who then becomes the prey of that spirit. It is when the hunter realises the spirit is also a person with desires, actions, a sense of self, that he is in danger of being subsumed by a cosmologically dominant point of view. The dream of *hamui-hera* there is a similar perspectival exchange of this most dangerous kind. The famous man is confronted with symbols of others more powerful than himself (tigers, Europeans, trains, guns) and is therefore reminded of his vulnerability. Fame and utterances eventuate this oneiric confrontation, but the remedy lies in sacrifice. Although the oneiric confrontation is caused by utterances, it is hard to see how it fits the existing anthropological literature on name taboo.

NAME TABOOS AMONGST THE ZEME

Taboos associated with names have had a canonical role in anthropology since its conception as a comparative project (Dowdy 2016 citing Benveniste 1971, Frazer 1996, Freud 1918, Haddon 1935, Wittgenstein 1993). And yet taboos of unmentionability are 'everywhere and nowhere', with untouchability taking precedence over unmentiona- bility in anthropological writings ever since (ibid. 4). *Hamui-hera* sits uncomfortably in the canon of name taboos as it is not the sufferer who has committed any cosmological or societal violation, and certainly not through a single utterance or action. Rather, the sin is a process of accumulation which leads to oppression for the bearer of the name. The act of violation stems from society's excessive use of a name and the sufferer is at fault for giving them cause. Names for the Zeme were a gift from society, not from immediate kin or through ritual feats[3]. In Zeme villages the elders named children. As children grew up they learned the importance of names and certain acts of avoidance, such as the unmentionability of their spouse's name, a taboo shared across other Tenyimia Nagas and many other South Asian communities (cf. Hutton 1921: 219).[4]

[3]For name giving rituals amongst other former headhunters (cf. Van Baal 1966)

[4]This taboo is still remembered and practiced by some members of the Zeme com- munity.

Amongst the Zeme, uttering names left the bearer of the name vulnerable to malevolent spirits. Souls could not be relied upon to stick with their associated bodies; they could get stuck, weakened, lured away, or simply wander off. A name uttered in a forest could act like a snare, trapping the bearer's soul and placing it under the domain of some spirit other[5]. One of the easiest ways to trap souls was through names. When the situation was reversed and the name of spirits was used, the situation was equally perilous with only the oldest of men in the village calling the names, as he had the least life to lose. The linkage between names and persons was cosmological; the improper uses of names could be discerned in various ways, and in the case of *hamui-hera* the improper use was discerned through dreams.

While *hamui-hera* is remembered in contemporary Zeme communities, it is not practiced as outlined here. A second historical difference is also key: Graham-Bower recorded a widespread belief that language united diverse selves around the Zeme both human and animal. This belief has since dissipated. For the remainder of this essay 'the Zeme' will refer to Graham-Bower's informants, as opposed to the contemporary community, unless stated otherwise. Like many colonial ethnographers she did not feel the need to anonymise her informants or their communities.

The notes this essay draws on are linked back to the communities of Laisong, Hangrum, Asalu, Guilong, amongst others, but particularly Laisong where Graham-Bower lived. I visited many of these villages in 2014 and then in 2016, though they now find themselves at the confluences of Assam, Manipur and Nagaland. The size of Zeme communities at the time of Graham-Bower's ethnography is important to the taboo, most villages less than a hundred households. Her field sites were selected because the Zeme communities near the British station at Halflong 'were dull and poor... split between Christian and Pagan...[and] their morungs were decaying' (1952: 58). In other words, these communities were deemed inauthentic or debased. Instead Graham-Bower focused on the hilltop communities spread throughout the Barail range of Assam.

THE SYMPTOMS OF OPPRESSIVE FAME

> To see a train, gun or european [sic] means the dreamer is suffering from hamui-hera-hera - the weight of being too much talked about; to see a tiger means the same thing.
> (Ursula Graham-Bower 1942)

[5]Ethnographies of other contemporary Tenyimia communities displaying similar reticence around the utterances of names near forests (cf. Heneise 2017: 78).

I begin with my most suggestive argument: the oneiric confrontation of *hamui-hera* echoes the logics of predation. More specifically I argue that the inclusion of tigers alongside Europeans and guns in the oneiric symbols of *hamui-hera* are connected to the logics of hierarchy and perspectival exchange. *Hamui-hera* is suggestive of a self-ordering logic amongst the unconscious where the unconscious groups together signs (Kohn 2013: 176-7 citing Freud 1999 and Levi-Strauss 1965). And I think it is useful to draw on Marshall Sahlins' work on structure and conjecture (1981) in order to avoid overstating the creative powers of colonialism. Here the signs are all dangerous, with the dangers of guns, Europeans and trains, as later additions to an existing cultural category. The colonial symptoms may well be new, but it is likely they were addition to older indigenous categories of reference -with the symbol of the tiger no doubt being the oldest. The equivalence of man and predator is found throughout forest dwelling communities globally where 'animals are people, or see themselves as people' (De Casteo 2015: 198) and this holds up well amongst the Zeme. However the Zeme did not extend perspectivism to all animals, but to a distinctive category of megafauna and particularly predators[6].

All perspectivism is historically located as it is contingent on certain types of ecologies (Kohn 2013: 96). And the perspectivism discussed here is rooted in a distinct period of political and environmental history. The Burmese invasions of Assam in the 18th and 19th century - the same invasions that brought British colonialism up from Bengal and into the Naga Hills - inadvertently created a proliferation of megafauna due to afforestation. As the armies of the Assamese, British, Burmese, Manipuri, Kacharis, brought widespread looting and marauding to the region, this in turn caused widespread depopulation and a breakdown in agricultural cycles and eventually afforestation (Cederlöf 2013: 191-3). In the generations before Graham-Bower's fieldwork the forests around the Zeme were teeming with elephants, hornbills, buffalo, deer, bears, monkeys, and feline predators. This proliferation of megafauna made certain types of perspectivism possible, and here is an illustration of a certain kind of perspectival logic amongst Zeme hunters:

> The ordinary word for tiger, Hradi, may not be mentioned in the jungle or the tiger will hear and be angry and carry off the speaker. The expression 'Makao' (= something) is always used when speaking in the jungle.

---

[6]This equivalence also shaped food taboos. Tigers, leopards, wild dogs, could only be eaten by old men. Hornbills too. Monkeys, with their person-like features, were again the preserve of old men -with women only occasionally allowed to partake. The equivalence between megafauna and persons was really just focused on male elders, who were the most famous and powerful men in the village, which is why they could eat what others could not.

The parallels between *hamui-hera and* the name taboo around *hradri* (tigers and leopards) are highly suggestive. Predators were bound by the same logics of personhood that governed Zeme society. Predators were persons much like hunters in their ways of thinking and the ways they approached prey[7]. Tigers had the rights to their quarry and sought revenge if it was taken by Zeme hunters. Tigers were also believed to be able to lure their prey by imitating the sound of the barking deer; much like human hunters tried to lure and manipulate deer (Graham-Bower 1941). When hunters used the term *hradri*, tigers were seen to react angrily to this appropriation. Such taboo utterances transformed the hunter into the hunted, forcing a radical shift in subjectivity mirroring the *hamui-hera* dream[8]. Predators knowing their killers could be dangerous.

> When a python is found, all dogs must be taken away and weapons hidden. The sight of either infuriates the snake. The bucks then move in close to it, the leader telling it that they wish to take it up to the village for everyone to admire. When he has finished his speech, they step up alongside it, one to the head, one to the tail, and one in the middle...On arrival in the village, the python is taken straight to the bucks' own morung. They have already announced what they carry by a special chant, and half the village will be there to see them come in. The python is released, and for half an hour or so allowed to slither at large about the hall and in among the spectators. During this lull, the old men - if there are any present who have the skill - look at the markings and foretell the future. Then a man chosen for the job comes up to the python slowly, a dao carefully concealed behind his back. At the last moment he whips this out and strikes off the snake's head at a blow.
> Ursula Graham-Bower (1939)

[7]Although the Zeme specifically rejected the notion that tigers could become men or vice-versa which set them apart from other Naga communities (cf. X).

[8]Instead of Hradri, the Zeme used the term Makao ('something') thereby avoiding the cosmological snare linking names and persons. An intriguingly similar predatory linkage comes from ethnographies of the neighbouring Angami Nagas. For the Angami when a tiger was killed, its mouth was wedged open and the head was placed in the stream so it could not tell the spirits the name of the man who killed him (Hutton 1920: 42). Again, this mirrors the change of subjectivities in the hamui-hera dream and shows a wider Teny-imia Naga logic relating to names and selves.

Ritual of divinations through pythons is one of the many instances in Zeme cosmology where fame is a foreshadowing of danger. So, let us explore the ritual above. First the python is respected; weapons are concealed; dogs are banished; chants are sung. Even the execution blow is hidden. The capture and death of the python marks a similar shift in subjectivity as when the hunter utters *hdrari* in the forest; the great predator suddenly slips from predator to prey - all without ever seeing the *dao* or the face of its executioner. During the ritual, it appears important that the python sees the Zeme in a certain way, not as potential prey or as predators but as other persons. The formulation is more like sovereign and people, or priest and followers, than captive and captors. When the python entered the village, and while charmed by its warm welcome, it was placed on softened earth so that its marks could be examined by the village elders. Elders would interpret the signs in the marks in much the same way they would interpret dreams[9]. After the python was killed its meat was eaten by the elders and the capturer hung its skull as trophy as a marker of his newfound fame[10].

The equivalence of man and pythons is deep in Zeme cosmology where pythons have a more prominent role than feline predators. In creations myths pythons are the last born child and the snakes were said to take human wives and have a king of their own. Python worship was also linked to the two anti-colonial prophets amongst the Zeme: Haipou Jadonang and Rani Gaidinliu. Jadonang kept several of the great snakes in his temple (which the British killed on his arrest), and Gaidinliu was said to have been anointed by a python, as well as having numerous other connections (Longkumar 2010: 107, 174, 176-7). So why do pythons relate to *hamui-hera*? Pythons offered an alternative form of second sight, they were subject to the taboos of fame, and as outlined above they were subject to a form of perspectivism that imagined python society like human society with language, prey, wives, and a king. Constrictors have often been interpreted as possessing this particular kind of charisma. For example, amongst the Runa of the Ecuadorian Amazon, the anaconda is held as the 'the predator hunters would like to be: one that is not initially recognised as such' (Kohn 122).[11] It is this type of charisma that the social value for the Zeme: the ability to draw others to you as fame and power

[9]The marks were given to predict the future of the man who captured the pythons: pug-marks foretold a successful tiger hunt; bear-tracks indicated a successful bear hunt; a girl's footprints meant success as a lover.

[10]Soppit's (1888) account also corroborates the Zeme habits of bringing pythons to the village and that tigers were a dangerous sign.

[11]This obfuscation is key and is suggestive of why the Zeme prized pythons so highly. Zeme hunters would tie gawang (a root) to themselves, its smell disguised their presence to the python, allowing the hunters to ensure their subjectivities did not shift from predators to prey. Pythons were predators of attraction and many Zeme warned Graham-Bower about their magical abilities to lure men to the deaths by drowning them in pools and rivers.

invariably do.

The presence of trains and Europeans, in the semiotics of hamui-hera help place the taboo in the colonial period. This indicates that the form of the taboo recorded by Graham-Bower reflected contemporary anxieties in Zeme society as opposed to some immutable tradition. Indrani Chatterjee's Forgotten Friends (2013) has helped to reanimate the complex networks of monks, mercenaries and traders, that weaved around Zeme lands in the 18th and 19th centuries, linking the gunpowder kingdoms of the Ahoms, Manipur, and Burma, with pan-Asian monastic orders and global markets. The Zeme had never lived in total isolation, no one does. In all likelihood the Zeme had already encountered some of the eclectic fair/white others who preceded the British. Merchants and mercenaries of Afghani, Armenian, and European, descent had long made their way up from Bengal into Assam to access the markets and courts of local rulers (ibid). However it seems unlikely that the taboo references these earlier interlopers as they had little effect on the Zeme. More likely it was whiteness invested with power that made the European an oneiric symbol.

The exact term Graham-Bower translated as European is unclear but it is likely to have been either kehame (white people) or sai kehaki (a white person of high rank). In the waking world Graham-Bower herself was misrecognized by a few Zeme as Rani Gaidiliu in European form and worshipped as 'Mother' and 'She-Spirit' (Graham-Bower 1952: 144). Misrecognition of this kind offers another piece of evidence for the structures of conjuncture (Sahlins 1981)as the category of powerful magical women appears an old one in Zeme cosmology (see Soppit on the Kachari witch 1885). More importantly however nearly all Zemes came to understand whiteness as being invested with power and danger as part of the racially hierarchical colonial system.

Trains were undoubtedly a newer symbol but why should they be deemed dangerous? There are no records of them being mystified as iron beasts or as any other anthropomorphised form. A more likely answer lies in older patterns of sovereignty and relation between states and forced labour (Scott 2009). Laying train tracks was just the latest form of corvée labour the Zeme witnessed, or had been forced participate in. The previous kingdoms of Assam and Manipur had extracted labour from hill communities for centuries to act as porters, soldiers, paddy workers, and in particular: road builders. Much like with the British, violence, or the threat of violence lay behind these extractions. At the time of Graham-Bower's writing in the 1930s, train tracks already bordered Zeme lands - though few Zemes had experienced train rides, and few train passengers had experienced Nagas.[12]

---

[12]The Zeme of Asalu lived just three miles from the nearest train station and had presumably seen the train at nearby Maibong for years. There is a humorous account of Namika, Graham-Bower's Zeme informant and assistant from Impoi, experiencing his first train journey and playing up Naga caricatures as savages and cannibals much to the

Alongside working as labourers the British had frequently conscripted the Zeme as porters to serve on military punitive expeditions. These expeditions all pretty much took same form: a long, brutal march to a distant set of hills; find the offending village; burn said village; and return. Before Graham-Bower's fieldwork a large number of Zeme porters from Hangrum - one of her key fieldsites - had died helping the British on punitive raids in what is now Mizoram. Many other Zeme had died in 1932 when they had participated in a wider Naga uprising against the British led by Rani Gaidinliu (for more information see Kamie 2004, Longkumer 2010, Samson 2012).

Monopolising violence in the Naga Hills had been a long-standing concern of the British dating back to their first encounters with Naga raids in the 19th century (see Angelova and Tinyi this volume) and by the beginning of the 20th century headhunting had abated amongst the Zeme. However, the subject is still worth dwelling on because of its connection with fame in Naga communities and its entangled relationship with colonial violence. C.A. Soppit, who published the first ethnography of the Zeme in 1885 recorded that: 'in the old days the Kachcha [Zeme] Nagas looked upon no male as worthy of the name of man, unless he had taken at least one head. Any head was sufficient to stamp a warrior, - an old woman's or a child's' (Soppit in Elwin 1969: 442). Headhunting was clearly linked with fame in the past. Raiding and ambushes often resulted in the same radical switch in subjectivity as hunting: from warrior to victim; from person to object. A raid was often met with a counter-raid from another village; again a dangerous encounter in the forest. Guns had radically transformed the last years of headhunting, making conflicts and feuding ever more violent.

Headhunting was still in living memory during Graham-Bower fieldwork due to a resurgence in the generation before. After the Kukis resisted colonial conscription to provide labour in the First World War, the British took the positions of tyrants everywhere: if you are not with us you are against us. Some Zeme communities took this opportunity to avenge old scores against the Kukis caused by land disputes and to take new heads[13]. At least five Zeme men had headhunting trophies in the 1930s (Graham Bower 1952: 41). This colonial-inflected form of headhunting might also have had repercussions for the symbolic value of heads taken as the victim did not appear to have undergone a final transformation from object to friend common throughout Southeast Asia (cf. McKinley 1976).[14] However, this lack of transformation does not seem to have impacted the heads' life-giving or fame-giving potential. Headhunting ornaments were still worn by the

---

terror of his fellow passengers and his own amusement (1952: 86-87).

[13]In 1931 the Kukis had their revenge during an uprising amongst the Zeme and other tribes as this time the Kukis had tacit colonial support.

[14]This is found amongst other Naga communities such as the Konyaks who fed captured heads rice beer (Fürer-Haimendorf 1969)

Zeme elders and stones associated with head-taking played key roles in the winter solstice.

In order to control headhunting the British controlled guns. When Soppit conducted his fieldwork guns were known and used in many Zeme villages (1885). Firearms had a deep history of flowing from the valley states into the hills, which was a cause for concern among the British, who saw firearms as their domain. Colonial resistance only furthered British restrictions[15]. Violence became monopolised which might help explain the role of the European in the dream of *hamui-hera*, superseding the danger of headhunting warriors or tyrannical rajas. The European, gun, and train, are all linked to what Karl Schmit called the ultimate power of sovereignty, a power which underpinned the colonial system: the right to conduct violence with impunity. However, despite this there was a sort of false equivalence the colonial system encouraged between the Naga elite and colonial administrators such as J.H. Hutton and Graham-Bower; many genuine friendships appear to have been created against a backdrop of implied force.

Dreams help to produce and maintain lifeworlds (Opas 2016), and *hamui-hera* reflects the lifeworld of the forest and maintain its logics, albeit in a colonial inflected way. *Hamui-hera* places the great hunter/warrior in a dreamscape where he is forced to confront his own mortality and is oppressed by his fame. This pivot, I argue, is identical to the pivots that shaped the logics of predation: the dangerous moments when an individual has left the village and is at risk of being transformed from predator to prey – a risk all hunters must face. In other words, the sufferer becomes simultaneously more conscious of *powerfulness* and *powerlessness*. The sufferer is also called to action: to undertake an act of subservience and a destruction of some portion of his wealth. And this part is key. While my unpacking of the dream is of course interpretive, the historical record shows sacrifices were made based on this dream. Famous men monopolised the resources of what had become increasingly poor communities, and sacrifices were a chance to lessen spiraling wealth inequality as the poor Zemes became poorer.

THE CREATION OF FAME

After dealing with the symptoms of the hamui-hera in the previous section it is now time to turn to its causes. How was fame acquired in Zeme society in the early 20th century? The previous section dealt with hunting, headhunting, and other forms of warfare, and this section focuses on the creation of fame within the village. This returns us to Graham-Bower's observation on the Zeme's proclivity for exchanging

[15]After Angami uprising of 1879, the Kuki Rebellion of 1917, and Naga revolt of 1931, guns in the highlands were increasingly controlled by the British. Such deep state control became ever easier with trains.

Figure 5. A Zeme man from Assam wearing a *nrupire ntun pai* shawl, 2016.
(Photo by Jelle J. P. Wouters.)

cash for honour - which in this case really means something more like fame. Fame could be acquired through elaborate acts of generosity and displays of verility. Fame was the value of Zeme society, but it came at a cost that was almost unsustainable.

Although Graham-Bower recorded nearly all aspect of Zeme life - even sexual relations and affairs - she rarely recorded what women said or thought. However, she also insisted that women were 'the real rulers of the communities' (1952: 78). Due to her privileged positions of whiteness and colonial service, she was placed amongst male notables and that is where she felt the action was. This obscured the intricacies of the lives of Zeme women from her research, a bias I have unfortunately reproduced here due the marginalised role of women -especially married women- in both the archive and in the public theatricality of fame in Zeme communities. This theatricality was built on women's labour: making shawls, transforming raw to cooked for feasts, and even creating wealth in the first place (cf. Strathern 1998).

Fame for the Zeme had generational divides. Only when a man left being a hangtingmi (householder) and became a katsingmi (village elder) could he display all the trappings of fame and become a true village gerontocrat. This is important as fame was acquired throughout a man's life but only great men, in this case elders, tended to suffer from a hamui-hera. Graham-Bower paints the young men as unburdened by work or responsibility. Much of their time was spent hunting, practicing games, and beautifying themselves by hunting for orchids to wear, or checking their appearance in the village trough. Like most Naga groups the young men had hangseuki (dormitories) more commonly referred to a morungs in other Naga ethnographies.

In the early 20th century, the Zeme were at the peripheries of a colonial market economy that had been transforming the landscape of Northeast India. Colonialism brought with it a tidal wave of radical environmental and social changes such as tea plantations and logging; new markets and goods; roads and railways; and the spread of Christianity. The paradox of a fame taboo amongst the Zeme, is that in the late colonial period nearly all excess wealth and labour was invested in celebrating and creating fame at a time when the Zeme were experiencing serious economic hardships brought on by famines, disease, and the substantial loss of agricultural lands. Furthermore, hamui-hera fueled the consumption of what little wealth there was due to the need for successively bigger sacrifices.

Most Zeme communities were poor in the 1930s. The cycle migrations practiced for decades had been restricted by colonial legislation and Kuki communities settling on once Zeme land (see Arktong 2010: 59-61). Rice was the primary source of wealth for the Zeme and the source of commensality in village life through drinking and feasting. Zeme women not only transformed raw to cooked but they were also tasked with the majority of agricultural labour. State patronage and labouring for neighbouring communities therefore became increasingly important alternatives to agriculture. Animal sacrifices, another key pillar of ritual life, became increasingly difficult. The price of mithun (semi wild bison, Bos Frontalis), the animal of choice for sacrifices, had become ruinous for all but the wealthiest individuals.

The colonial authorities tried to improve the quality of life in Zeme villages through medical programmes, and by persuading the community to adopt wet rice cultivation - one of the first cash for development schemes amongst the Zeme. Like the development schemes that followed it directed the flow of resources into the hands of a few male community representatives - usually the famous men among the Zeme. What wealth could be gained through trade, labour, or colonial patronage, was quickly spent. Wealth was never accumulated for wealth's sake, rather it was spent on feasts, ornaments, and other expressions of fame. Zeme feasts of merit where the most spectacular forms of expenditure. These feasts appear to have been largely uncompetitive when compared with other examples in the anthropological canon, with no accounts of shaming or expectations in return (cf. Boas 1921).

Most feasts of merit were directly linked to aristocratic actions or aspirations. If a man desired to build a large house called kumarumki, kapeoki, or hekuiki, each required successively more elaborate feasts of merit, with the latter two feasts being so expensive that they were rarely, if ever, performed by the early 20th century (Longkumer 2010: 70). Similar feasts were required for monolith raising, pond digging, and a host of other village constructions. Feasts were usually accompanied by the rights to adopt certain adornments or shawls. Where fame is often an intangible form of capital, the case is rarely so in Naga communities. The Zeme were among the most theatrical Naga communities and had an elaborate system of recording famous deeds through visual tallies. Tufts of red fur attached to shields to display how many heads were taken by the owner of the shield, or, another example would be carved rice beer mugs, each shaped differently depending on feasts given. Even sexual conquests were tallied in this way.

Who is sleeping with whom tends to be a universal societal interest, at the very least in the domains of gossip and rumour. However very few societies are interested in making such sexual conquests visible and legible. Even rarer is the desire to monumentalise an individual's lists of conquests in formal and excessive ways. And yet the Zeme did just this. When a man became an elder (katsingmi) he could reveal his conquests and begin to celebrate them in a theatrical way. Younger men (rahangmi) were set up for seduction. They were excused most agricultural labour, given good clothes by their parents, and their days focused on drinking, gossiping, making baskets, playing music, bathing and grooming, so as to attract the girls returning from the fields. Young men cultivate fame; women cultivate.

The symbolic links between sex and eating is found throughout anthropology and Zeme male elders had privileges in both domains. When certain types of sex, such as sex as conquest, are conflated with eating, sex fails to seem reciprocal as 'eating is an inherently one-sided relation' (Graeber 2007: 19 discussing Levi-Strauss 1966). And I think this is a useful way of thinking about sexual conquests and fame amongst the Zeme-who is doing eating, and who is being eaten. Becoming an elder opened up a whole set of privileges regarding the consumptions of tabooed foods: tigers, wild dogs, hornbills and monkeys;[16] an elder also gained the privilege to display what he has consumed sexually. The more difficult the conquests, the more fame it would create and the more theatrically a man could celebrate his conquests. Examples of fame generating conquests are as follows: if the man had conducted a simultaneous affair with a mother and her daughter (without either knowing); an affair with two sisters (without either knowing); or deflowered two or more virgins. This insistence on secrecy and tabooed conquests are premised on the man's perspective of an inherently two-person act.

The semiotics of sexual conquest filled Zeme public life: headdress, ornaments, clothes, and monuments, were awarded to great lovers. Assemblages of stones were erected in Zeme villages called *herem-leo*, each stone representing a conquest.[17] These

---

[16]The reasons why the above animals were tabooed is they had some essence in form, substance or soul that could affect the eater. Most of the tabooed animals were precisely the types of megafauna that were seen as possessing varying degrees of personhood.

[17]Graham-Bower recorded a fine example in Hajaichak and years later Christopher Furer-Haimendorf filmed a memorial in Laisong. The Pitt Rivers Museum in Oxford contains numerous examples of artefacts drawn from Tenemia celebrating individuals who colonial ethnographers deemed casanovas (Mills 1937b). These radically different sexual codes fascinated colonial ethnographers whose own mores were rooted in British Protestantism. Furthermore such sexual practices presented a strong contrasts to the

sites are so numerous that it is possible all Zeme villages had some type of memorial celebrating seduction. The example from Hajaichak documented by Graham-Bower featured thirty-six individual stones each equating a woman -all-the-more impressive considering the small size of Zeme villages.[18] Add these memorials to the trophies from hunting, headhunting, feast-giving, megalith raising, and pond digging, and the picture emerges of a society thick with fame.

Sexual fame was taken so seriously that cultural measures were created to foil cheats. The *heleomi gi kalang* was a cotton thread a Zeme girl gave her lover to prove the act took place (Longkumer 2010: 226). Sexual conquests were so highly competitive that rules and proof was required to differentiate the boasters from the genuine lotharios.[19] The gift of a cotton thread mirrors hunting rituals, and the python and tiger trophies discussed before. Successful hunters and lovers became famous by displaying their ability to transform persons into objects by drawing others to them and demonstrating their powers of chase, pursuit and virility. Artefacts made achievements visible and helped enforce the social logics of a gerontocratic society, the old men's political dominance was mirrored by their material culture. This material culture can roughly be divided into two forms: those that celebrated the transfer of essences and ability to best other selves (sex, hunting, war) and those that marked the ability to command labour (houses, ponds, megaliths, shawls, ornaments).

Alongside sex, game-like rituals offered chances for merit and kept the young men of the village entertained. These competitions were tied to the ritual calendar of solstices, harvests, and other yearly occurrences. And, much like sexual conquest, these games provided relatively egalitarian access to social capital - although doubtlessly the rich would have more time to perfect play and seduction. Being an able-bodied man was the only prerequisite to partake in these games. At hgangi, the festival at the winter solstice, young men took turns jumping off the hazoa, a sacred

---

communities in the plains adjacent to the Naga Hills. While the scholarly lacuna on Naga sexuality could be placed at the door of missionaries, and the subsequent Christianisation of Nagaland, the colonial ethnographers Hutton and J. P. Mills were interested in Naga sexuality. Nevertheless, they still failed to produce anything close to Malinowski's The Sexual Lives of Savages (2006) or Verrier Elwin's excessive descriptions of Bagia procreation (1939).

[18]Similar constructions exist amongst some, but certainly not all, Angami villages in the same period (Hutton 1921: 151, 162)

[19]The Rengma Naga employed a considerably more confrontational strategy to the same effect. The man with wounded pride would approach the woman who denied their moment of intimacy and say "Iza rhamkho" which translate as 'eat my private parts'. This had the implicit challenge to the woman to swear an oath regarding the nature of their romance (Mills 1937a). Rape was also one of the three capital crimes in Zeme society (Graham-Bower 1952: 107).

stone at the centre of the village under which headhunting trophies were buried. Structurally there are some basic shared facets to all Zeme games: they were highly theatrical; were conducted at the centre of the village, and had male and female audiences. The winner of the hazoa competition was the man who jumped the furthest, each competitor stretching-out their legs to land at the greatest distance. Power, speed and agility were needed, mirroring the attributes of warriors. The reward? An immediate surrendering by the winner of his clothing to the surrounding crowd - merit in exchange for wealth. Ritualised chases of pigs and mithuns brought forward similar rewards. Winners would be quickly 'de-kilted, by any elder present, on the grounds that "anyone so gifted by nature can spare ornaments for those less gifted"' (Graham-Bower 1952: 95) - a good line indeed, but tellingly, it is the elder who takes from the young and thereby maintains the gerontocratic position of dominance. A python visiting a man's house of its own choosing was another blessing that required the blessed to give back to the village (see Soppit on pork feasts 1885). The formulation honour exchanged for wealth is yet again demonstrated.

The ritual that mirrored humui-hera most closely also contained the same shift in subjectivities discussed in the previous discussion on perspectivism. Mpe-kap-pe-ngi was the wood-striking-ritual of the Zeme at the winter solstice. The material here is drawn from Graham-Bowers writings in the 1940s, although I have been fortunate enough to witness a similar festival in 2016. The ritual began as follows. Young men go into the forest and cut down a tingsap ching (king tree) which is to have the central symbolic sacrificial role. Like many sacrificial victims, the tree must have no defects, in this case knots or holes in the wood. Once transformed from tree to timber, it is placed in a fenced enclosure to protect against wandering mithun, dogs, and chickens – the polluting touch of animals. Even rain can defile it and make it unusable. The mpe is then transformed into a person with alternating patterns representing teeth, eyes, hearts, and a shawl. More villagers join the ritual as the mpe temporarily becomes the prominent person in the village - literally standing taller than all other persons, beautified with flowers and banana leaves.

Once the mpe is erected it becomes subject to taboos around purity, again highlighting its importance. A period of avoidance is enacted in the village and men and women separate; the sexes eating together is taboo, so was sex. But the mpe's good fortune cannot last. Just like the python, its adulation foreshadows its demise. The men of the village gather, sing the chants associated with headhunting, and throw reed darts into the mpe bringing about its destruction. The darts are both literally destructive, going into the flesh of the mpe and also an act of sympathetic magic transferring sin away from the throwers. If enough darts stuck, it was a sign of good fortune. Unblemished pigs are sacrificed, eaten, and the village sleeps. If the villagers have bad dreams the process is repeated until satisfactory. Dreaming well was the acid test of the success of any ritual.

The normal cure for bad dreams was to have a bath and cut off locks of hair, as though the essence of the dream was attached to the sufferer. However, the essence of fame was harder to expedite. Fame lies with society and it needed a different resolution: a sacrifice and its related feast. In a society where every aristocratic material ambition needed a license from either a colonial administrator or society then it is perhaps unsurprising fame needed to be licensed in a similar way. Famous men need a sort of societal consensus to wear the best shawls; erect the best monuments; eat the best food; drink the most rice beer; and boast about their successes in hunting, war, and love. All this came at a cost. Society demanded that this good fortune was shared through a myriad of cultural mechanism with hamui-hera being the most unusual mechanism.

RESOLUTION

It is difficult to read and write about *hamui-hera* without thinking of contemporary wealth inequality in Northeast India. During fieldwork in Assam, Nagaland, and Meghalaya (2012-17), I often heard the lament that local leaders "no longer care about us", or that wealth was being hoarded at the top of society. I imagine such complaints are familiar to most readers. Inequality of this nature has become a global problem and recent studies such as Thomas Piketty's *Capital in the Twenty-First Century* (2014) and David Graeber's *Debt: The First 5000 Years* (2014) have helped uncover inequality's historical roots. I believe the reason to study *hamui-hera*, and anthropology more generally, is because it reveals the possibility of other forms of social, economic, and political life, and how other societies addressed issues like inequality. Zeme society in the early 20th century was structured such a way that very few men could meet the conditions needed to be both wealthy and famous. Such questions of how best to constrain and confront the powerful have been foundational to anthropology as discipline and indeed writing more broadly.

The first work of literature, the Mesopotamian epic of Gilgamesh, opens with the question of how the King of Uruk, Gilgamesh, should be constrained. Born of a goddess, Aruru, Gilgamesh is richer, stronger, and more powerful than any other man. But he has abused his gifts; like a wild bull he tramples his citizens, crushing them until they could take no more. The citizens cry out to the gods, who, in response, make a mirror image of Gilgamesh, the wild man Enkidu. Although Enkidu fails to defeat Gilgamesh, the confrontation was sufficient to launch Gilgamesh on another path -his quest for fame- and deliver the citizens of Uruk from their oppression. While the Zeme spirits could not create mythic doubles for each famous Zeme man, they did place such doubles in their dreams: the tiger, European, and the symbols of colonialism. Encountering dreaming as a radical and non-violent power in society, capable of confronting the rich and encouraging exchange, is what makes *hamui-hera* worth studying; it present one answer to common questions posed by humanity: how do we confront each other better?

One of the foundational books in anthropology Mauss' The Gift (2016), is a kaleidoscopic look at humanity and how acts of exchange facilitate confrontations and negotiations of power between people. The book helped make the concepts of kula, hau, and potlatch canonical to anthropology. Less well known are Mauss' attempts to extend the logics of Americas and Melanesia to India, such as his expositions on Brahmin gifting and his interpretation of the Mahabharata as a gigantic potlatch hidden beneath its theological and literary forms. Mauss also thought that ancient India was 'doubly the land' of potlatches (ibid. 159), being found in both Hindu gifts and in the tribal communities of Assam and tribal communities of Munda origins[20]. By Assam Mauss meant Naga for the most part. Mauss even reviewed W.H. Furness' erratic overview of Ao, Miris (Mishing), Semas, for the journal L'Année sociologique. And although Naga culture is a passing reference in the text, it shared many of the forms of exchange Mauss discussed, principally aristocratic gifts and feasts of merits.

The Gift was written in the aftermath of the First World War, a catastrophic tragedy that claimed the lives of many of Mauss' students and colleagues. Northeast India was pulled into the vortex through the Naga Labour Core and Kuki Uprising. Despite all the suffering Mauss had witnessed he still maintained the hope that man was perfectible, and that anthropology and sociology could provide vital inspiration. Mauss wanted his peers in Europe to contemplate the possibilities of different forms of social organization and learn to 'confront one and other with massacring each other, and to give to each other without sacrificing themselves to the other' (2016: 197).

I think Mauss would have been fascinated by hamui-hera. The spirt of the gift Mauss re-traduction of the Maori "hau", the force that returns to initial bearer, was in all forms of fame for the Zeme. The preferred form of reciprocity in village life was the aristocratic feast, which is the resolution of hamui-hera which melded together the economic, religious, political, and oneiric, life of the village. One of things missing in The Gift, which subsequent authors have importantly highlighted, was how colonially inflected many of exchanges practices carried out by indigenous communities had become. The potlatches Kwakwaka'wakw when Franz Boaz recorded them not only distributed blankets and baskets but Singer sewing machines; one of Bronislaw Malinowski's later regrets about his book the Argonauts of the Western Pacific was his erasure of the kula's colonial context in his monograph.

The colonial context of hamui-hera, as I hopefully demonstrated, is vital to understanding it. Feasts of this kind, and the deliberate consumption of huge amounts of wealth as opposed to monetarized accumulation, appear time and again amongst societies living at the edges of bureaucratic market economies (Graeber

---

[20]Mauss viewed these communities as remnants of once much larger populations in keeping with theories of Aryan conquest that were popular at the time.

2013). For example, there are intriguing parallels amongst the grand dream-guessing festivals of Iroquois and their relation to the colonial market economy in North America (see Graeber 2011: 151-58) It is in part the continual refusal of many of the cultural values of the bureaucratic market economies that bordered the Zeme – the Kachari kingdom, the Manipuri kingdom, and British colonialism- that helped shaped Zeme culture. While their cultural forms could be refused, their power and demands for suzerainty often became unavoidable.

> If a man falls ill and suspects it is due to "hamui", he takes a piece of ginger, puts spittle on it and throws it outside the house last thing at nighttime after addressing the spirit responsible and promising to perform the right ceremony if cured, but assuring the spirit that he will not offer anything if he does not get better he will not offer anything if he does not get better. If his dreams are bad that night he repeats the throwing the following night.

Out of all the people who could be struck with *hamui-hera*, *dobashis* (colonial liaisons) and *gaonburas* (village heads) were the most vulnerable. These men had the best of everything their communities had to offer: honour, sex, wealth, ornaments, food, rice beer, and hundreds of other privileges big and small; they were also responsible for their communities in the eyes of the colonial state and were expected to ensure British edicts were carried out, just as the previous generation of *gaonburas* and headman help similar positions for the rajas of Kachar and Manipur and, on occasion, the Angami Nagas (Aphun 2008: 81-85).

When the British came looking for taxes, porters, labourers, or soldiers, *dobashis* and *gaonburas* were the men they came to extract resources from communities and to create new treaties and agreements. Naga headman became entwined with the colonial state to help facilitate labour (Dzuvichu 2014). If they proved cooperative, they were gifted shawls, money, development contracts, and further administrative roles in the colonial state. Once their positions of power were recognised by the British, local elites' roles were quickly solidified by a colonial system that prized stability above all else. The refusal of such gifts and boons was both dangerous and unwise, especially as some other rival in the locality might come forward as willing alternative for colonial patronage.

The very reasons *hamui-hera* entered Graham-Bowers research is that her assistants, the men most willing to work with the colonial authorities, suffered from this condition. This is an important point: hierarchy in most Zeme villages was fixed by powers outside the village. Violence against headmen who abused their position was barely an option considering their colonial protection. The growth of capitalism and the colonial market threaten to distort village hierarchies further. Instead the best way to limit inequality was through ritualised confrontations such as *hamui-hera*. And who carries out the confrontation? The dream analysts: kith and kin – and the spirits.

END NOTE

Hamui-hera depended on the spirts, after all, they were the ones who received the sacrifice. But the spirits days were numbered. By the time Graham-Bowers conducted her fieldwork Christianity and Heraka (the seeds of which had been sowed Haipou Jadonang and Rani Gaidinliu) had led many Zeme villages to embrace new forms of religious practice and abandoned the older traditions. This process hastened after the Second World War. Now the village of Laisong, which was for a long time Graham-Bower's fieldwork base is divided between into colonies based on faiths: Heraka Presbyterian, Catholic, Baptist. The last few Paupaise communities have had to find new spaces for their rituals and beliefs. When communities started moving away from worshipping the spirits much of the culture around fame and *hamui-hera* was abandoned.

Perspectivism experienced an equally sharp decline. Megafauna became virtually extinct in Zeme lands due to overhunting and deforestation, which has lessened the power of pythons and tigers to affect the imagination and the subconscious. New religious practices brought other ways of thinking with animals; Heraka increasingly framed human animal relations through Vashnavite traditions of non-violence and vegetarianism; Christianity offered a radically different lexicon of animals: lions, sheep, and donkeys, to think with through the Bible. Arkotong Longkumer has argued that it was partly the burden of these sacrifices and taboos that led many villages to abandoned them (2010). The dominant cosmologies have now become those of world religions and this has changed dreaming. However many of the other old oneiric symbols still remain -as they do in other Naga communities (Heneise 2016).

Both Christianity and Heraka forbade animal sacrifices, albeit for radically different reasons. Both also strove to curtailed the excessive consumption of rice beer that marked Zeme feasts, with Christianity, unsurprisingly, being far stricter. Sex became equally problematic. The sexual competitions that brought fame for Zeme elders, the prestige of sleeping with a mother and her daughter, was replaced by the valourisation of chastity and marriage. Shawls and ornamentation linked to status have been maintained, although their forms have changed due to material and restrictions have been loosened. The importance of women's labour in celebrating feasts and making shawls has remained a constant.

Although many cultural forms unique to the Zeme in the 1920s have been lost, many changes have been for the better. Colonialism has been replaced by participation in the world's largest democracy and voting has become a new way to challenge the powerful and redefine social order. Such democratic practices have transformed the Naga tradition of feast giving, a good example of how cultural forms adapt (see Wouters 2015). The effects of capitalism are more ambiguous, as it would be hard to deny that financial inequality has not grown in Assam and across Naga communities. And it remains difficult to see how such inequalities will resolve themselves in the coming decades. The question is perhaps now turned to us: how do we confront the rich, powerful, and famous better, when the spirits no longer control their dreams? That is the challenge set by *hamui-hera*.

▪ ▪▪ ▪▪

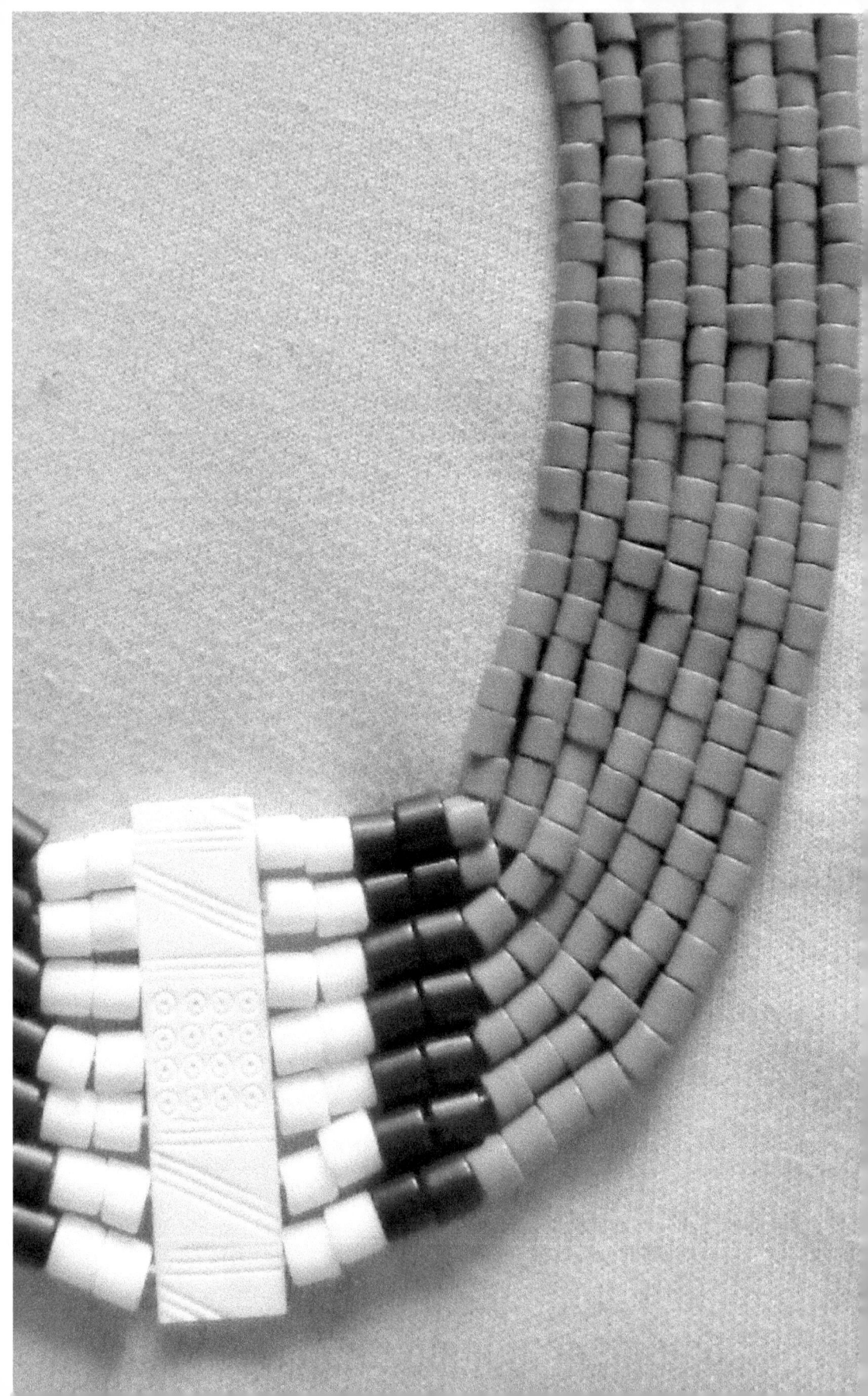

04

COLONIAL RULE, CHRISTIANITY AND SOCIO-CULTURAL (DIS)CONTINUITIES AMONG THE SUMI NAGA

Iliyana Angelova

> It is curious that the large and important Sema tribe [...] should have attracted so little attention during the early [colonial] period.

— Elwin 1969: 371

This acute observation with which Verrier Elwin starts his introduction to his short entry on 'The Sema Nagas'[1] in his edited volume *The Nagas in the nineteenth century* (1969) poignantly indicates the general scarcity of written accounts (both

---

[1] A note on nomenclature: the ethnonym 'Sema' was codified in colonial writing and was in widespread use until recently, when it was replaced by the ethnonym 'Sumi' as an indigenous term by which the 'Sema' denoted themselves. In reality, both ethnonyms are currently used interchangeably, but since 'Sumi' is considered the more politically correct one, I will retain it throughout this chapter. Necessarily, any discussion of earlier written sources on the 'Sema' will be used without correction.

in the colonial and post-colonial period) on one of the most numerous and geographically dispersed Naga 'tribes'.[2] The diverse peoples inhabiting the Indo-Burma borderlands came to be known as 'Naga'[3] in the early nineteenth century when the first British military officers-cum-administrators, surveyors, topographers and explorers surveyed the area for its geostrategic location between the newly discovered tea gardens in Assam to the north, the Kingdom of Manipur to the south and Burma to the east. Soon after that, the first accounts of the 'exotic' Naga customs, political and social organization, religion and languages started appearing in the form of field diaries, reports, memoirs and articles that seem to have generated significant interest among readers in Britain and the wider world (cf. Butler 1855, Peal 1874, Johnstone 1896). While 1832 is considered the official year of first colonial contact between the British and the Naga, it took the British several decades to start consolidating their rule in the Naga areas. In 1878 they established their headquarters in Kohima (Angami Naga area) with a sub-division in Wokha (Lotha Naga area), and the separate Naga Hills District within the British Province of Assam was established in 1881. In 1888 another sub-division was established in Mokokchung (Ao Naga area) (Elwin 1961: 24). Within these administrative arrangements, the growing number of Sumi villages that fell under the administrative and political control of the British in the ensuing decades were divided between the Kohima division and the Mokokchung division. As the effective border of the Naga Hills District kept moving further east and ultimately came to be designated at the Tizu River, by 1906 all Sumi villages on the western bank of the river came under direct British administration whereas all Sumi villages on the eastern bank of the river remained within the so-called 'unadministered Naga areas' until 1947 (Sema 1992: 22-6).

It is clear that the presence of the British Raj and its administrative and military structures in the Naga-inhabited areas has had a profound impact on

[2]Whereas the term 'tribe' has been largely discarded in anthropology in favour of 'ethnic group' in an attempt to overcome the Eurocentric bias implied in it, its use in India is distinctive because it is a legal category of the Indian Constitution (Scheduled Tribes). The members of the social groups that are recognised in this way, such as the Naga, are entitled to certain privileges (government jobs, university places, political representation) within the system of positive discrimination offered by the reservations policy. Inasmuch as the Naga themselves subscribe to the term 'tribe', it will be retained throughout the present chapter without further qualification, while recognizing the ethnographically contingent status of its use anywhere, including in India.

[3]'Naga' is a generic ethnonym of foreign origin, which is used to denote a number of tribal groups in Northeast India and Northwest Burma, which share discernible cultural and linguistic affinity. Prior to being designated as 'Naga' in the years of initial contact with the British, these people usually referred to themselves by the names of their respective villages.

changing worldviews, modes of life and customs among the Naga, even if some of their lands might have remained outside the scope of direct political control. The British introduced a number of innovations which had multiple implications for the political, economic and socio-cultural life of the Naga. In political terms, the British introduced new forms of political organisation in the offices of *gaonbura*[4] and *dobashi*,[5] which transformed power relations and the construction of authority in Naga villages. Another political innovation was the establishment of courts of law as a supreme judicial authority, which started settling disputes habitually settled by the village councils (Ao), the village chiefs (Sumi) or the whole community (Angami). In economic terms, the British introduced a money economy, which gradually substituted the local barter economy and had serious implications for the transformation of economic relations and modes of accumulating wealth. Another major impact of British colonial rule over the Naga was the prohibition of the religious and cultural practice of headhunting,[6] which was widespread among all Naga tribes as an institutionalised way of achieving social status and prestige based on one's ability to kill 'enemies'.[7] With the strict enforcement of the ban on headhunting among the administered Naga tribes, trade and other relations between Naga villages thrived as it became safer to travel, and stronger alliances were formed. However, the prohibition of headhunting had crucial implications for the socio-cultural and religious practices of the Naga: the role of the boys' dormitory (or *morung*) as a focal point of community life gradually diminished, numerous symbolic artistic forms related to headhunting fell into a gradual decline (e.g. woodcarvings, house decorations, ceremonial dress and ornamentation, body tattoos etc.), and the ceremonies, feasts and customs associated with headhunting were gradually neglected, to varying degrees.

It should be noted, however, that such socio-cultural transformations do not appear to have been the explicit agenda of successive British administrators in the Naga Hills as they were more often than not genuinely interested in Naga cultural practices, which they described in a number of papers and reports. Necessarily, and in line with the prevalent spirit of the day, the information provided in these early accounts was often marked by what would now be considered a patronizing attitude characteristic of the Victorian era and its mission to 'civilise' the various tribes encountered by the British in India.

---

[4]*Gaonbura* - a village headman appointed by the British.

[5]*Dobashi* - an Assamese-speaking Naga who acted as an interpreter and intermediary between the British government and Naga villages.

[6]Headhunting was premised on the notion that bringing the head of a killed enemy to one's village would bring prosperity to the whole community in the form of many children, abundant crops and numerous cattle (cf. Hutton 1965, Mills 1926).

[7]This category was loosely defined and shifted on a regular basis as villages formed and broke alliances.

Nonetheless, British administrators appear to have been sympathetic outsiders in positions of power who introduced a number of protective policies in the Naga Hills.[8] These policies, even if not entirely altruistic but driven by broader political interests, undoubtedly motivated by the geostrategic position of the region, enabled the Naga to preserve control over their lands and customary practices in times when large sections of the tribal population of Central India were being deprived of their ancestral lands and subjected to great exploitation in huge land alienation scams, as described most eloquently by Fürer-Haimendorf (1982) and Padel (1995), among others.

While 'civilising' the Naga was certainly an important aspect of British colonial policy in Northeast India, arguably the biggest agent of socio-cultural change were the American Baptist missionaries who established their first permanent mission stations in the lands of the Naga in the 1870s, and initiated the process of Naga conversions to Baptist Christianity. As conversion rates gradually increased in the following decades and the Naga began to articulate and experience their identities in Baptist Christian terms, many aspects of 'traditional'[9] Naga culture started losing their prominence and symbolic value. At the same time, the forceful incorporation of the lands of the Naga into the Indian Union in 1947 and the subsequent decades of Naga armed struggle for their right to self-determination and independence have certainly left an indelible mark on the experiences and identity constructions of generations of Naga.

One often hears the argument that the Naga were drawn too quickly into the vortex of world affairs and Western modernity by the collective operation of all these power actors, and that they have lost much of their cultural heritage in the process. Drawing on extensive periods of ethnographic fieldwork in Nagaland and archival work carried out at the Pitt Rivers Museum (University of Oxford), the Nagaland State Archive in Kohima (Nagaland) and the mission centre of the Council of Baptist Churches of Northeast India (CBCNEI) in Guwahati (Assam),[10]

[8]The most prominent ones among these were the 1873 Bengal Eastern Frontier Regulation (the Inner Line Regulation) and the 1880 Frontier Tracts Regulation II, which broadly guaranteed that the Naga areas would be administered differently from the rest of British India, and that Naga land ownership and customary practices would be protected against outside influences.

[9]The terms 'traditional' and 'tradition' have been used throughout this chapter to denote the pre-Christian (Sumi) Naga religion and culture with the clear understanding that precepts, customs and ritual practices change over time and are always in a process of creatively making, re-making and influencing each other. With this necessary qualification, the terms will be used without quotation marks hereafter.

[10]In addition to the ecclesiastical archive of the CBCNEI, I also consulted the online editions (1873-1909) of the *Baptist Missionary Magazine* published by the American Baptist Missionary Union and accessed via the Oxford University Library Services. However,

the present chapter will present a contextual analysis of some of the major transformations and (dis)continuities that Sumi society has experienced since the beginning of the twentieth century, and especially as a result of Baptist mission work among them. The chapter will start by reviewing the available knowledge about this 'large and important' tribe, to borrow Elwin's words above, in the early colonial encounter. It will then proceed with a discussion of the dynamics of conversion among the Sumi and the several mass movements that are recorded to have occurred within this community. The chapter will then offer some general highlights on the contemporary significance of Baptist Christianity to Sumi self-ascriptions and identity constructions, and discuss how this is inter-related with ongoing grassroots projects of reviving and preserving some 'good' aspects of Sumi cultural heritage that have been demonized in the course of earlier conversions. In order to weave all these aspects together, this chapter will seek to demonstrate that while Christian conversions have indeed effected a number of changes and discontinuities in the socio-cultural traditions of the Sumi, much more has remained as a substratum of cultural reproduction than conventionally acknowledged even by the Sumi themselves. As a result, I suggest that it is analytically more fruitful to view Christianity not merely as an external agent of change, but as an intrinsic part of contemporary Sumi identity, an indigenous form of religious expression and meaning-making, which is being firmly embedded in Sumi socio-cultural tradition and history.

EARLY COLONIAL ACCOUNTS ON THE SUMI

As Elwin rightly observes, written accounts from the colonial period dedicated specifically to the Sumi are scarce. They feature briefly (as 'Sehmah') in the second lecture given by Colonel R.G. Woodthorpe to the Royal Anthropological Institute and published in its Journal in 1882 as 'non-kilted Naga' (along with the Ao, Lotha and Rengma Naga). Woodthorpe was typically interested in physical appearance, matters of personal hygiene (or perceived lack thereof), village layout and fortifications, the ritual treatment and disposal of enemies' heads etc. His account is understandably generic and often describing a vague 'Naga' category. There is also some brief mention of the Sumi in Robinson (1841) and in Mackenzie

---

despite the availability of a wealth of information on missionary strategies for converting the Naga, general reflections on and experiences of missionary work in the Naga Hills and personal correspondence, not much information on the Sumi was contained in these resources, undoubtedly due to the later beginning of American missionary work among them. It is acknowledged that a future research project will benefit immensely from an extended stay at the archives of the American Baptist Historical Society in Atlanta, Georgia (USA) where more relevant information on the Sumi is bound to be found.

(1884); the latter reproduces a paper written by Captain John Butler in 1873 in which there is the following short text on the Sumi: 'North and north-east of the Angami we come upon the "Sehmah Nagas", regarding whom we at present know very little beyond the fact that they possess five villages on the left bank of the Doyeng, and probably extend across to the other bank as well' (Mackenzie 1884: 85). This indicates that in the first few decades of the colonial encounter the British knew very little about the Sumi. Despite these sporadic contacts, however, the Sumi are listed as one of the 'four races' inhabiting the Naga Hills District of Assam, alongside the Angami, Lotha and Rengma Naga in the 1881 Assam Census Report (Mackenzie 1884: 549).

The 1891 Census of India, compiled by A.W. Davis, then Deputy Commissioner of the Naga Hills (1891: 246-8) and reproduced in full by Verrier Elwin in his *The Nagas in the nineteenth century* (1969: 372-6), provides the most comprehensive information available at the time about the Sumi under the rubric of 'The Sema Nagas'. The report starts by explaining that only nine Sumi villages are reported to be within the administrative control of the British, with seventy villages (or more, as the data is not conclusive) lying beyond the administrative boundary. It then details information on geographic location, physical appearance and dress, hereditary chiefs, village site, marriage customs, funerary customs, origin of the tribe, religion, village customs and general remarks. These sections are of varying lengths ranging from two-three short sentences to longer paragraphs of ten-fifteen sentences or more. Davis starts by noting that the people in question called themselves 'Simi', but were known to the British 'by their Angami name of Sema' (Davis 1891: 246). It is noteworthy that throughout their rule in the Naga lands the British have chosen to retain this foreign ethnonym when interacting with or writing about the Sumi instead of using indigenous names such as 'Simi' or 'Sumi'. I hold this to be an indication of the general lack of familiarity and close contact with this tribe in addition to parochial colonial attitudes. Davis then proceeds with his description of which I will only present certain highlights here. He notes that the Sumi differed from all other known Naga tribes in that their villages were governed by hereditary chiefs who had numerous wives. He also observes a particular type of migration and village settlement among the Sumi whereby the elder sons of village chiefs left their ancestral villages in order to establish villages of their own. Thus, Davis concludes, 'Sema villages are small as compared with the villages of the other Naga tribes' (1891: 246). He also points out the particular Sumi custom of disposing of the dead by burying them just outside the house. He closes this census entry by noting: 'The Semas are the most barbarous and savage tribes with which we have yet come into contact in these hills' (1891: 248).

While these early descriptive accounts on the Sumi offer some important, albeit rudimentary, information about their culture, religion and lifestyles, they are necessarily fragmentary in scope and patronising in tone. Moreover, the information provided in them should be treated with caution, as Elwin warns us, because they contain a lot of factual errors and misunderstandings of custom and were sometimes 'heavily marked by personal bias', some being no more than 'obviously guess-work' (Elwin 1959: xv). Moreover, they were general accounts which lacked ethnographic detail and often confused the names of villages and tribes or simply used the generic 'Naga',[11] which makes it difficult to determine which Naga tribe they were discussing.

This tradition of British colonial writing changed in the early twentieth century with the publication of a series of ethnographically rich classical monographs on the Naga written by erstwhile colonial administrators of the Naga Hills. These include *The Sema Nagas* (1921b) and *The Angami Nagas* (1921a) by John H. Hutton, and *The Lhota Nagas* (1922), *The Ao Nagas* (1926) and *The Rengma Nagas* (1937) by James P. Mills. *The Sema Nagas* remains the most comprehensive and authoritative account of Sumi customs, culture and religion to date. It follows the conventional structure of all classical monographs from this period, namely general notes on habitat, cultural affinities, origins, appearance etc.; domestic life, including village site, house layouts, art, livelihoods etc.; social life, including social organisation, marriage rules, property, dispute settlement etc.; religion; language, and folklore. The monograph confirms the validity of some of the information about the Sumi that is found in the 1891 Census of India entry, especially in relation to inheritance, settlement patterns and village sites and layout. In addition, Hutton provides a wealth of comparative material that I found useful in my own work – e.g. naming rules, ritual celebrations of traditional festivals, marriage and funerary rites etc. Prior to writing this monograph, Hutton toured the Sema country extensively in his capacity of Deputy Commissioner of the Naga Hills stationed in Kohima. His field diaries from this period provide very rich information about the way of life of the Sumi, their material culture, religion and customs as well as a chronology of the inter-village disputes (incl. some disputes between administered and trans-frontier Sumi villages) that Hutton had settled and the various judgements he had passed. The diaries also contain rich photographic material on various aspects of Sumi material culture, e.g. textiles, grave decorations, house decorations, Y-shaped wooden posts commemorating feasts given by men of prominence to the whole village (described in the anthropological literature as 'feasts of merit') as well as many personal photographs of village chiefs and other dignitaries in full formal attire.

Despite its undoubtedly great ethnographic value, Hutton's monograph and tour diaries about the Sumi should of course be treated critically as historical documents representing the perspective of a sympathetic outsider writing from

---

[11]Elwin warns that the indiscriminate use of the term 'Naga' to denote a hillsman or a tribesman has caused much confusion, especially since the people whom the early authors called 'Naga' are not always classified as such nowadays (Elwin 1959: xxxii). And, as already mentioned, they did not ascribe to the term themselves in the years of initial contact with the British.

a position of power. Maybe inadvertently, The Sema Nagas helped create and reinforce an image of Sumi tradition based on Hutton's conception of what it meant to be a Sumi by accentuating some cultural features and neglecting others. In line with the prevailing ethos of the colonial ethnographic tradition, his writing also idealised an imagined 'golden past' and promoted the image of the Sumi as a 'noble savage' whose 'authentic' culture was threatened with impending extinction in its sustained contact with Western modernity. Despite some well-justified criticisms of his approaches and conclusions as well as his choice of often derogatory descriptive terms, however, Hutton remains very well-respected within the Sumi community.[12]

BAPTIST CHRISTIANITY AMONG THE SUMI

The first foreign missionaries arrived in the Province of Assam in 1835, inspired by the missionary zeal of the Second Great Awakening in America and at the invitation of Captain Jenkins, then Commissioner for Assam (*Baptist Missionary Magazine* Jun 1901: 207). These were American Baptist missionaries belonging to the erstwhile American Baptist Missionary Union.[13] From the American missionaries' point of view, the Assam mission was to serve as a strategic outpost to aid in reaching the Shan of northern Burma and southern China, but that project was never carried out (Downs 1992: 70). Instead, from their mission stations in Assam the American missionaries came into contact with Naga tribes inhabiting the hills surrounding the Brahmaputra valley, and it was the Naga conversion story that would become one of the greatest successes of American Baptist missionary activity overseas.

The first permanent mission stations with resident American missionaries on Naga soil were established in the Ao area in the 1870s and in the Lotha and Angami areas in the 1880s (cf. Downs 1992: 82). Soon after that the first two mission schools were opened at Impur (Ao area) and Kohima (Angami area). By contrast, because of funding problems and their remoter geographical location in

---

[12]For a contemporary critique of J.H. Hutton and his legacy among the Sumi, see Chophy (2015). For a critique of Hutton's practice of collecting Naga artefacts, see Ngully (2015).

[13]The Union was established at the beginning of the nineteenth century under the name of the General Missionary Convention of the Baptist Denomination in the United States for Foreign Missions. In 1845, as a result of the Civil War and the growing dissension within the Convention on slavery-related issues, the Southern Baptists split away to form the Southern Baptist Convention. Baptists in the North restructured their programme as the American Baptist Missionary Union. In 1910 it was renamed the American Baptist Foreign Mission Society (ABFMS), and since 1973 it has been operating under the name of the American Baptist Board of International Ministries (Brackney 1990).

the interior of the Naga Hills, the Sumi did not have a resident American missionary until the late 1940s. The absence of American missionaries, however, did not hamper conversion work among the Sumi: initially, they received the Gospel from itinerant Ao evangelists from the north and itinerant Angami evangelists from the south. Students and teachers from the mission school at Impur, for example, are reported to have undertaken regular evangelising trips during vacations and at weekends to different Sumi villages, where they sang, preached and gave 'an example of the Christian life', which might have influenced some Sumi families to send their children to school (Ao 2002: 36). In this way, Sumi boys started joining the mission schools in Impur and Kohima and, having completed their studies there and returned to their home villages, they became the first Sumi school teachers and evangelists.

The official birth year of Christianity among the Sumi is held to be 1904 when Ghopuna and Ghosuna, *gaonburas* of Ighanumi village, were baptised by Revd Rivenburg in Kohima. In 1906 Revd Dickson became the first American missionary to be given official licence to work among the Sumi, and he briefly toured some of the Southern Sumi villages from Kohima before his return to America in 1908. He was succeeded in the duty to preach among the Sumi by Revd Bailey and Revd Longwell in Impur and Revd Tanquist in Kohima. In November 1928, the ABFMS passed a formal resolution to open a new mission field for work specifically among the Sumi, but it could not designate any funds to sponsor it, and no work actually commenced (Anderson 1978: 29). Finally, in 1936 Revd Anderson was assigned to supervise mission work among the Sumi and was placed in charge of building a Sumi mission centre at Aizuto in Zunheboto District, the traditional headquarters of the Sumi. Although Revd Anderson resided at the new mission centre briefly from 1949 to 1950, the first permanently resident American missionary for the Sumi was Revd Delano, who served in the newly established Aizuto mission station from 1949 to 1955; his family was also the last American missionary family to leave the Naga Hills when the Indian government expelled all foreign missionaries from the turbulent Naga areas.[14]

Many evangelists from different Naga tribes are acknowledged to have made an invaluable contribution to early conversion work among the Sumi (cf. *NBCC Platinum Jubilee Souvenir* 2012 and Anderson 1978: 29). However, by far the greatest credit for Sumi conversions is owed to the Sumi themselves. With only sporadic external support, as obvious from the above discussion, within the first three decades of the twentieth century Sumi conversions gained much momentum through a grassroots Christian movement. Pioneer Sumi evangelists such as Ashu

---

[14]This expulsion was the result of security concerns shared by the new Indian government that the American missionaries in Northeast India could be connected with the nationalist struggles of the hill tribes in the changed geo-political environment of the 1950s.

Kushe of Chishilimi village,[15] Inaho Kinimi of Lumami village[16] and Revd Yemhi of Lazami village[17] have gained an almost legendary status among the Sumi because of their contribution to spreading the Gospel. These individuals, together with many others who remain in the memories of their respective fellow villagers, contributed to a mass movement of the Sumi to Christianity in the 1920s and 1930s, which is recorded to have happened in a rather distinctive way: without sustained American missionary work, without mission funds, despite very poor connectivity between Sumi villages and opposition to preaching the Gospel on the part of non-Christian Sumi.

While touring Sumi villages in those early years, the American Baptist missionaries witnessed and documented this 'spontaneous movement' of the Sumi towards Christianity. According to Revd Tanquist, '[t]he way this genuine Christian movement was started among the Semas with practically no direct influence from without, and the way it has progressed in spite of gross neglect on our part as a Mission, is a marvellous thing indeed. [...] The Sema work is conducted in true 'faith mission' style. The money has been coming, we hardly know from whence' (Minutes 1936: 41). Similarly, Revd Anderson also writes of the immense promise of the underdeveloped Sumi mission field:

> The Semas are the most fruitful of our Christian Communities in the Assam Baptist Mission fields but they have not received the attention they deserved during the past year. [...] We must concentrate on teaching this great mass of new Christians the word of God and on establishing churches in their villages. During the last ten years, the increase in membership has been on mass movement proportions. In 1925 we had 500 Sema Naga Christians; now we have 6,500 and more are coming. (Report 1936: 43)

---

[15]Ashu Kushe is remembered as the first Sumi prophet (*tungkupu*), who converted not through any human preacher but through his direct encounter with God in a dream in 1922. He spent his life working as an itinerant evangelist to Sumi villages and made a contribution to spreading Christianity among neighbouring Naga (see Chishi Swu 2004).

[16]Inaho was a *dobashi*, who was notorious for persecuting Sumi Baptists and American missionaries until he had a Pauline experience and converted in 1927. He was one of the leading activists in the creation of an independent Sumi Baptist Association in 1929 and spent most of the rest of his life as an itinerant evangelist (*NBCC Platinum Jubilee Souvenir* 2012: 188-9).

[17]Revd Yemhi became the first ordained Sumi pastor in 1926 (*NBCC Platinum Jubilee Souvenir* 2012: 193).

Whereas early Naga conversions are usually attributed to missionary strategies in translating the Gospel, the provision of medical services at the mission stations and the establishment of mission schools which provided opportunities for social mobility and government employment (cf. Joshi 2012, Downs 1992, Eaton 1984), this mass movement among the Sumi that Revd Anderson talks about can also be understood in the context of Sumi social organisation that previous colonial sources had described in some detail. It can be plausibly suggested that Christianity also spread among the Sumi through their kinship networks and especially through the conversion of village chiefs that often entailed the conversion of their whole families and clans. In this way, being a Christian gradually came to be associated with prestige and authority (for a detailed discussion of conversion motivations among the Sumi, see Angelova, forthcoming).

The second wave of mass Sumi conversions to Baptist Christianity in the 1950s coincided in time with arguably the most turbulent period of Naga political history, which witnessed the extension of Indian sovereignty over the erstwhile British dominion in the Naga Hills. As the Naga resisted this process and advanced claims to their right to political independence, the Indian government deployed thousands of military and paramilitary personnel in the Naga Hills in an attempt to supress the Naga nationalist movement. In the course of the ensuing armed hostility, the civilian Naga population suffered unprecedented acts of violence, loss of human life and mass destruction of material culture (for a detailed account, see Maxwell 1980, Luithui and Haskar 1984, Iralu 2009), which created an environment of precarity and fear. Among the Sumi these experiences were exacerbated by the fact that after the expulsion of Revd Delano and his family from the Naga Hills in 1955, the young Sumi Baptist churches were left to cater for themselves without external support and guidance. As the churches strived to consolidate their membership and sustain their fellowship amidst this general feeling of loss and a lack of direction across the Naga areas, the 'miracle of [evangelical] revival came like a wildfire', according to my elderly informants. The revival spread spontaneously and quickly among all Naga areas in the late 1950s, and it was during this revival that many Sumi committed themselves to Christ. These later conversions were undoubtedly the result of the spiritual fervour of these times, but they can also be seen as a political statement of resistance to the oppression of the Indian nation-state, especially since the Naga nationalist movement was increasingly being conceptualised in Baptist Christian terms (on the relationships between Christianity and Naga nationalism see also Longvah, this volume). In the mid-1970s, influenced by a worldwide charismatic revival wave, another great evangelical revival spread across Nagaland, which brought about a renewed focus on world evangelism and missionary outreach in Naga Baptist churches. My elderly informants narrated that this revival began in a highly charged way with what they described as an 'unprecedented outpouring of the Holy Spirit' that saw thousands of people recommit their lives to Jesus amidst abundant stories of miraculous healings and prophecies and visions coming true. These two evangelical revivals have had a decisive impact on Sumi conversions as the community firmly declared its commitment to Christianity, in its Baptist conservative or more charismatic varieties.[18]

The Baptist church currently has the most members among the Sumi and has emerged as one of the most powerful institutions in their society. In its age- and gender-specific departments (children's, youth, women and general department) it encompasses all community members, at least officially, thus providing a sense of belonging and a stable network of social support while at the same time ensuring the involvement of the whole community in its activities and collective worship. The church building is the most prominent building in Sumi villages and a focal point of community life. The annual programme of each church department is interspersed with various activities and events which aim to engage the community not only in regular worship but also in other forms of sociality which strengthen the feeling of group cohesion and fellowship. The church in the village where I resided, for example, conducted regular Sunday school classes and organised an annual Vacation Bible School and a picnic for the children; the young people were engaged in regular Saturday evening services, but also took part in an annual retreat and a Music Night Show, among others; and the adult congregants attended general Sunday services in the morning and evening while a special service for women was conducted on Thursdays. In addition, numerous prayer programmes, special celebrations and of course the normative community celebrations of Easter and Christmas saturated the church programme. The other Baptist churches that I visited in different Sumi villages had similarly rich annual programmes for their young and adult congregants.

Through such varied activities and pedagogical strategies, Sumi Baptist churches not only transmit Christian knowledge cross-generationally to their young members, but also create certain dispositions in them in order to prepare them for a life of active devotion and service, which is highly esteemed in Sumi society. In the process of socialising children and young people as religious persons, the church instils and nurtures in them a certain form of religiosity which, through sustained religious instruction and ritualised practice, over time becomes an embodied religious habitus in the sense that Mauss (1979) and Bourdieu (1977) use the term. As a result, Sumi children and young people learn to internalise and enact accepted forms of socio-religious practice throughout their lives. Recent anthropological work has similarly argued that religiosity is not an inherent characteristic of human beings; rather, it has to be taught, learnt and reiterated through various pedagogical strategies and ritual behaviour (cf. Berliner and Sarró 2007, Luhrmann 2012). This, in turn, guarantees that the majority of the community members participate in the various events and services organised by local churches, that Christian morals

[18] For a more detailed discussion of evangelical revivals among the Sumi, see Chishi (2003) and Angelova (2015); for a general account of evangelical revivals across Nagaland, see *NCRC Souvenir* (2012).

are inculcated and that Christian knowledge, drawn from the widely reiterated Bible stories, is passed down the generations. By engaging everyone in such regular forms of fellowship, the Baptist church has become inextricably interwoven into the fabric of Sumi social life, and its ritualism permeates private and public events in clearly observable ways. For example, all life-cycle events in the life of a Sumi individual – naming ceremony (*Aje kuku*), marriage, funeral – are structured like church programmes and feature an invocation prayer by the village pastor or another church executive, accompanied by intercessory mass prayer by everyone present.

BAPTIST CHRISTIANITY AND SOCIO-CULTURAL (DIS)CONTINUITIES

Historical conversions to Christianity among the Sumi have undoubtedly entailed the demonization and prohibition of many core aspects of their traditional culture, such as headhunting and all ritual observances, songs and dances related to it,[19] many of the elaborate house decorations, the practice of drinking of rice-beer (a staple to Naga diet), polygamy, among others. In the early years of Christian conversions, a Sumi would be excommunicated for performing such cultural forms, participating in the celebration of calendrical rites and tribal festivals or drinking rice-beer. Such instances of 'backsliding' and 'reverting back to heathen ways', as abundantly documented in missionary correspondence, were a major concern in this period. Indeed, severing ties with and distancing oneself from the 'old' religion and culture was promoted as a value in itself that was crucial to the experience of conversion as many young Sumi churches sought to establish themselves and strengthen their membership. Realties on the ground were, of course, often more complex. Touring some Sumi villages in 1947, W.G. Archer, erstwhile sub-divisional officer in Mokokchung, observes that the seemingly mass conversion of the Sumi to Baptist Christianity has had varying degrees of impact on their traditional way of life. He notices that Sumi men of prominence continued to decorate their houses in traditional fashion, with many of them still adorning their houses with *mithun*[20] skulls and woodcarvings. But, he writes, 'instead of performing certain prescribed gennas [i.e. ritual prohibitions], a Sema, wishing to put up carvings must now

---

[19]Headhunting was one of the first cultural practices that was banned by both the American missionaries and the British colonial authorities.

[20]*Mithun (Bos frontalis)* - a type of semi-domesticated buffalo, which is still widely reared by the Naga. In the past it was used as a sacrificial animal in ritual ceremonies; nowadays, it is slaughtered for important community feasts such as Christmas, tribal festivals and weddings.

give two or more big feasts at Christmas. When he has done this, he proclaims the fact through carvings in exactly the same way as was done in earlier times' (Archer 1947). Such practical accommodations to the precepts of the new religion have been common among Naga converts as continuities of socio-cultural custom survived in various guises.

The contemporary study of conversion in anthropology is often accompanied by analytical discussions of issues of rupture, radical discontinuity with the past and a total culture change induced by mission Christianity's version of modernity (cf. Robbins 2004, Engelke 2004, Keane 2007). It is indeed often the case that the foreign missionaries who worked among non-Christian communities, such as the Naga, wittingly or unwittingly set out to effect a total change in culture among local populations by condemning and demonizing many aspects of their traditional culture as antithetical to their Christian understanding of morality and truth. Contrary to such totalising discourses and practices perpetuated by foreign missionaries and their local converts, however, and as the above example demonstrates, very often continuities of social and cultural custom have been maintained to a greater extent than initially anticipated. Therefore, in some cases it seems analytically more useful to interpret conversion not as a rupture, but as an ongoing process in which some earlier cultural ideas and practices might be suppressed but others survive to inform the trajectory of the local form of Christianity into the future (cf. Cannell 2006, Hefner 1993, Mosse 1999). In discussing Sumi conversions, therefore, I prefer to analyse religious change first and foremost as a matter of a changed sense of belonging and a new alignment of loyalties in the changed socio-political order to which the Sumi had to adjust in the late colonial and post-colonial periods.

This re-alignment of loyalties and re-articulation of identities among the Sumi and other Naga often involved symbolic acts of severing ties with their 'heathen' past, which might appear as ruptures. This usually took the form of a public burning of one's traditional insignia. My elderly informants remembered, for example, that during the First Great Revival of the 1950s Sumi Christians were told to throw away and burn all their traditional insignia (e.g. spears, headgear, loincloths, shawls, *mekhlas*,[21] jewellery etc.) for its alleged satanic qualities, with the urging that 'you are Christian now, leave everything that was before', denounce your past as head-hunters and, most importantly, repent. As a result, much of Sumi material culture appears to have been physically destroyed by over-zealous Sumi Christians in this period.[22] The magnificent *Ashothi chipa*, *Achikuhu chipa* or *Tamla chipa* necklaces, for instance, which were made of several lines of tubular cornelian stones and ivory and were passed down as heirlooms within families (see Figure 8),

---

[21]*Mekhla* - a woven wraparound skirt worn by Naga women, which bears tribe- and status-distinctive designs.

[22]Admittedly, much cultural heritage has also been lost as a result of the burning of Sumi villages by the Indian Army in the course of the armed Indo-Naga struggle.

are very hard to find in Sumi families nowadays. Most of them have been 'lost' in the past, as one elderly informant lamented:

> Actually...that was happening: after accepting Christ, we were allowed not to wear our own traditional dresses, because those of the treasures that we are now using as our traditional [attire], *mekhla* and all these things, the history said that it [was] copied from the works of the devil. Since it is copied by the devil, we should not wear it. And all our ornaments, they were neglected like anything, no one is preserving during that time when they became Christians. So, we lost many of our cultural and traditional things.[23]

My informant, Mr Kiyevi, talked about the ways in which traditional 'treasures' of Sumi material culture, such as jewellery and textiles, appear to have lost their symbolic value for the articulation of Christian Sumi identities. As a result, many of them had been neglected and destroyed as they were thought to be 'the works of the devil' and therefore unbefitting for Sumi Christians. Textiles and ornaments were destroyed by Sumi believers in their attempt to adopt a new, Christian identity, which was signified, among other things, by the clothes one used to wear.

Significantly and despite this apparent rupture with tradition, however, the cultural knowledge related to the production of such 'treasures' has been preserved and is currently being re-enacted in the creative reconstruction of Sumi jewellery and textiles with new materials and new designs. Undoubtedly, these processes are driven as much by local attempts to recreate and maintain a continuous cultural link with the past as by the increasing market demand for such cultural items due to intensified domestic and international tourism. All elderly women in the family with whom I lived, for example, had learnt how to make traditional Sumi necklaces as young girls, and often made them for their children and even for myself. But instead of using semi-precious stones that are now hard to find and very expensive, they used commercially-bought coloured beads. Each of them also owned an original *Achipu* necklace (made of only one line of cornelian stones, see Figure 9), which they had received as a gift from their parents upon marriage. At the same time, the short booklet on traditional Sumi textiles and jewellery that I bought during the 2011 Hornbill Festival (Achumi 2011) quickly became a reference point in jewellery-making in the whole neighbourhood, which to me was an indication of the continued interest in preserving this traditional handicraft.

The same attitude is discernible in the desire to preserve the traditional handicraft of weaving, especially shawls of various lengths, which bear motifs

---

[23]Formal interview with Mr Kiyevi Awomi (church deacon), conducted on 22 September 2012 at his residence.

distinctive of the Sumi. Some elderly women in the village where I usually resided were skilled weavers of small-sized male and the female Sumi shawls (respectively referred to as 'mufflers' and 'stoles'), and some were transmitting this knowledge to their daughters and grand-daughters. The latter showed varying degrees of interest in being engaged in such lessons on a regular basis. Because of their more intricate designs and the greater time and skill required to make them, *mekhlas* and full-length shawls were usually purchased either from shops in Dimapur, the commercial centre of Nagaland, or, whenever possible, from villages in the interior of Zunheboto District where textiles are produced by Sumi women as a form of livelihood. Traditional stoles and *mekhlas* were worn by the village women at formal church services, when they had to perform as part of a singing group in church and during the celebration of tribal festivals. Men would occasionally wear mufflers and full-length shawls during formal church services and village celebrations. In recent years Sumi men have also started wearing waistcoats instead of shawls and mufflers: the waistcoat is an innovative piece of clothing, which bears some of the symbolic designs of a shawl and is worn by young and old alike. These examples demonstrate that, despite the large-scale destruction of original jewellery and old textiles in the course of Sumi history, and despite common perceptions that culture is dying out and everything is 'lost', cultural knowledge has not only been preserved but attempts are also being made to transmit it to the younger generations.

This renewed active interest in Sumi cultural heritage is directly related to larger processes of so-called *cultural revivalism* within Naga society, which have been an observable socio-cultural phenomenon since the 1980s. Initiated by Naga community and church leaders, the cultural revival discourses and projects have sought to revive and preserve some valuable aspects of traditional Naga culture that have been rejected as 'unchristian' in the course of earlier conversions (e.g. some songs, dances, handicrafts etc.). With the re-evaluation of the cultural significance of this inheritance, traditional Naga culture has been discursively described as either 'good' or 'bad'. This selective bias reflects the complex nature of cultural heritage as a cultural, political and economic resource which is inextricably interwoven in processes of identity construction. As such, cultural revival projects are heavily underpinned by issues of power because they assign contemporary meaning and value to certain inheritance from the past and determine its future uses while at the same time delegating other aspects of this inheritance to the oblivion of the past (cf. Tunbridge and Ashworth 1996, Graham and Howard 2008, Smith 2006). Across Nagaland, cultural revival initiatives have attempted to reconstruct the collective Naga identity by reclaiming pride in 'good' cultural heritage and resituating it within the dominant referential frame of Baptist Christianity. Consequently, the revival of culture is underpinned by the tacit understanding that 'good' culture is what does not contradict the Biblical message and the accepted form of Baptist ritual and moral practice, while 'bad' culture is what does (the latter being primarily associated with the propitiation of spirits and their natural abodes). Against the moral sanction of Christianity, therefore, the 'good' cultural practices that are being revived (e.g. tribal dances, games, ceremonies) take a distinctly cultural rather than ritualistic form.

Within this discursive and power paradigm, my elderly Sumi informants talked about reclaiming 'good' culture and bridging the allegedly growing socio-cultural disconnect between the generations. For most of them 'good' culture consisted in continuing the culturally significant practices of weaving and jewellery-making (as already described), preserving Sutsa (the Sumi language) for the younger generations and celebrating Sumi festivals, such as Tuluni (the festival of abundant crops celebrated in July) and Ahuna (the harvest festival celebrated in November). While participation in these festivals would entail the excommunication of those participating in them in the past, they are nowadays important community events in which the village pastor often plays a central role, not only by offering the invocation prayer at the beginning of each celebration but sometimes also by taking an active part in the festivities. In one Sumi village that I visited during Tuluni in 2012, for example, the pastor had taught the young boys the dances and indigenous games for the cultural programme that accompanies the formal celebrations and took the lead in the head-hunters' dance (*aphilekuwo*). The performance of games and dances related to headhunting constitutes an essential part of contemporary cultural and festival celebrations among the Sumi. My informants, lay believers

Figure 6. *Achipu.*(Photo by Illiyana Angelova.)

and church executives alike, did not seem to see anything 'unchristian' about such cultural displays largely due to the fact that they are believed to have been stripped of their ritual significance and to have become 'innocent culture', as I was told. The function that this 'innocent culture' performs is not instrumental but rather serves to support symbolically and accentuate Sumi identity. The pastor in question, who was leading the head-hunters' dance, simply explained: 'This is our culture, na, how can we not know?'. On further probing it became obvious that the pastor had been actively involved in the student union of his village when he was young and had learnt the traditional games and dances while participating in cultural programmes organised by it. Another interview that I took with a senior church executive revealed a more theologically nuanced explanation of how the revival and enactment of 'good' culture intersects with the contemporary practice and experience of Baptist Christianity among the Sumi: 'it [traditional culture] was all created by God and therefore it cannot be wrong; tradition is not wrong because God made it'. This illustrates the fact that the Sumi Baptist Church is not ideologically opposed to the ongoing promotion of certain aspects of traditional Sumi culture in public and private life, and there is a growing understanding across church leadership that the display and practice of traditional cultural forms should be encouraged because it is constitutive of Sumi-ness, the condition of being Sumi.

At a macro-level, political discourses on the need to preserve and exhibit certain aspects of Naga tradition, especially performative Naga culture (dances, games, tribal festivals etc.), have been circulating in public space and in the local media most pronouncedly since the early 2000s. These discourses are indicative of a shift in political thinking which places a new emphasis on the need to make Naga culture more visible by creating opportunities for its display or 'showcasing', as the popular expression goes. The resultant commodification of this vibrant and visible part of Naga cultural heritage is then used by the state government for the purposes of promoting tourism and drawing political dividends from it while also generating some revenue. At the same time, however, it also exoticises the image of the Naga as brave warriors and of Nagaland as 'The land of festivals'. This is particularly obvious in state policies to promote domestic and international tourism in Nagaland via the annual Hornbill Festival, which has been organised in the first week of December since 2000. The festival is held at Kisama, a specially constructed heritage village near the state capital Kohima, and has become a mega tourist event in recent years, described by the Government of Nagaland as 'The festival of festivals' and as a 'cultural extravaganza' that attracts hundreds of foreign and local tourists to Nagaland.

Such commodification of indigenous culture for touristic purposes is certainly not a unique innovation of the Government of Nagaland. Each year it generates much public controversy and often heated debates in daily newspapers and on social media on the rationale of hosting such a 'cultural extravaganza' in the state, on the logistic burden it poses on the state's economy and the limited revenue that it actually generates, and on the 'authenticity' (or not) of the cultural forms

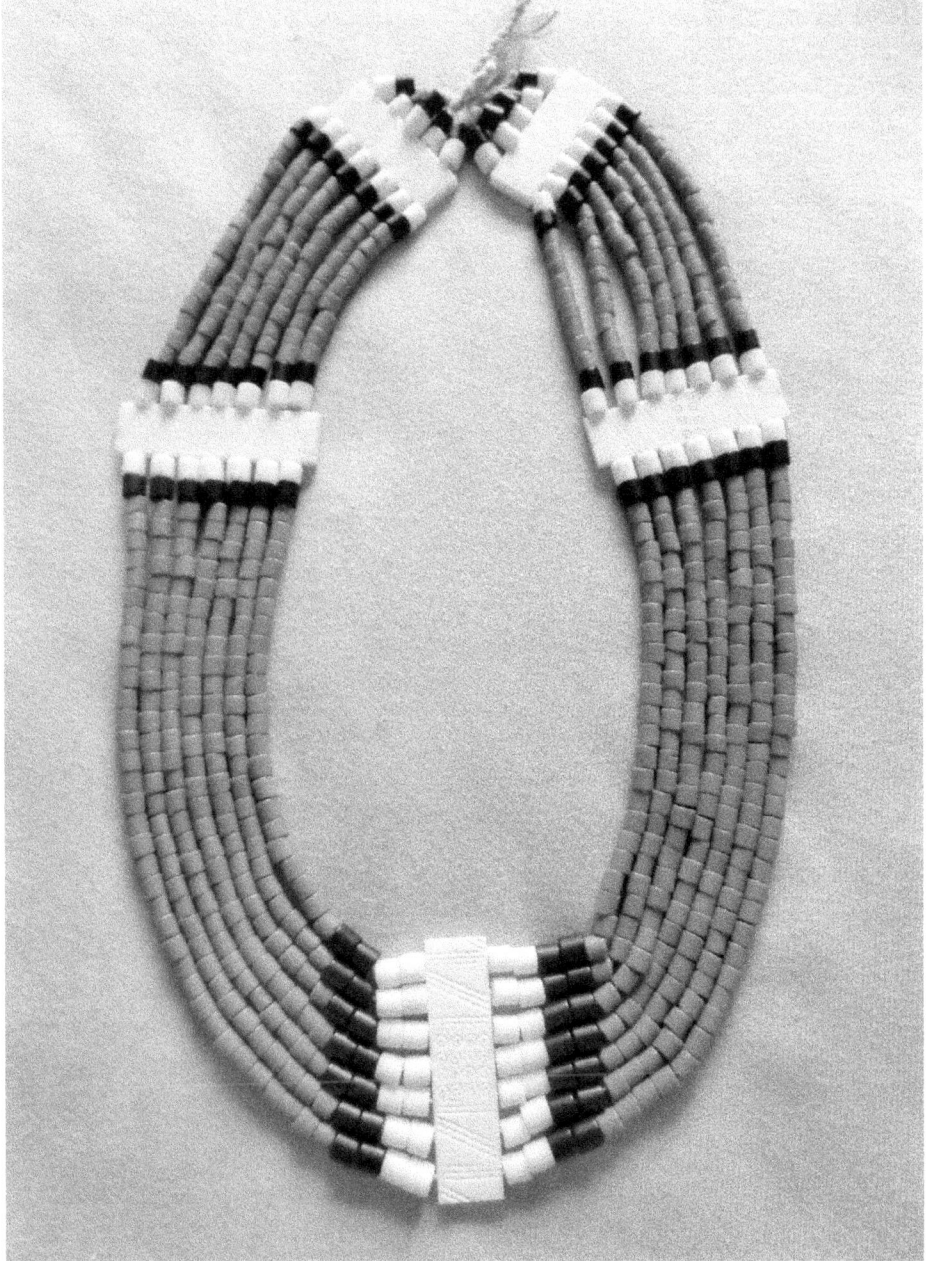

Figure 7. *Tamla chipa.*(Photo by Illiyana Angelova.)

displayed during the festival and their appropriateness (or not) for 'true' Christians. These debates, which intersperse the weeks preceding the Hornbill Festival each year, are significant because they reflect public sentiments and power dynamics within Naga society. It seems equally important, however, that the Hornbill Festival is underpinned by larger political and symbolic significance which, when analysed in its complexity, can shed some light on current processes of identity formation among the Naga and their political aspirations. Longkumer (2013) usefully suggests that the Hornbill Festival should be viewed not as a micro-event but as embedded in larger cultural, political, economic and religious processes that are shaping the present and future of the Naga. The consistent portrayal of the festival as 'indigenous', for example, serves as a political tool for procuring international legitimation for the Naga political claims for independence based on their distinct culture. Similarly, Stockhausen and Wettstein (2008) argue that the Hornbill Festival is a political tool through which the Naga declare their uniqueness and distinctiveness to the world, and thus legitimise their nationalist movement. Moreover, the authors interpret the coming together of various cultural groups representing different Naga tribes, who would otherwise not have much sustained contact between each other, as a powerful demonstration to the outside world that the Naga wish to be seen as one people, one nation. This indicates a desire to create and maintain a pan-Naga sense of solidarity and collective identity as well as constitute new forms of meaning-making among the Naga (cf. also Longkumer 2013 and Patnaik 2014).

Similar arguments can be advanced in relation to the nature of the other 'official' tribal festivals,[24] such as Tuluni among the Sumi that I have described above. On the one hand, the celebration of Tuluni serves an important function in sustaining the cultural memory of the Sumi and their experiences as one people through the customary narration of its story (*Tuluni ghili pini*). On the other hand, it is also often predicated on consumerist considerations which often prevail in village decisions on whether to organise a community celebration at all or not. Due to the high financial costs associated with the organisation of a community feast and a cultural programme, in some Sumi villages Tuluni is currently celebrated at the community level only if a chief guest (a patron to the celebration) or foreign guests are present. Despite this apparent lack of performative festivity, however, it is nonetheless significant that Tuluni is still widely observed by the Sumi in more intimate ways: by customary exchanges of pork meat and *anagho*[25] between family

---

[24]In the past, the celebration of the major tribal festivals among all Naga took several days to a week to complete. In the current political situation, the Government of Nagaland has fixed only one official date for the celebration of each major tribal festival. For the Sumi this is Tuluni, which is celebrated on 8 July.

[25] *Anagho* (from *ana*, 'cooked rice' and *agho*, 'a gift') is a special gift people exchange on Tuluni: it contains cooked rice and very big chunks of boiled pork wrapped up in banana

and friends and by shared meals and visits between family members. One of my elderly female informants explained these intimate celebrations in the following way: 'We just invite close close relatives OK, we have food together once and that's it. If I give this year, you will give next year, like this…'. This underscores an important cultural continuity in the contemporary celebration of Tuluni: it continues to represent a symbolic reinforcement of kinship and community ties, as it had done in the past, because the sharing of meals is central to the way in which Sumi kinship is constructed and experienced.

Necessarily, the contemporary meaning which is attached to the re-enactment of traditional cultural forms, such as performative Naga culture and handicrafts, is different from their original cultural context and hence open to reinterpretation, reinvention and continuous improvisation. As Patnaik (2014) demonstrates in relation to the Sumi, these improvisations are underpinned by an aesthetics which operates differently depending on its target audience: the local or the national/international market. Moreover, Patnaik contends that while driven by consumption demands, the aesthetics of cultural reproduction is also underpinned by the strong undercurrents of 'the refiguration and thus revaluing of cultural artefacts' by those who produce them (Patnaik 2014: 235). I would like to take this argument further by suggesting that this revaluation of cultural heritage is directly correlated to ongoing processes of identity reconstruction among the Sumi and other Naga, which seek to creatively constitute a 'new tradition': one which draws its symbolic resources both from certain aspects of historical cultural heritage and from Christianity.

The presence of a strong substratum of cultural reproduction and continuity in this 'new tradition' is particularly evident in the everyday lived realities of my Sumi informants, despite widely shared sentiments that culture is 'lost' or on the verge of being 'lost'. The distinctive social organisation of Sumi society, for example, has remained largely unaffected by their conversion to Christianity. Arguably, this could be attributed to the fact that neither the British colonial administrators nor the American Baptist missionaries interfered actively in this aspect of Sumi tradition as well as to its socio-cultural salience for Sumi identity constructions. For example, while polygamy is no longer practised, the hereditary right of succession to power within chiefly lineages has remained intact, and customary laws are still being followed in relation to the settlement of land disputes, village feuds and the inheritance of property. Some traditional rites of passage are no longer observed (e.g. the piercing of the ears of infant Sumi boys), but many others have retained their symbolic value, even though they are nowadays transformed and celebrated with Christian ritualism. The naming ceremony (*Aje kuku*), for example, continues to form an important rite of passage in the life of a Sumi individual; the selection of a spouse follows customary rules which prohibit the intermarriage

---

leaves and given to friends, neighbours and relatives.

of closely related clans; in accordance with Sumi custom, wedding invitations for close kinsmen are accompanied by big chunks of pork meat; and the preferred place for burying deceased family members continues to be the house compound. Admittedly, an important Christian innovation in the cycle of Sumi rites of passage is, of course, the ritual of believer's baptism, which is crucial to the construction of one's Christian personhood.

In addition, contemporary attitudes to illness and affliction among the Sumi also exhibit a strong continuity of cultural tradition. While the initial response to illness is the combined application of biomedicine and Christian prayer (especially in the form of collective prayer meetings organised on behalf of the afflicted by their family members), traditional healers are also occasionally contacted for certain persistent ailments. There are various types of such healers: masseurs, bone-setters, herbalists etc.[26] All of them specialise in the treatment of certain ailments and combine their healing powers with prayers; some of them are believed to see visions in dreams, which help them heal their patients. In this way, the healers are held to be in a sustained contact with the divine and thus able to channel its support for the benefit of their ailing patients. Some traditional healers are famous and are frequented by numerous patients from far and wide; others practise on a smaller scale in their villages. For example, the mother in the family with whom I lived was a traditional healer specialising in the treatment of muscle cramps and nerve inflammations. As a rule, she helped relatives and friends only, and her method of treatment included massaging the patient with mustard oil and pressing down very hard in the direction of the nerve/muscle. She explained to me that her healing was a gift from God, and she had inherited it from her mother. In addition, she was an active member of the village Baptist church and participated regularly in all prayer meetings, signing competitions and special functions organised by the church. The accommodation of such traditional healers in the life of the Baptist church is yet another example of the 'new tradition' that is currently being constituted among the Sumi and other Naga.

Last, but not least, the preservation and continued use of Sutsa, the Sumi language, represents a socio-cultural continuity, which has important implications for the construction of Sumi identity. With their first biblical translations in the beginning of the twentieth century, the American missionaries and their Sumi assistants promoted the codification of the hitherto oral language of the Sumi to writing and initiated a long and vibrant literary tradition. Nowadays, the Sumi Cultural Association and the Sumi Literature Board in Zunheboto are sponsoring or otherwise supporting various publications, especially targeting the promotion of the Sumi language, thus facilitating the continued growth of a strong body of indigenous literature. The burgeoning interest in traditional Sumi culture that

---

[26]See Joshi (2012) for a detailed discussion of the types of traditional healers with a special reference to the Angami Naga.

this chapter has sought to present is also reflected in some recent publications by Sumi authors in Sutsa (cf. Zhimomi 1985, Yeptho 1991) and in English (cf. Assumi 2009, Yeptho 2011, Achumi 2011), which complement other works focusing on the history of Christianity among the Sumi and its socio-cultural impact (cf. Aye 2005, Kiho 2004, Chishi 2003, Zhimomi 2012 etc.). This indigenous scholarship has not only provided a wealth of information about Sumi culture and traditions but has also filled in a significant gap in knowledge about the 'large and important Sema tribe', to borrow Elwin's words yet again. It has also made an important contribution to contextualising Christianity and embedding it firmly in Sumi cultural tradition and history.

CONCLUSION

The construction of the contemporary Sumi identity has been a long process of rejection, incorporation and creative transformation of cultural elements belonging to Christian and non-Christian religious traditions against the background of specific historical and political circumstances. British colonial rule and American Baptist missionary activity since the early twentieth century and the contested incorporation of Sumi lands into the independent Indian nation-state in the mid-twentieth century have served as important agents of change, which have left their imprints on the ways in which the Sumi constitute their identities and engage with their cultural heritage. With a particular focus on the history and contemporary significance of Baptist Christianity among the Sumi, the present chapter sought to demonstrate that even though Christian conversions have entailed certain discontinuities in the socio-cultural traditions of the Sumi, a number of continuities have persisted and come to shape the ways in which contemporary Sumi identity is being reconstituted. This chapter argued that, as a result, Christianity should not be viewed merely as a major agent of socio-cultural change among the Sumi, but rather as an intrinsic part of their contemporary identity and, more importantly, as a vital constitutive part of a 'new tradition' that is currently in the making: one, which is creatively embedding Christianity within a solid substratum of cultural reproduction.

It is clear that in the conversion process some important village institutions, such as headhunting and the *morung* system, have been abandoned while others have been continued and preserved. The distinctive social organisation of the Sumi, for example, has remained largely unaffected by their conversion to Christianity, and customary law is still practised in matters pertaining to the settlement of land disputes and the inheritance of property. While some rites of passage (e.g. the piercing of the ears of infant Sumi boys) have lost their symbolic significance and are no longer performed, others (e.g. naming ceremony, marriage and funeral rites) have remained strongly rooted in tradition although they are nowadays marked by

Christian ritualism. Necessarily, the rite of believer's baptism has become a new rite of passage central to the constitution of Christian Sumi identities.

It is also acknowledged that many items of Sumi material culture (e.g. jewellery, *mekhlas*, shawls, weapons, headgear) have been destroyed in the course of Christian conversions for their symbolic association with a 'heathen' past that the new converts wished to distance themselves from in their adoption of a new, Christian identity. However, the fact that the cultural knowledge about these items has been preserved and some of it is currently being recreated in cultural revival projects clearly indicates that their symbolic value for the construction of contemporary Sumi identity is being re-evaluated. With the tacit sanction of the Baptist church, various local initiatives have therefore sought to revive, preserve and promote certain inheritance from the past, such as performative Sumi culture (e.g. dances, songs, indigenous games) and some handicrafts (e.g. weaving, woodcarving, basket-making). Some of the village elders with whom I interacted were also taking concrete steps in teaching the younger generations this cultural knowledge in practical attempts to bridge an allegedly growing socio-cultural disconnect between the generations. To borrow Daniel Miller's (2003) terminology, the Sumi seem to have preserved and perpetuated those aspects of their traditional cultural heritage which *matter* to them because they are perceived as salient cultural symbols and resources infused with sentimental and symbolic value. At the same time, through the creation of new *mekhla* designs, innovative pieces of clothing such as the male waistcoat and new types of jewellery that still bear distinctive tribal colours and design patterns but are more affordable than their traditional counterparts, the Sumi seem to have creatively reinvented and re-imagined their cultural heritage in a process of traditionalisation in which the cultural value attached to tribal textiles and jewellery has been retained while their form has changed.

For my informants across Sumi villages, being Sumi meant a number of things: preserving *Sutsa* (the Sumi language), promoting the production and wearing of traditional textiles and jewellery, performing Sumi rites of passage and perpetuating the custom of community festivals and feasting, among other things. In the context of larger cultural revival initiatives which are ongoing across Nagaland, these have been deemed as 'good' culture, and therefore worthy of being preserved and transmitted to the younger generations. From my experience, young people were overall quite interested in engaging more deeply with their cultural heritage. In the process, traditional culture becomes commodified to a certain extent, especially for the purposes of promoting national and international tourism, but this need not obfuscate the significance of the personal meanings and motivations attached to it for those who are engaged in reproducing it. While the suppression of certain elements of cultural expression in the past has been perceived as essential to adopting a 'true' new Christian identity, their creative re-enactment in the contemporary period reflects the shared understanding within Sumi society that these forms of cultural expression represent the uniqueness and distinctiveness of their community and as such they cannot be antithetical to their

Christian identity. As I have sought to demonstrate here, this suggests that a 'new tradition' is currently being creatively constituted by the Sumi, and it draws its symbolic resources and strength from an equal engagement with Sumi cultural heritage and with Christianity.

■ ■■ ■■

05

PRAYERS FROM THE KUKI-NAGA CONFLICT: LIVING THROUGH VIOLENCE IN MANIPUR

Asojiini Rachel Kashena

Growing up amongst survivors of the Kuki-Naga conflict that raged between the years 1992 to 1998, I am drawn to explore how people continued their lives after experiencing the trauma of losing loved ones. I want to understand their post-conflict lives better. My exploration of this question entailed meeting people from both Kuki and Naga communities living in the villages of the Kangpokpi region in Manipur.[1] Although Kukis and Nagas living in Kangpokpi region interact through

[1]Kangpokpi was still a sub-division of Senapati district at the time I conducted my research in December 2015. It has now become a district. The Kukis involved in my research resided in Kangpokpi town. Both Kukis and Nagas inhabited the town before the conflict but now it is populated by Kukis who were displaced from Tamenglong, Ukhrul and Chandel districts during the violent ethnic conflict. On the contrary, Nagas who were settled in Kangpokpi town before the conflict and in villages around the town like Thangal Surung and Makeng left in large numbers, and now mostly reside in Senapati town. The Nagas who were involved in my research resided in the villages around Kangpokpi town, as they did prior to the violent ethnic conflict.

economic and political relations, most of their social and civic lives are conducted separately. During the conflict, Kangpokpi was regarded as the most dangerous region. People were pulled down from buses and shot. Some others were hacked to death. Recollecting the memory of the conflict from the years 1996 to 1998, when I was a child, I remember the everyday routine of running for cover whenever there was a shootout nearby. Families would hide in underground shelters, which were usually hand dug, located with an entrance underneath their bedroom floor or behind their houses. During wintery nights, every family sat on the cold floor of their bunkers and maintained complete silence, fearing that enemies might detect their hideout. Adult male members from each family would take guns and guard the village every night.

Anthropologist, Kimberly Theidon (2006), in her work on communities in the Ayacucho region of Peru, discusses what it is like to live in a post-conflict society where people formerly enacted violence on each other. She remarked: "Co-existence is based upon a complicated alchemy of remembering, forgetting and remembering to forget" (2006: 98). Such a process is also visible in Manipur. In the absence of communal reconciliation,[2] some Kukis continue to observe September 13 as 'Black Day' to commemorate the killing of 87 Kukis on the 13th of September 1993 at Tamei in Tamenglong District of Manipur.[3] The objective behind the commemoration is complex. For example, some people use the day to remember their loved ones, others use it to demand justice and some use it to instigate hostility. While some Nagas also individually commemorate their loved ones during annual death anniversaries, others chose not to observe this.

THE KUKI-NAGA CONFLICT

From 1992 to 1998, the violent ethnic conflict between Kukis and Nagas spread in places across Northeast India.[4] Manipur witnessed the most violent clashes, which claimed hundreds of lives, while they also displaced thousands.[5] Writing about the Kuki-Naga ethnic conflict is a complicated task given the multiplicity of causes, incidences of violence, as well as its manifold consequences and after

[2]The lack of political consensus, land disputes between Kukis and Nagas, and the negligence of both the central and the state governments remain hurdles for a communal reconciliation between the two groups.

[3]While other accounts claim different figures, I will use the figure of 87 Kukis that were killed on the 13th of September 1993, based on the responses given by many Kukis during my fieldwork. Also, see Aheibam Koireng Singh, 2008) and SR Tohring (2010).

[4]The Kuki-Naga conflict affected the states of Assam, Manipur and Nagaland.

[5]Within Manipur, the ethnic violence concentrated in the districts of Chandel, Senapati, Tamenglong and Ukhrul.

effects, which members of both communities faced after the violent ethnic conflict came to an end. The scramble for land, however, remains a dominant narrative. The beginning of the Kuki-Naga conflict can be traced back to at least the time of the British colonial era. However, intermittent disputes in the form of inter-village raids existed between Kukis and Nagas even before the colonial era.[6] Guite (2013) posits that such raids were conducted when negotiations between villages failed, or when there was a failure of payment of tributes. He holds that such raids were usually accompanied by plundering and the taking of captives. The colonial land re-arrangements and the policy of divide and rule bred further animosity between Kukis and Nagas. In 1840, McCulloch, the then Political Agent, resettled some Kukis in the front lines of the British territory and amongst Nagas for them to act as a buffer against the Burmese, the Nagas and the Lushai tribes (Dena, 2007: 184).[7] In this way, the British as well the Rajas of Manipur used Kukis against Nagas. This strategy was also employed the other way around. For instance, when Kukis revolted against the British in 1917 by refusing to be recruited for the Manipur Labour Corps and be sent to war trenches in France, Naga warriors were deployed to suppress the uprising. Similarly, Kuki warriors were recruited to suppress the 1930 uprising, which was led by Jadonang, who was a Naga.[8]

During those days, both Kukis and Nagas formed organisations to socially and politically represent themselves.[9] Some of these political organisations went underground in the postcolonial era after the Indian government denied their political claims and instead retained the colonial legacy of divide and rule, which continues until today. Kabui (1994: 17) remarked how the Indian government displayed the colonial mentality by instigating one tribe against another. "The greatest casualty", he writes, "is the credibility of Indian security forces, especially

---

[6]This does not mean that Kukis and Nagas always had antagonistic relations towards each other. In the past, they would often make peace or maintained tributary relations. In addition, Kukis and Nagas conducted raids within their own respective tribes, too. Moreover, when the British attacked them, it was natural for the Kuki and Naga tribes to help and protect each other. Elwin (1961) and Guite (2013) state that Kukis and Nagas also conducted raids on the British as acts of resistance against the encroachment of the colonial tea planters on their territory.

[7]The resettlement of the Kukis caused many disputes between Kukis and Nagas on the question of land and territory.

[8]Jadonang was a Rongmei Naga, social and religious reformer whose intention was to drive away the British. He launched a political movement by mobilising the Zeliangrongs in 1930 (Longkumer 2010).

[9]The Kukis formed an organisation called the Kuki National Assembly (KNA) in 1946 and later an underground unit called the Kuki National Front (KNF) in 1988. Naga political organisations such as the Naga Club and Naga National Council (NNC) were formed in 1918 and 1946 respectively.

the Assam Rifles and the Assam Regiments who were alleged to have been involved in the conflict instigating one against another."

The consolidation of the Kuki and Naga ethnic identities began to emerge during the colonial period and it hardened with their respective demands for territorial integrity during the postcolonial era. The violent conflict during the 1990s was a consequence of both communities in Manipur making overlapping territorial claims for several decades.[10] The immediate cause of the conflict in 1992, however, was the desire of the respective ethnic armed groups (Kukis and Nagas) to control an important trading town called Moreh located along the international border between Manipur and Myanmar.[11] The Naga armed group, the National Socialist Council of Nagaland-Isak/Muivah (NSCN-IM), levied taxes that created resentment among the Kuki communities living in Indo-Myanmar border villages. In retaliation, the Kuki armed group, the Kuki National Army (KNA) began to demand tax from Naga villages in Chandel district. Initially, the clash was between these two non-state armed groups. However, due to the ethnic alliances (as Kukis and Nagas) civilians soon became deeply entangled in the violence. The people from both the ethnic communities formed village guards to protect their homes. While members from the various Naga groups of Manipur were involved in the conflict, not all Kuki tribes were involved.[12]

By 1993, the ethnic conflict was at its peak and the most brutal forms of violence were recorded that year.[13] The dead often bore multiple wounds and cuts; bodies were cut into pieces, to the extent that some victims could no longer be identified. To explain what drives 'ordinary' people to participate in such macabre violence, scholars have argued that the categorisation of groups based on fixed

---

[10]On one hand, the National Socialist Council of Nagaland (NSCN-IM), a Naga armed group fighting for a Naga homeland asserted the integration of all the Naga inhabited areas of Arunachal Pradesh, Assam, Manipur, Nagaland and parts of Myanmar to form the 'Greater Nagaland'. On the other hand, the Kuki armed groups that is the Kuki National Front (KNF) and Kuki National Organization (KNO) demanded for a 'Kuki Homeland' within the state of Manipur.

[11]The Kuki and the Naga armed groups as well as the government of India and Manipur desired to take control of the border town because this trade point of Myanmar generates considerable sources of income.

[12]The Kuki tribe involved in the conflict was the Thadous, one of the major tribe within the larger Kuki-fold.

[13]Some of the major incidences of violence, which most scholars have reported are the Khallang Massacre on the 8th of August, 1993; the Gelnel Massacre on the 13th of September, 1993; the Tamei Massacre on the 13th of September, 1993 (also remembered as the Joupi Massacre); the Toloulong Massacre on the 21st of September 1993. There are other violent incidences that occurred on the 29th of September, 1993; the 1st and 16th of December, 1993 and in October, 1994. See Aheibam Koireng Singh, 2008.

and rigid identities can lead to negative perspectives about the others (Mamdani 2001; Kriedie & Monroe 2002), so preparing the grounds for communal violence. Mamdani (2001) and Peterson (2002) explain how fear and obedience can drive, in particular circumstances, individuals towards violent actions. The people I interacted with pointed out that those civilians involved in violent acts were guided by armed groups and often feared becoming victims themselves. Thus, they enacted violence in the belief that this would produce safety for themselves. In addition, rumours about the cruelty of the violence enacted by 'the other' created resentment and fear, eliciting fantasies of revenge among survivors. During my fieldwork, several people from Kangpokpi region said, "The clash died down when a sense of realisation of the severe damage arose in the minds of both Kukis and Nagas." While over two decades have now passed, many of them still fear that the conflict has a possibility of resurfacing because of the continued aspirations for ethnic homelands propagated by the respective armed groups.

By presenting prayers from the Kuki-Naga conflict in the chapter, I also ask the following broader questions. What constitutes faith and healing in militarised societies?[14] What kind of spiritual crisis do survivors undergo after witnessing violent killings? In what ways can we understand attributes that are defined as "good and bad" as people of Christian faith share their experiences of violence? In order to examine these questions, this chapter is divided into four sections. First, I explore how Christianity came to Kukis and Nagas of Manipur, which subsequently led to spiritual and moral transformations in their societies. Next, I present personal narratives of individuals who lost their spouses during the Kuki-Naga violence. Sections three and four subsequently analyse how these individuals experienced the process of healing through prayer and forgiveness, which in turn elucidates how a particular understanding of faith and Christianity exists among survivors of the Kuki-Naga ethnic conflict. I submit that such an exploration contributes towards ongoing conversations about everyday experiences of enduring violence, processes of reconciliation and notions of justice, and healing in conflict societies not just in Manipur, but across Northeast India and beyond.

[14]In Manipur, like most of the north-eastern states in India, the presence of heavy paramilitary forces and the long history of armed conflicts has created a highly militarised situation in the society. For instance, there is one-armed personnel to every five individuals in Manipur. Kikon (2004; 2005) wrote that the Indian state manifested its presence in the north-eastern region through military expeditions, thus developing an increasing emphasis on military power. As a result, militarisation has brought about a "fundamental distortion of the region's social and political institutions" (2004: 12).

SITUATING CHRISTIANITY IN CONFLICT AREAS

Colonial sources and texts on tribal communities in the North East region of India, and particularly in Manipur and the Naga Hills, show how Christianity and conversions transformed societies immensely.[15] Today, the portrayal of Christian faith among tribal communities is presented either as a modernizing element that brought education and institutionalized religion or as a subversive element from the west that incited tribal communities to break away from India.[16] According to my fieldwork experiences, neither of these dominant frameworks captures the everyday experiences of people who profess a faith they define as Christianity.

Christianity reached Kukis and Nagas of Manipur in the early parts of the twentieth century. William Pettigrew, a member of the American Baptist Mission Society, started his work among the Tangkhuls of Ukhrul district as early as 1896. The activities of the Christian missionaries among the Kukis began with the establishment of a mission school in a Kuki inhabited part of Ukhrul. However, it was only in 1912 that mission work among Kukis became active with the arrival of Rev. Watkin Robert of the Welsh Presbyterian Missionary and Dr. G.G. Crozier, a member of the American Baptist Mission Society. These two missionaries worked among the Kukis in Kangpokpi (Senapati district) and Churachandpur

[15]Adopting Christianity meant adopting not just a new religion, but also a new mode of life. Downs (1993) explains how Christianity was emphasised as a life style by the Protestant missionaries. In addition, Elwin (1961: 16) notes that the concept of "personal salvation in Christianity has introduced a new individualism in place of the former community spirit..." Conditions were laid down for the church members to renounce their traditional religious practices. For instance, Longkumer (2013) pointed out how the early Christian missionaries made a clear distinction between the traditional religion as 'false religion' and Christianity as 'true religion'. Consequently, the animistic worldview was subordinated. While many practices like head hunting and fear of evil spirits of the indigenous people were abandoned for good, many valuable parts of tribal heritage such as songs, dances, poetry and festivals have diminished after Christianity was introduced. In this volume, however, Angelova, in her exploration of contemporary identities among the Sumi Nagas, argues that Christian conversion should no longer be interpreted as a social and cultural rupture but as an agent that plays a significant role in the ongoing process of reinventing new Sumi identities.

[16]Longkumer (2013: 4) throws light on the analogy of how the Sangh Parivar believes that "Christianity poses a challenging threat to the territorial integrity of Bharatvarsh. The Sangh regards this 'challenge' as territorial 'secessionism'; their aim is to prevent this and unite the country." In the context of the Naga Movement, Nuh (2006), Thomas (2016) and Elwin (1961) point out how Christianity became a symbol of resistance to the military campaign of the Indian government subsequently contributing towards the further strengthening of the resolve of the Nagas to preserve Christianity. In preserving so, Longvah, in this volume, illustrates how Christianity made a significant impact to the development of the Naga consciousness for a common political identity.

district. The Catholic missionaries also started their work among the hill tribes of Manipur in 1912 under the leadership of Father Ansgar Koenigsbaver, a German Salvatorian missionary. Although, the primary aim of the Christian Missionaries was to proselytise, they also took to propagating love and brotherhood among the hitherto warring tribes. Ultimately, however, it was largely through medicine and education that the missionaries won the confidence of the hill people.[17]

For missionaries, educating the hill people meant first and foremost teaching them how to read the scriptures. This was effective in making them understand the ways of Christian living. Downs (1993) and Mohan (2016) point out how prayer had a prominent place in missionary teachings. The reading of scriptures in the schools was accompanied by the learning of prayers. The lives of newly converts began to be increasingly governed by the time of prayer. For instance, congregations would assemble every evening to learn prayers. It was through the learning of prayers, that hill people acquired an understanding of the need to repent for their sins and seek forgiveness from God. For instance, Iralu (2000) notes how the precolonial practice of head hunting amongst hill tribes, including the "avenging of a murder", was governed by a code of honour where "the failure to avenge a relative's murder was the most shameful thing on the part of the living" (Cited in Joshi, 2012: 254). However, after embracing Christianity, Kukis and Nagas developed an approach towards forgiveness and abstinence from revenge based on the Christian theological notion of reconciliation.[18]

Mohan (2016: 46), in his study of the role of prayer among the Dalit Christians in Kerala posits, "The ideas and metaphors that the Dalits have learned through prayers were fundamental in transforming their social and cultural practices."

---

[17]Vibha Joshi (2012) explains how the missionaries envisaged hill people's interest in education as an opportunity to gain access to them. Besides education, the medical services provided by the missionaries was another effective way of gaining acceptance among the hill tribes. The missionaries often combined evangelism with medical care because diseases such as cholera, malaria, small pox, dysentery, tuberculosis and leprosy were prevalent in the Manipur and the Naga Hills in the early twentieth century.

[18]Christianity-based civilian organisations such as the Forum for Naga Reconciliation (FNR) have made appeals for reconciliation between the various Naga nationalist factions that have carried out recurring acts of vengeful killings. The theme for reconciliation was laid out with the hope that through prayer; the armed Naga nationalists as well as lay people would apologise and ask for forgiveness. There were a number of cases in Nagaland where families or clans reconciled as a result of this. However, despite the rhetoric surrounding the need to forgive and forget, there are few expressions of apology or regret on the part of the alleged perpetrators of the rival factional killings (Joshi, 2012, pp. 252, 253). Similarly, in the absence of an apology between Kukis and Nagas, the process of reconciliation becomes difficult. It prevents what Veena Das (2007: 218) considers central to reconciliation, which is that: "Public acknowledgement of hurt can allow new opportunities to be created for resumption of everyday life."

The Protestant missionaries introduced prayer books to the Dalits in Malayalam, which was used for everyday prayers. In the course of time, some individuals became experts in composing 'extempore prayers' and they assumed leadership in the community. Similarly, the missionaries who were working amongst Kukis and Nagas introduced prayer books while also translating the scriptures in local languages. Today, following the footsteps of the early Christian missionaries, Kuki and Naga pastors, priests and nuns continue to teach their respective congregations about how to pray. Prayer books are also distributed to church members. Those Kukis and Nagas belonging to the Baptist and Revival denominations within Christianity have resorted to 'composing extempore prayers' based on their own context and understanding. However, most of the Catholic Kukis and Nagas recite given spiritual prayers, for instance, the Lord's Prayer, taught to them by the church.

For Christians, prayer is regarded as food for the soul. Or as Sproul (2014: 1) writes, "Prayer is to the Christians what bread is to life." Christians believe that prayer builds their relationship with Jesus while also helping them determine God's will and overcome temptations. In light of the fundamental role played by Christian prayers in the lives of Kukis and Nagas, I will now present stories of how survivors of the Kuki-Naga conflict pacified themselves and dealt with the trauma they faced through their passion for prayer.

STORIES OF LOSS AND TRAUMA

Storytelling, a part of human experience, helps people to relate to other persons more intimately. Stories also work to build bridges between the past and the present. It is through story telling that the narrator can express emotions of pain, anger, happiness and hope. La Capra (1999) suggests that in post-traumatic situations, when one relives (or acts out) the past, distinctions tend to collapse, including the crucial distinction between then and now. Larson (2009: 185), in her exploration of forgiveness and reconciliation in the years following the Rwandan genocide points out that the process of learning to tell stories of loss, especially about the sudden loss of loved ones, helps victims in coming to terms with their emotions. It helps them overcome emotions of anger, frustrations, distress, grief and feelings of helplessness in the wake of 'sudden violent death' of loved ones. Similarly, Thiranagama (2013), through her ethnographic exploration of the Sri Lankan Civil War, affirms that the narratives of the 'wartime self' generates channels of coping. Likewise, I observed that survivors of the Kuki-Naga violence received some comfort from narrating their stories to those willing to listen to them.

In the narratives that follow, I have given fictional names to the survivors who participated in the research to protect their confidentiality.[19] As I began my

---

[19]The names were derived from the kind of qualities I saw in them. At the same time, I

research, I introduced myself as a survivor of the conflict. I shared my story and asked them if they would be comfortable to narrate their experiences to me. They opened up their home more easily because we shared similar experiences of the conflict. I posed the following set of questions to them:

> I would like to start by asking you to tell me in your own words the story of your life. I want you to tell me about your life, your struggles, the challenges you faced as if it is a story. Tell me about the experiences of your transition from a wife to a widow/husband to a widower. Tell me about the future of how things will look for you. Do not be bothered that I am going to write it down so the story should be told in this way or that way. Just tell me in a way that is most comfortable for you.[20]

KHANGTHEIDUI'S STORY

One winter morning in December 2015, my father, a local guide, and I went to the home of Khangtheidui, an 85-year-old Naga woman. Her daughter together with Khangtheidui's youngest son and his family received us. On stating the purpose of my visit, her children worried that their mother was very old and had started to lose her hearing ability. They were not sure whether she would be able to recollect memories of the Kuki-Naga violence. Moreover, they were sceptical about her ability to speak 'Meiteilon.'[21] As she came out of her room, we shook hands and she sat down beside me. In Thangal Naga, the community she belongs to, Khangtheidui means 'the enduring one.' Despite the scepticism of her children and her advancing age, she recollected many vivid memories of violent incidents that took place in 1995. In fluent Meiteilon, she narrated the incidents.

It was sometime in May 1995 when Khangtheidui was weaving a shawl in a corner of the veranda of her home, when her husband said that he was going to fetch firewood from the

---

have tried not to stray too far away from the meaning of their original names. I have named them based on their ethnic affiliation.

[20]Some of the questions were adapted from, Goodman, 2004. Coping with Trauma and Hardship among Unaccompanied Refugee Youths from Sudan. Qualitative Health Research. p. 1180.

[21]*Meiteilon* was used as the medium of communication during the interviews.

forest as well as take their buffalo for grazing. Khangtheidui protested at his idea of venturing out into the forest because of the prevailing ethnic tension. She asked him to stay back at home but, as a hardworking man who never liked to sit idle, he would not agree. He set off to the jungle assuring her that no harm would come to him and that, in any case, he would not go far. When he did not return until late in the night, doubts began to rise and Khangtheidui informed her neighbours of his missing. Some people gathered to search for him and found his body hacked into pieces with a machete. Pieces of his body were found lying around in the forest. They collected the pieces and carried them home. Those who killed him had also taken away his buffalo. The search party did not allow Khangtheidui to look at the body. They told her: "It looks like meat cut into pieces. It would be better if you do not look at it." A funeral service was conducted and his body was buried in the church's cemetery. Khangtheidui said, "I was devastated but I told myself that I should not dwell on the loss. I had to stay strong for my children. I tried not to think too much and I prayed to God for the strength to cope with the loss."

JOB'S STORY

One evening, in December 2015, I listened to Job, a 57-year-old Naga pastor, teacher and a father of three children. His name is taken from the Biblical character Job, as the pastor's words and way of understanding the blessings and tragedies of life resembled that of Job.[22]

On Friday the 14th of July 1996, Job and his wife decided to go for a stroll and check on the paddy that was growing in their fields. Having done so, Job told his wife that they should head back home. It was time to feed the infant who was being looked after by a baby sitter. Job also was to evaluate the half-yearly exam papers of his school students. Job told her that they could come back the next day, if need be. His wife

---

[22]In the Bible, Job is presented as a prosperous family man who encountered a terrible loss of his family, wealth and health. He struggled to understand his situation and simply put it as God's will. The pastor quoted Job saying, "The Lord has given and the Lord has taken away" (Job 1:21 NIV). Therefore, I ended up putting Job as the fictional name of the pastor.

agreed. However, she insisted that she would first check on her mother's paddy fields before they would leave. On the way, she spotted some mushrooms and asked Job to collect them while she went ahead to check her mother's fields.

Some moments later, Job heard a gunshot. He stood up and saw some smoke curling up in the air. Immediately, he suspected that his wife had been shot. Job started running towards his wife but then a thought crossed his mind. "I should not go towards her now. What if the man is reloading his gun?" A little later, he could hear other people shouting and running in the direction of his wife and himself. At this moment, Job saw his wife lying dead on the ground. Recollecting the incident, Job said, "She must have tried to run towards me after seeing the man hiding in the bushes with a gun. The bullet went into her from the left side of the body and it pierced her heart."

The man who shot Job's wife ran up to the hill after he heard people shouting. Job realised that nothing could be done even if he had chased after him. His wife's body was carried home with the help of the people from his village. He said:

> I was filled with rage, traumatised and could no longer think straight. People from my village and I wanted to stop vehicles that passed by on the National Highway running through our village. Fortunately, no vehicle passed by. Otherwise, some Kukis would have been killed that day. I was aware that repaying evil with evil is not the way to right the wrong. However, in that moment of anger, I wanted to avenge the unjust death of my wife. Later, I prayed to God to give me the strength to endure and keep me away from revengeful thoughts. I would never find any peace if I had taken revenge that day.

HATNEIKIM'S STORY

I managed to fix an appointment with Hatneikim, a Kuki woman, taking the help of my local guide. As I arrived to listen to Hatneikim's story, I found her already waiting for my arrival. Hatneikim is 49 years old and lives with her four children. She is actively involved in the local church that she and her husband established. Additionally, she is engaged in informal business from time to time. Hatneikim means 'the plucky one' in Thadou Kuki. "Where do I start or how do I even tell you? Well, let me narrate it to you this way", she started her narrative. On the day Hatneikim's husband died, she had asked him to take rest because he was feeling unwell. However, he went off to cut firewood in the forest regardless. She told me: "I made some *rotis*, and prepared tea in a kettle and gave it to him, so that he and my eldest daughter could have it later in the day." Sometime in the afternoon, Hatneikim heard a gunshot and she ran out of the house to see what had happened. She realised that the gunshot was fired from the direction where her husband and her daughter had headed off earlier that morning. After a while, her daughter came home running and told Hatneikim that her father was injured. Leaving her children behind at home, she ran to the forest. The only thought in her mind was to take him to the hospital, even though she feared he might already be dead.

People had already gathered at the place when she reached. They cut down some branches of trees and tied these together in the form of a makeshift stretcher to carry her husband to the hospital. Sadly, he died on the way. Hatneikim murmured: "I... did not have the strength to look at him. I felt that my husband was carried like an animal that had been hunted down. I went mad, I lost consciousness..." After a long pause, she uttered, "*Yam...nungaite...*" (it was such a very painful feeling). When her husband was carried home, two elderly Naga women and a man came down from the hill carrying firewood on their backs. That moment, Hatneikim thought of killing them. "I was very angry... at that particular moment; I felt that I had the strength to kill anyone. I became fearless... I wanted to grab a machete and hack them to death but suddenly...." Hatneikim paused while she gazed at the floor in deep thought.

> I heard a voice inside me saying that God would not be happy with me if I caused any harm to the innocent people who did not know anything about what had happened. I felt a sense of power controlling me.

After the death of her husband, Hatneikim's biggest worry was to look after her four children. With a deep sigh, she looked up, rubbed her face with her hands, cupped it, paused for a while, and then spoke:

> Then, the next morning I woke up... and I prayed to God and spoke with Him at length about the challenges that awaited me. I felt a sense of relief, a sense of happiness after I prayed. I told myself that I should stop crying over the death of my children's father. I should be strong for their sake. I started earning once again with the determination to find every possible means to look after my children.

RECOLLECTING TRAGIC LOSS

These stories were narrated to me about 20 years after the events had taken place. What nevertheless struck me was the vividness in which they were told. I was astonished by how memories could seemingly just flow from the past into the present. This brought to mind what Maria Konnikova (2015: 1), drawing on her study of 9/11 survivors in New York, had to say about emotional memories: "Shocking emotional events tend to leave a particularly vivid imprint on the mind almost leaving a scar upon the cerebral tissues creating a cognitive impression called the flashbulb memories."[23] When I reflected upon Job and Hatneikim's responses to their encounters, it seemed that anger was the strongest emotion they felt in the aftermath of the violent act. They were filled with rage.[24] Angered by the injustice, they wanted to exert revenge in the name of their beloved one(s). Over time, however, it seemed that their anger was transmuted into a remarkable rationality

---

[23]Similarly, in relation to recalling memory, Butalia (1998: 24) formulated that, "Often, people find it difficult to disentangle what they remember: the memory of violence, the victimhood and the many years that has passed. It is surprising how memories of the past can easily flow into the present and how remembering also meant reliving the past from within the context of the present."

[24]Abrams (2013: 58, 48) in her study to understand parental loss wrote thus: "Feeling of helplessness can often turn to feeling of intense anger which is a natural reaction to a harrowing event. Rage and helplessness are two sides of the same coin." Similarly, Elisabeth Kübler-Ross (1969) in her postulation of "The five stages of grieving" in *On Death and Dying* indicated that anger is a necessary stage, an important element in the process of grieving. She added, "Anger is strength and it can be an anchor, giving temporary structure to the nothingness of loss. The anger is just another indication of the intensity of your love" (Kübler-Ross 1969: 63).

shaped by their realisation that, despite the violence enacted against their spouses, harming others as a response to their emotional state would be equally wrong.[25]

The trauma of losing their spouses led to a transition of their selves. The survivors articulated the experience of their transition as that from a wife to a widow and from a husband to a widower. One of the many challenges, for them, was to appropriate the role of the lost one. This was an overwhelming experience for them. For instance, Job, suddenly a single parent, pointed out how difficult it was for him to run the household on a daily basis. Hatneikim and Khangtheidui expressed how the death of their husbands led to a major downturn in family finances. Adding to the narrative of their struggles, they said, "As widows, we were often isolated." In patriarchal societies like those of the Kukis and Nagas, one common challenge faced by widows is that they are often left alone to fend for themselves.[26] Although some widows are fortunate to receive extensive support from family members, some are not.

When I reflected upon the survivors' narratives, I noticed that they developed certain strategies in order to cope with their loss. I perceived that through prayer, among other strategies, they were able to mitigate their experiences of loss and regain a positive attitude towards life. They acknowledged this by saying, "We were able to find the assurance to move on and to not dwell on the loss."

PRAYER

I asked the survivors about the role of prayer in their lives, especially in view of the loss they had experienced at the hands of ethnic violence. Both Khangtheidui and Hatneikim expressed the divine love they experienced from the firm conviction that God listened to their prayers. Job said thus:

> In prayer, I am consoled; I get more courage and faith. In prayer, I learned to forgive, I get peace and my sorrows are lifted. Prayer has been my armour in all these 20 years since my

[25]Nevertheless, this rationality might only be applicable to the informants and not necessarily to all the others involved in the violence. Many, indeed, did take revenge, and which inflated the violence.

[26]For instance, a widow has no right over her deceased husband's property and pension funds. She may receive a portion of the land and paddy to support her children (Barooah 2002). As a result, it becomes extremely difficult for the widow to sustain her family especially if she entirely depends on agriculture for livelihood, therefore, she has to look out for other means. There are many cases of women being sent away from marital home by the in-laws if the widow has no children from the marriage to look after (Kikon 2002).

wife had passed away.

Prayer, then, helped the survivors reflect on their thoughts and actions. It was through prayer that they could place the dramatic event that occurred in their lives in the hands of God, believing that it must have been God's will. "What has happened has happened. What can I do? Alternatively, what could I have done to change fate? God knows. It is God's will." These lines echoed in the narratives of the survivors I spoke to. Attributing the loss to God offered the survivors a kind of comfort and consolation.[27] Furthermore, I wanted to know how they prayed in their difficult times; Job thus articulated his prayer in the following words:

> I beseech you, O Merciful Father, God of Compassion,
> Have pity upon my sorrows,
> I pour out my grief to you.
> Lord, at this moment, nothing seems to be able to help the loss I feel,
> I am broken and my spirit mourns,
> I beg you to listen to my pleadings.
> Nourish me with your strength,
> Nourish my soul with patience in this difficult moment.
> Help me to conquer this suffering with love.
> Help me to forgive the person, who killed my wife,
> Remember him in mercy; help him to be good again and give him peace. All I know is that you will protect those who acknowledge you, I will lean on you and your faithfulness.

At a broader level, I was curious to know how Kukis and Nagas prayed in times of war and difficulties. A Naga pastor from Manipur who actively worked for peace during the conflict told me how he would go to Kuki villages and prayed with them in their churches.[28] He explained that many village churches were kept open so that anyone could enter and pray for peace, to pray for the cessation of the violence, and to pray that nobody, be they Kukis or Nagas, faced death or misfortune. "Prayer created a sense of understanding between members of both the communities and the intensity of violence was reduced", said the pastor. Noteworthy, too, is the role of the Kuki Women Organization (KWO) and Naga

---

[27]Janice H. Goodman in her study on the coping strategies of young refugees from Sudan pointed out that attributing incidents to the will of God avoided the participants from struggling with questions about why would this happen to them. "It provided an easy answer and enabled the participants to avoid thinking about the reasons for or the meaning of sufferings all around them" (Goodman, 2004: 1187).

[28]Some Kuki pastors performed similar activities.

Women's Union of Manipur (NWUM), which took the initiative to open up a channel of communication between the two communities.[29] In addition, the All Manipur Christian Organisation (AMCO) and Manipur Baptist Convention (MBC) went at great length to encourage mass prayers and peace initiatives in order to reduce the intensity of violence.[30] The Baptist World Alliance also helped in bringing the churches of Kukis and Nagas together to initiate a process of reconciliation. Similarly, civil society groups such as the Kuki Inpi Manipur (KIM) and the United Naga Council (UNC) also formed the Committee for Restoration of Normalcy (CRN) with the motto – 'Let there be no ill-will' to work for the return of peace and normalcy.

What I understood from my interactions with both Kuki and Naga survivors is that prayer provided them with succour and was a means by which they created a relationship with God. Prayer also served as a medium for constant conversation with God. For the survivors, prayer became very personal and did not have to be necessarily articulated into audible words. It became a part of their everyday lives. The narratives here illustrate how praying "signifies to give and to forgive without reservation" (Andrews 2005: 197). Prayer thus gave them the strength to forgive (in the case of some survivors) and to reconcile with their trauma.

FORGIVENESS

> In acts of forgiveness, we are saying here is a chance to make a new beginning because without it there is no future
>
> Desmond Tutu, No Future Without Forgiveness. 1999

When I asked Job how he sees the killer of his wife now, he replied:

> I forgave the man who killed my wife but I will not forget what had happened. Once, I saw the person who killed my wife at the market. Another time, I met him on the riverbank. He did

---

[29]Similarly, reflecting on the power of prayer, Abigail E. Disney and Gini Recticker (2008) in their documentary movie, *Pray the Devil Back to Hell*, shows how women from different religious background gathered to pray for peace during the civil war that started in 1989 in Liberia. In prayer, they found successful ways for reconciliation, peace and courage to bring out more innovative ideas to fight injustice and violence.

[30]AMCO convened emergency meetings during the conflict and made fervent appeals to the two warring tribes, Kukis and Nagas to forgive the wrongs done in the past. Different churches, such as Sadar Hills Baptist Association, Rongmei Naga Baptist Association, Mao Baptist Association and Manipur Catholic Association appealed to people to observe social harmony by not yielding to false rumours (Dena, 2010).

not know that he had shot my wife. He asked me, "Brother, are you cultivating rice here?" I replied, "Yes I am. Where are you off to?" Then I whispered in my heart, "I forgive you."

Job's reflections made me wonder how exactly does one forgive? What made him forgive the person who had so deeply wounded him? How did he find the strength to extend forgiveness? As I began my efforts to explore these questions, I observed that Job recalled the hurt by trying to see how the event would have unfolded from the offender's point of view. He said, "The person who killed my wife was also seeking revenge for his niece who had been injured. Why bring further grief to his family members like he brought to mine?" He then empathised with the family of the offender. By trying to see the events from the point of view of the man who shot his wife, Job extended the altruistic gift of forgiveness. With conviction in his voice, Job told me, "Forgiveness means I hold no grudge against the offender. I have buried what had happened. Of course, it is impossible to forget."[31] While trying to grasp Job's process of coming to terms with his situation and to bestow forgiveness, I found Everett Worthington's principles of forgiveness very relevant. Worthington used the acrostic REACH to teach forgiveness: "Recall the hurt, Empathize, Altruistic gift of forgiveness, Commit publicly to forgive, and Hold on to forgiveness" (Larson, 2009: 91). For Job, forgiveness became a lived experience, not just an extension of theological teaching. Similarly, when I asked Khangtheidui about her view of the wrongdoers, she said,

> I cannot tell whether I have forgiven the wrong doers or not.
> I do not even know whether I have grudges against those who killed my husband. Nevertheless, I stopped my sons from taking revenge. I only prayed harder for strength.

Larson (2009: 88) noted that it is very unhelpful and unwise to make someone feel guilty about not being able to forgive. She holds that, in order to understand forgiveness, one has to understand what forgiveness is not.

> Forgiveness does not mean that what happened didn't matter. It isn't saying that the crime was a misunderstanding. It isn't saying that the crime did little harm. Forgiveness isn't forgetting. Forgiveness isn't usually a one-time act, but more commonly a lifetime commitment, especially of deep wrongs. Finally, and most importantly, forgiveness is excruciatingly difficult and should not be demanded.

---

[31]By not forgetting, it does not imply to evoke anger or revengeful feelings; I feel it is a reminder of people's strength in being human.

Forgiveness is one of the most difficult things to accomplish, almost impossible in the human experience. Yet, it is regarded as a mandate for every Christian. The New Testament places much emphasis on forgiveness.[32] In Christianity, forgiveness has two dimensions: one vertical, the other horizontal. The vertical dimension refers to forgiveness from God and the horizontal dimension refers to forgiveness from and to human beings.[33]

Khangtheidui, Hatneikim, and Job also spoke about their views on revenge. Their narrations reflected the teachings of their faith (Christianity) wherein God does not approve of vengeful thoughts. For instance, Job quoted the New Testament about the disapproval of seeking revenge.[34] He then interpreted the biblical teachings about abstaining from revenge and seeking the peace of God in the following words,

> The priests used to tell me that I would be no less than the perpetrator if I seek revenge. I was advised, "Control your anger and pray for your wife's departed soul instead. Pray for yourself and the perpetrator too." I would be filled with rage when I think about what had happened to my wife. However, I tell myself that I have no right to take his life. What would I gain by taking his life? I could have sought revenge but I left it to God to decide the judgement for the perpetrator.

Similarly, Khangtheidui voiced, "We were all devastated. My sons wanted to avenge their father's unjust death but I warned them not to do so by saying, Our Lord Jesus taught us not to take revenge or they would lose their lives instead." I noticed that Hatneikim also had the same approach when she thought of avenging the death of her husband, as I mentioned earlier. She stopped herself from inflicting harm on someone with the thought that God would not be happy with her. Thus, I infer that the teachings of their faith actively prevented them from committing a revengeful act.

[32]For instance, Mark 11:25 (NIV) says, "If you hold anything against anyone, forgive them, so your father in heaven may forgive you". To cite a few more instances, Colossians 3:13, Matthew 18:21 and James 5:16.

[33]This insight is derived from a conversation I had with Melvil Pereira on December 20, 2016.

[34]"Do not repay anyone evil for evil. Do not take revenge, my friends, but leave room for God's wrath, for it is written: "It is mine to avenge; I will repay," says the Lord. (Romans 12: 17&19, NIV)."

CONCLUSION

In this chapter, I explored the lived experiences of survivors of ethnic violence in Manipur and demonstrated the centrality of prayer in their lives. Through their everyday prayers, they were able to endure and forgive. I witnessed that the faith professed by people living in Manipur's militarized society largely helped them in rationalising tragic events in their lives. The strength of their resilience also helped them to construct positive attitude towards life.

While I believe that these survivors trusted the mercy of God, I am equally convinced that their strength of character to imbibe Christian teachings and to put these into practice exemplifies that they live out what is preached locally. I, however, do not claim that all Kukis and Nagas succeeded in this. Members of both communities, after all, were involved in violent acts. The paradoxical Christian life among Kukis and Nagas also maintained the status quo of the protracted conflict. On one hand, Christianity preaches 'agape'[35], which is sacrificial to the extent of self-denial for the sake of another, while on the other its Kuki and Naga followers were not devoid of violence between themselves at a communal level and along ethnic and sectarian lines.

However, the stories of survivors, their experience of forgiveness and reconciliation validates humanity and it sets an example for us all. I addressed reconciliation with the concept of healing; a healing of an individual's wound created by the violent Kuki-Naga conflict. This healing, which is a lived experience re-humanises the survivor and restores hope. Noteworthy is Lederach and Lederach's (When Blood and Bones Cry out: Journeys through the Soundscape of Helaing and Reconciliaiton, 2010) work on their quest for nurturing spaces of healing and reconciliation after Liberia's civil war. They asserted, "Healing restores voices of individuals and communities through interaction and interplay of voices" (Ibid.: 110). Through the stories of the individuals, I realised that it is important to share stories in order to nurture spaces of healing and reconciliation. More broadly, among Kukis and Nagas, an undertaking of a communal exploration of the common grounds of empathy, compassion, sympathy, respect, and altruism would facilitate much needed communal reconciliation.

---

[35]The Greek word agape is often translated 'love' in the New Testament. The essence of agape love is goodwill and benevolence. Unlike the English word love, agape does not refer to romantic love nor does it refer to the love of close relationships. *Agape* involves faithfulness, commitment and an act of will, distinguished from other types of love. Accessed at: https://www.gotquestions.org/agape-love.html on 05-01-2017.

ACKNOWLEDGEMENTS

Analysis and research presented in this chapter are further elaborated in my monograph *Enduring Loss: Stories from the Kuki-Naga Conflict in Manipur* (North Eastern Social Research Centre, 2017). It builds upon my M.A. dissertation, which was completed under the guidance of Yengkhom Jilangamba who directed my cathartic journey of taking forward my personal experiences and of moulding them into a work that lends a voice to those that were affected by the Kuki-Naga conflict. I thank Melvil Pereira and Walter Fernandes of North Eastern Social Research Centre (NESRC) for providing the academic space and materials required to write this chapter. I express my sincere gratitude to Dolly Kikon and Xonzoi Barbora for constantly encouraging me with their insightful comments in many drafts, while their home provided me with the stimulus and environment to write this chapter. Joel Rodrigues, for patiently meeting my demands on his time; his feedback on early drafts of this chapter has benefited it immensely. The comments of the two anonymous reviewers also benefitted this chapter substantially. I express my heartfelt gratitude to the two editors, Jelle J. P. Wouters and Michael Heneise for the dynamic discussions with valuable suggestions, ideas and comments, for being considerate and providing useful related materials. I thank two local guides for their kindness in giving so much time and helping me meet the survivors to learn their stories. I remain indebted to the men and women, whose stories I tell here. I cannot express enough gratitude to them for speaking to me and opening up their painful, yet powerful, experiences. I sincerely hope that I have not reduced their overwhelming experiences to a mere pile of words, for they are, and will always remain far more than that. My deepest gratitude to my father for being my interpreter and my companion all throughout the course of my data collection, his deep understanding of the nuances of the languages and local cultures helped me connect to my participants and understand them better. The usual disclaimers apply.

■ ■■ ■■

06

WHO SINGS FOR THE HORNBILL? THE PERFORMANCE AND POLITICS OF CULTURE IN NAGALAND

Arkotong Longkumer

This chapter reflects on the annual Hornbill Festival celebrated by the Nagas of Nagaland in Northeast India. It provides an ethnographic account of the various activities and the different actors involved in the Festival, and examines what makes this a compelling tourist destination. The state of Nagaland capitalises on the colourful image of the Festival as an 'exotic' location, which plays on the warrior and tribal identity often associated with the Nagas; ideas of 'traditional' culture; and the mountainous and pristine landscape. While the region has witnessed over fifty years of armed conflict between the Indian state and different Naga nationalists demanding independence, the Festival provides a creative public space where all sections of society – urban/rural; students/politicians/administrators; Indian army/Naga nationalists – can freely mingle, a temporary lull from the otherwise pervasive militarised landscape.

From the vantage point of the tribal Naga Kachari morung (traditional youth dormitory), I am mesmerised by the vivid colours of the different tribal attire. I hear myriad voices as throngs of people huddle around crackling bonfires with their bamboo jugs of hot tea and rice-beer, as dusk brings the unwelcome December winter chill in Kisama. It's the end of the first day of Hornbill Festival

2012. Just above me, amidst the orange glow of the evening sun, the white letters 'Naga Heritage Village', a copy of the iconic 'Hollywood' sign, are faintly visible in contrast to the faded green of the hillside. On the hilltop, a familiar Christian cross was foisted, I was told, to remind people that this is Nagaland, and like in most Naga villages, it is a central symbol: of Christ as redeemer. Each tribal morung is arranged according to the geographic map of their location within Nagaland. During the course of the Festival they entertain various visitors in their morung by performing their songs and dances, and exhibiting the different material culture.

The Festival over the years has mushroomed into a mega state event that includes stalls that sell food, clothes and artefacts encouraging local, regional and national entrepreneurs to participate; it also hosts a number of indigenous games like Naga acrobatics, pig-chasing, and Naga chilli (the hottest in the world!) eating competition. It has introduced Rock, Fashion and Art shows and a bizarre World War II car rally that is an attempt to cater to a variety of audiences both within and outside Nagaland.

Access to Nagaland has been difficult primarily due to the fifty-year-old independence struggle with the Indian state that has seen the rise of several Naga movements: the Naga National Council (NNC), the two National Socialist Council of Nagaland (Isak-Muivah; and Khaplang), and other variants of these factions (see Longvah, this volume). The peace process between these groups and the Indian state in 1997 ushered in relative calm, making travel and tourism easier. However, 'official' access to this region is still enforced in the form of the Restricted Area Permits (RAP) for foreigners and the Inner Line Permits (ILP) for Indian citizens outwith Nagaland and Northeast India. In 2011 the RAP was lifted while the ILP remains. Some Indian citizens I met from the Indian states of Uttar Pradesh and Maharashtra were irked by this duplicity that denies them access to regions within their own country. As a sign of protest, they have 'infiltrated' Nagaland without ILPs.

Speaking and interacting with various people gives me a sense of the truly global dimension to the Festival that has grown in leaps and bounds from its earlier conception. Its origins coincided with the International year of the World's Indigenous People in 1993. It was called 'Naga week' and held between 1st- 5th of December in the local Kohima ground, organised by the Naga Peoples Movement for Human Rights (NPHMR) and the Naga Students Federation (NSF). 'It was a difficult time for us', reflected Neingulo of NPHMR because factional clashes between the two NSCNs, along with Indian Army operations made the situation very tense 'on the ground'. Using the slogan and rhetoric of the 'world's indigenous peoples' year', the NPHMR and the NPF appealed to the two NSCNs to cease fighting. Calm pervaded throughout the week when around twenty-seven Naga tribes from the Indian states of Nagaland, Assam, Manipur and even Burma came and constructed their morungs and celebrated their 'indigenous' cultures, creating a momentary safe space where they could come as 'one' Naga nation.

For Neingulo, this was a 'real' celebration of indigenous Naga culture because

Who sings for the Hornbill? The performance and politics of culture in Nagaland   ▪

109

Figure 8. Sangtam Naga women performing outside of their *morung*.
(Photo courtesy Michael Heneise.)

there was a spirit of solidarity, amidst the chaos and violence, that encouraged cooperation between different Nagas from all over. He laments that the Hornbill Festival in its current avatar is a poor imitation of the 1993 event. He says that the Government of Nagaland has made it into a commercial 'state' Festival that involves only its official seventeen Naga tribes. Many people I spoke to seem to agree with this sentiment. In fact, two officers from the tourism industry tell me separately that the Festival is about 'selling' Nagaland to the outside world. They say that the success of the Festival is down to the presence of international tourists who come with cameras and are busy interacting with the various Naga troupes of performers. In fact, I do notice the active (and sometimes aggressive!) camera flashes are from their lenses. Most international tourists come to the Festival as 'cultural tourists' who frequent festivals in many indigenous hotspots. One couple from Germany tell me they recently attended a similar Festival in Papua New Guinea and heard about the Hornbill on their way to Bhutan. Such cosmopolitan tourists makeup the majority of those who come to Nagaland. I interact with four of them from England. Johnny and Sabina weren't sure if the 'Nagas' were 'Indians' – they said that Nagaland feels more like Southeast Asia. For Johnny, the Hornbill Festival represents the expression of an 'authentic Naga national identity'. He is particularly impressed by the parade of bagpipes and drums with its accompanying material accoutrements. Perhaps this is a nostalgic reminder of Britain's colonial rule? Indeed, the odd conflation of tartans kilts amidst the sea of Naga traditional clothes makes the event slightly bizarre if not mildly entertaining.

Sabina is more critical. Having lived in Northern Thailand, where similar festivals were common, she observes that whereas in Thailand it was less organised and more spontaneous, the Hornbill was highly choreographed and managed. It gives one the impression that it is more of a 'show', than a 'genuine' Naga festival. Haley agrees. She contrasts the Hornbill Festival with those of neighbouring Garo and Khasi tribal festivals that were more 'genuine'. Mike is more academic in his approach and says that he really enjoyed the Hornbill and this is the 'real deal'. He is wary of comments of 'authenticity' – which authority decides its criteria? He is unequivocal in his stance that if the Nagas say that they are attempting to preserve and display 'authentic' Naga culture than who are we to say otherwise?

Authenticity is what drives many tourists to the Hornbill. I meet a group of tourists from Bangalore who are part of a photography course. Priya, Sandesh and Ashwin came across Peter van Ham's coffee table book on the Nagas and were fascinated by the vivid picture of 'traditional-authentic' Nagaland. I ask them if such representations are highly 'exotic' and problematic? They react positively and say that the 'exotic' element is one of the reasons why they came in the first place (see also Tinyi, this volume). Of course, coming here, they realise that things are different between 'image' and 'context', but nevertheless it is the motivating factor. Our conversation drifts to ideas of indigenous peoples' rights, the Hornbill Festival and the Naga national movement for sovereignty. Hema, an ecotourist, says that through this Festival she can see the unique 'indigenous' and strong national culture of the Nagas. Before she was wary of such intellectual tropes, but now she

Figure 9. The panoply of tourists, mixed with local participants, represents the sea of humanity (Photo by Arkotong Longkumer.)

Figure 10. *Nagaland: Land of Festivals* billboard.(Photo by Arkotong Longkumer.)

can see why the Nagas want to be left alone: 'self- determination' is a right. Malini disagrees and says that Nagaland is an integral part of India – even if they gain independence, how would they sustain themselves? These questions are at the back of the minds of many national tourists from outside Nagaland, due to its long history of violent insurgency in the region.

The visible presence of the security forces, both the Naga police force who provide security at Kisama to VIPs and delegates, and the throngs of Indian Army *jawans*, officers and their families, are a constant reminder that issues surrounding 'Naga independence' are hotly contested. One Kashmiri stall owner says that it is striking to compare Kashmir and Nagaland due to the overt and visible military might on show. The Indian Army even has a separate, cordoned off plush seating area for their officers and families. The co-mingling of the forces of exclusion and inclusion is what makes the paradox of nationhood striking: the uneasy relationship between the Nagas and the Indian state, even though it is funding from New Delhi that enables such a festival. On the other hand, questions of indigeneity provide international legitimation that allow the Nagas to perform and represent a 'distinct' Naga culture and link with United Nations ideas of indigenous people's rights of cultural uniqueness, self- determination, and sovereignty. These debates circle each Naga *morung* in the Hornbill though couched in a different, and sometimes ambivalent, language.

'Nagas are not Indians' is a common sentiment one often hears in the Hornbill (and elsewhere in Nagaland). Some Nagas say that this idea becomes even more coherent when international tourists (mainly) recognise such disjuncture of the territorial imprint of the Indian state and the national imaginary of the Nagas. The jarring of these two ideas is evident during the opening session of the Hornbill Festival. The event starts off with the Indian national anthem that is greeted with indifference by the largely Naga audience (a number of tourists also told me that it felt rather forced). This message of national integration of the Indian Republic is further extolled in speeches made by the Governor and Chief Minister of Nagaland. Yet, some of the Naga public are uneasy with such rhetoric because for them Naga sovereignty is non- negotiable and the intrusion of the Indian state (read Indian Army) in such national festivals is flexing muscle – to 'show who is boss'. Other Nagas favour being in the Republic because it brings economic development – Naga independence anyway is a far-off dream! Some are not fully aware of what it even means to be 'Naga' let alone Naga sovereignty.

Khiamniungan Nagas from places like Noklak in Eastern Nagaland (near the Burma border) told me that the Festival is a chance for them to see other Nagas. They have only 'imagined' and heard of the Angami and Chakhesang Nagas, now they can actually see them. The constructed and dynamic nature of Naga identity is played out interestingly in the Hornbill Festival. For some it allows a visual glimpse of other tribes, while for others it's an opportunity to be included into the Naga fold. Many Kachari, Garo, and Kuki people told me that even though they are recognised 'officially' by the Government of Nagaland as 'Naga', the other Naga tribes don't. Having a *morung* in the Hornbill is helpful and legitimises their claim to be 'indigenous' inhabitants of Nagaland – for them territorial indigeneity is the

Figure 11. Tourists with their cameras.(Photo by Arkotong Longkumer.)

Figure 12. A day out in the sun, with a group of Indian tourists. (Photo by Arkotong Longkumer.)

sole marker of Naga identity, not blood, language or customary practices. Although they have kin relations elsewhere: the Garo (in Meghalaya); the Kachari (in Assam); and the Kuki (in Assam/Manipur/Mizoram), they say they are Nagas and have nothing to do with their kin (although cultural ties are strongly maintained through marriage). When one Kuki lady said that they are not 'Naga', she was quickly reprimanded for her foolishness. The politics of the moment necessitates their inclusion into the Naga fold.

While the political dimension of the Festival clearly resonates with the larger project of national identity, especially when one digs deeper, the cultural aspects of the Festival are also significant. What is 'culture' is often asked when interacting with the many performing artists and tribal delegates in the *morungs*. For some, they haven't changed one single song or dance routine, it's 'original' they say. Others confess the painful tattooing process and vow never to do it again, and point to cohorts' tattoos that have been painted using ink (some even wear plastic Hornbill feathers due to its rarity). Amongst the Nagas, they comment that the 'wilder' you are, the more tourists you attract. So, the Konyak, Yimchunger, Chang, and the Khiamniungan *morungs* are busier than most. Some, like the Phom *morung*, are largely empty while the Lotha *morung* serve mainly food. The Ao *morung* involves a lot of joking and jesting around one Ao comedian who is being recorded on mobile phones to show to their villagers upon returning home. The idea of 'tradition' and 'modernity' are part and parcel of the surroundings and there is no denying that the two often go hand in hand when discussing the politics of 'culture'. This particular dimension has become significant in the past few years and the future of the Hornbill signals the happy co-mingling of both the local and the global.

Speaking to Abu Metha and Himato Zhimomi, both distinguished officers in the Government of Nagaland and organisers of the Festival this year, one gets the sense that the Festival is expanding its reach in terms of the scale of organisation, variety of programmes; making this truly a mecca of Festivals both nationally and internationally. 'Why can't we make the Hornbill Festival like the Edinburgh Fringe?' Abu told me as we stood inside the venue of the Naga Art Exhibition. He said that along with the Chief Minister of Nagaland, Neiphiu Rio, they came to Edinburgh during the Fringe and were in awe of the scale, infrastructure, organisation, the events on display, and its reputation. He wants to make the two festivals more alike and even showed me the Hornbill catalogue of events that resembled the Edinburgh Fringe one. Such is the vision, but not shared by all. Some see the Hornbill as a waste of time, money and exercise, which needs to be reduced to three days – it takes immense human labour, inconvenience (traffic during the Festival is a nightmare), and expenses that don't justify its scale. One tourism officer told me that the investment far outweighs the return, and it is unsustainable for the long run. Church leaders are equally sceptical. They see the Hornbill as encouraging drinking (Nagaland is a Christian dry state!), sexual freedom and partying (most of the local youths emerge only during the night entertainment of music, fashion and drink). One young Ao pastor told me that the Nagaland Baptist Church Council

Figure 13. Army personnel and tourists co-mingle at Naga Heritage Village, Kisama. (Photo by Arkotong Longkumer.)

(NBCC) held a day walk around Kisama praying against the evil and licentiousness the Hornbill was encouraging amongst the youth. The church holds that reviving traditional Naga culture mustn't clash with Christianity – the famous 'Christ and culture' debate is being rehearsed in many church corners.

Instead of viewing the Hornbill Festival as a micro-event, it is more useful to think of its links to the larger economic, cultural, religious and political processes that have wider consequences for the future of the Nagas. A sort of ethnographic 'thick description' has been attempted through the Festival that tells multiple stories with many actors and audiences. Its success has truly put Nagaland on the map in terms of its global outreach and tourist destination, but difficult questions are also being asked that involve many sections of the society with ideological positions in the global arena of fluid connections on the one hand and the increasing crystallisation of its boundaries and identities on the other. A balance between the two is most prudent but also the most difficult.

Sitting around a warm fire outside the Kachari *morung*, Joseph, a Kachari elder, and I are in deep conversation when one of the Kachari youth come up to him and ask if he could change into his 'proper clothes'. Joseph laughs and asks why, and the youth says because it's cold in my Kachari traditional clothes! I left the Hornbill thinking that there are many ways this puzzle can be completed, it's just that I still haven't found all the pieces.

■ ■ ■ ■ ■

07

THE HEADHUNTING CULTURE OF THE NAGAS: REINTERPRETING THE SELF

Venusa Tinyi

Introduction

It is a fact of history that Nagas practiced headhunting. What is unfortunate about this fact, however, is that it has come to be essentialised as the defining identity of the Nagas.[1] Nagas believed and practiced many other things but for reasons

[1]The use of the terms 'headhunters' and 'headhunting' without italics in this paper is deliberate. Throughout this paper, I will use them interchangeably with warrior. Just as the term 'Nagas' has been accepted by us, as our ethnic identity though popularized by the colonizers, Nagas have by and large accepted this description of former headhunters as well. In this regard, I agree with Longkumer (2015: 60) who observes 'that viable continuities exist between the colonial and postcolonial situation, and one must appreciate the way images [referring to headhunters and primitive], once deployed for colonialism's purpose, continue to shape the current landscape as an attractive medium for tourism and identity in the global arena.' He goes on to argue that such exotic images enables Nagas to forge a distinct national culture.

of their own, many colonial writers choose to overlook these and priviliged the 'headhunting culture' as the fundamental representation of Naga identity.[2] In this chapter, I will endeavour to present an understanding of what headhunting culture means to Nagas themselves, and from the view point of a native[3]. I then proceed to explain this culture in relation to some core traditional values and beliefs of Nagas. The discussion in this paper is expected to give some native insights from a contemporary Naga perspective about why we were the kind of people we were in the premodern time and also, to some extent, why we are the kind of people we are today.

ANALYSING THE TERM 'HEADHUNTING' VIS-À-VIS 'TROPHY HUNTING'

Let me begin with what is familiar to me. 'Headhunter', as a term, was not a self-referential expression and its equivalent meaning is difficult to find in the context of the Chakhesang Nagas. Similarly, Tezenlo Thong opines that Nagas never called or thought of themselves as headhunters (Thong 2012b). However, there are some notable linguistic similarities between the use of the terms headhunting and animal hunting. The first is related to the use of the syllable 'ga' (kill) in the Chokri language spoken among the Chakhesang tribe.[4] 'Ga', a suffix, is used to describe and qualify the act of killing animals (thi-ga) during animal hunting and the killing of 'other people' (mi-ga) during raids or wars.[5] 'Ga' has no moral connotation or implication unlike 'dothri' (kill or murder) which usually comes with a moral judgment. There is yet another significant parallel between the two in Chokri:

---

[2]Among others, the two important reasons worth noting in the context of this paper are (1) the urge of colonial writers to construct the notion of the 'exotic other' to satisfy the imagination of their readers in their home-countries and (2) the necessity of maintaining and justifying their colonial notion of power relations based on civilizational superiority. For a detailed criticism of stereotyping Nagas as headhunters, see Thong (2012b).

[3]In general, views expressed in this paper reflect a local view from the perspective of the Chakhesang tribe, the tribal community I belong to. However, care has been taken throughout the paper to ensure that the context of discussion will make it clear if I am writing from the perspective of a Naga in general or from the perspective of a Chakhesang, in particular. It may be noted that the Chakhesang tribe is one of the recognized tribes in Nagaland state. It is constituted by three main linguistic groups, namely, Chokri, Khuza/Kheza and Zamai. Some Chakhesang villages also contain Sema/Sumi speaking people.

[4]Chokri is my mother tongue.

[5]It is important to note that no Naga tribe has the practice of taking heads from within the same village. So, headhunting was expected only on people belonging to other villages or to non-Nagas.

thiri-hu and thi-hu. While the former literally means 'war-chase', the latter means 'animal-chase'. The common suffix for both the terms is 'hu', meaning chase. In this sense, the term 'thiri-hu' can be used very loosely to mean headhunting and 'thi-hu' to mean animal hunting. Derivatively, thirimi or thirimavemi may be seen as a translation of 'headhunters'. While thirimi generally refers to a group of people armed for war, thirimavemi is very specific; only those warriors who succeeded in taking a head from another village are called 'thirimavemi'.

Having discussed the meanings in Chokri, I however doubt that the colonial writers were aware of these linguistic connotations and accordingly decided to use the term 'headhunting' for the custom of cutting heads during raids and wars. On the contrary, it is highly possible that the employment of these terms by them was influenced, at least partially, by an elitist component of popular, colonial culture back then, that of trophy hunting.[6] Trophy hunting in Africa and the Indian subcontinents – then colonies of European powers - had become a fashionable recreational and sportive activity variously engaged in by colonial officers during their spare time. To cite just one instance; it is being recorded that King George V, after being enthroned in 1911, bagged 39 tigers, 18 rhinoceros and 4 bears in Nepal in one of his hunting trips along with his retinue in 1911.[7] The general practice of trophy hunting was to kill wild animals, not for their meat, but for pleasure and prestige and to keep selected parts of killed animals such as heads, teeth, tasks and horns as souvenirs. The selected parts of animals were generally displayed as trophies in a special room called 'trophy room' or 'game room' in which the weaponry of the hunters were also normally displayed. Animal trophies also of course served to represent the courage, skill and success of the hunters.

With this colonial European culture of trophy hunting at the back of our mind, it is not difficult to understand why colonial writers described the Naga custom of head-taking in wars and raids as headhunting. For instance, one colonial writer stated, 'When the enemy is caught unprepared, they rushed upon them with

[6]According to the International Union for Conservation of Nature Species Survival Commission (IUCN SSC), the term 'trophy hunting' is used to refer [animal] hunting that is ... 'usually (but not necessarily) undertaken by hunters from outside the local area (often from countries other than where the hunt occurs)'; see IUCN SSC Guiding principles on Trophy Hunting as a Tool for Creating Conservation Incentives. Ver. 1.0. IUCN, Gland. P.2. (https://cmsdata.iucn.org/downloads/iucn_ssc_guiding_principles_on_trophy_hunting_ver1_09aug2012.pdf: accessed on 24/04/2017). Synonymously, trophy hunters are also referred to as sport hunters or safari hunters in the contemporary time. Trophy hunting was practiced by kings and great hunters on the Indian soil since at least the medieval time, much before the advent of colonial raj.

[7]The details of this event was recorded by Baron Hardinge, who was the then Governor-General of India (1910-1916), in the Historical record of the Imperial visit to India, 1911, (pp.231-233) and the same was published by John Murray for the Government of India in London, 1914.

great ferocity, and tearing off the scalps of all those who fall victims to their rage, they carry home those strange trophies of their triumph.' (Robinson 1969: 538: emphasis mine). A. W. Davis reported in the Census of India (1891), 'In the front verandah are collected all the trophies of war and of the chase, from a man's skull down to a monkey's, most of them black with the smoke and dust of years' (Davis 1969: 399: emphasis mine).[8] It is interesting to note that Davis used the term 'chase' here, a term I have used earlier in the context of giving literal interpretations for the Chokri expressions, viz., 'thiri-hu' and 'thi-hu' respectively as 'war-chase' and 'animal-chase'. T.C. Hudson commented along similar lines, 'A raid in order to get a head is a religious business, and not lightly undertaken, whatever its motive. They may think killing 'fine sport', but they prepare themselves for the sport with solemn rites.' (Hudson 1991: 122: emphasis mine). Going by their language use, it is quite possible that colonial officers, at least some of them, perceived our ancestral custom of head taking in wars and raids as some kind of sporting activity or trophy hunting. Perhaps due to the influence of colonial writings of Nagas, even contemporary Naga writers in general seem to portray no qualms in describing the heads taken in past wars and raids as trophies.[9]

It may be pointed out that Nagas were not the only people who practiced headhunting and that it may be too quick to generalize from the foregoing account that the then usage of the term 'headhunting' was influenced by the colonial practice of trophy hunting.[10] However I posit that, as a term, 'headhunting' or 'headhunter' was not commonly used as an identity term or descriptive term with reference to the Nagas by the colonial writers in question until the later part of the colonial era. For instance, the seminal work on the Nagas by Verrier Elwin – The Nagas in the Nineteen Century – which is a compilation of a large number of articles/reports actually used the term 'head-hunters' only once, and so by A. W. Davis in the report mentioned above although Elwin himself used it a few

---

[8]In the same book, edited by Elwin, few others also freely used the term trophies to describe the heads/skulls preserved by the Nagas in their writing of the Nagas; they are, Lieutenant-Colonel R. G. Woodthorpe (63-83); Capt. Vetch (92-96); E. T. Dalton (440-442); W. Robinson (530-540). J.H. Hutton, one of the well-known authors on the Nagas has used the term 'trophies' to title his paper, 'Divided and Decorated Heads as Trophies' which was published in Man, Vol. XXII, No. 67 (1922).

[9]Despite Nagas' use of this term in their writings, I highly suspect that they would be using this term in the same sense as the colonial writers would. I have been asking lately if there is any equivalent term for 'trophy' in the Naga languages but to my surprise, none of my Naga correspondents could provide me with an adequate one. I assume therefore that Naga writers, at least some, have been using the term 'trophy' for want of a better term.

[10]Temsula Ao cites the work of Robert Heine-Gelden which claims that headhunting culture was prevalent in vast regions of Europe, Central Asia, Egypt and Near East, not forgetting the recent ones in Africa, South East Asia and Oceania (Ao 2014: 14-15).

times for structuring the book. Many authors, it must be qualified, alluded to the headhunting culture of the Nagas but without using the word explicitly. It became a common referential term mainly in the twentieth century. This seems to suggest that either the colonial writers then were not very familiar with the discourse on headhunting culture of other peoples, or that the term was not commonly used as a referential term for the Nagas as indicated above. In any case, the language of describing the headhunting culture during the initial encounters with the Nagas shows that the colonial writers interpreted headhunting from the perspective of their own culture, certainly not from a Naga point of view.

If headhunting was understood primarily as a form of trophy hunting from a colonial perspective, then it is not difficult to understand why they employed negative images to construct Naga identity.[11] It is certainly savage and immoral from the perspective of any modern civilizational sense to kill another human being just to collect his or her head as a trophy, as an item of display. But the question is this: Did our Naga ancestors who practiced headhunting actually prized human heads as mere trophies? My answer is that they did not. It may be noted that not all colonial writers gave a negative portrayal of the Nagas on account of this practice. Some like J.P. Mills, J.H. Hutton, and Christoph von Fürer-Haimendorf provided a more sympathetic account of headhunting by trying to give religious or mystical interpretations of its practice.

As far as the oral narratives of my tribe are concerned, our ancestors did not 'hunt' people to collect their heads for the sole of purpose of display, even though it is certainly true that they would return with the heads of the enemies after killing them. But the taking of enemy heads was not the primary reason for killing others, unlike trophy hunters or hunters for whom taking specific parts of animals or the meat of the animal for food constituted the very reason for hunting. Nagas, however, went to war or executed raids primarily in order to settle scores or to assert the power and supremacy of their village. Though some went to war for reasons of fame and honor, their personal ventures served the interest of the village. So unlike trophy hunting, which basically serves the interest of only some in the society without any direct connection to established customs and traditions, the practice of headhunting was deeply rooted in core values and beliefs of the people, and which were vested in the village. Headhunting in this sense was institutionalized,[12] an integral part of the social structure.

Although, it cannot be denied outright that the taking of heads has something in common with trophy hunting, such as the desire to display the heads as 'trophies'

---

[11]Whether or not their more sympathetic accounts are acceptable and justifiable is left to the readers to decide at the end of this paper. I for one do not think highly of their positive interpretations though their views are neither implausible nor inconsistent.

[12]Ao observes that because headhunting was an 'institutionalized' way of Naga life, it was surrounded by elaborate rituals and ceremonies (Ao 2014: 22)

to symbolize the courage and prowess of the warriors, the desire to prove oneself as worthy warriors would hardly constitute the main explanation for displaying heads in the case of Nagas. In other words, a human head is not prized for its own sake like an animal trophy. Rather it has some other purpose to serve, the end purpose of which does not require a human head as a necessary condition. Let me cite a couple of reasons from the context of my tribe, the Chakhesang Naga. If a warrior is unable to bring the head of the slain enemy (because he was not in a position to outrun the enemy warriors with the head or heads taken by him, or for any other reason), he is allowed to bring the right ear as a proof of his kill. This apparently was an acceptable custom even among the Semas/Sumis. Inato Yekheto Shiku (2007: 21) writes:

> It is deplorable and yet titillating to learn from my father, Yekheto Shiku, that my grandfather, Shokiye Shiku, was one of the headhunters who brought home the hacked ears of the enemy. He could not bring home the enemy's head because he had to trek a far distance from home and also had to escape his enemy.

Besides, the head of the slain can be taken back from the warrior by the villagers of the slain on request through recognized mediatory channels. For instance, legend has it that when the most well-known headhunter from my village (Kikruma) by the name Niho (famed for taking above 70 heads, some even say 100) was killed by warriors from neighbouring Phesachodu village, his head was given back to my village on request after necessary rituals had been conducted. The fact that there were such exceptions offer evidence that a human head is not prized as a trophy for its own sake. It is interesting and worthwhile to note that unlike some other Naga tribes, my tribe would not generally display heads in morungs,[13] on war drums or on sacred poles or trees or rocks;[14] heads would be hidden behind the village gates and entry to specific village gates, whose passage would be restricted to outsiders or travelers for some fixed period of time when fresh heads had been put in those gates.[15]

From a different trajectory, Thong has aggressively argued that colonial writers misrepresented Nagas as headhunters in a derogatory and abusive manner. He writes:

[13]The dormitory for grown up boys/young adults is called morung. It is in the morung that the boys would generally get all their traditional schooling for life's lessons.

[14]For more details on the sacred locations of keeping the heads by different Naga tribes, see (Mills 1935: 418-428).

[15]I owe this information to Mr. Veswuhu Vero, a respectable elder from my tribe. He further explains to me that this was done for security reason.

The term 'headhunting' is a colonial construct, which has become synonymous with the word Nagas. Headhunting refers to the practice of decapitation in warfare, which has been often understood and described out of context. This misconstrued stereotype implies that the Nagas had and have an innate and bloodthirsty nature. As a consequence, they are often referred to in colonial texts as 'wild' Nagas, 'bloodthirsty savages', etc. (Thong 2012b: 608).

The point Thong is trying to drive home perhaps can be framed like this: 'Colonizers are guilty of making us look like barbarians by misrepresenting us as headhunters; don't you see that we are as normal as any other human being?' Thong basically analyses the practice of headhunting in relation to war and then goes on to argue that war is not a part of the normal life of the Nagas, rather unlike the exaggerated versions of the colonial writers. He aptly discusses the customary rules related to wars in the context of the Nagas and provides a very non-savagery and non-barbaric picture of traditional Naga warfare. Reading Thong's essay gives an impression that war and headhunting incidents were so minimal that they remain better seen as stray cases. However, he does not explain why our ancestors practiced headhunting as part of warfare in the first place, even as he seems to disagree with different views on the explanation of headhunting.[16] As such the reader is left with little clue as to how one ought to make sense of the headhunting culture of our ancestors. Moreover, due to his attempt to associate headhunting only with wars, Thong does not discuss the practice of raids.[17] It may be pointed out, however, that raids were actually more common than wars in the context of the Nagas and that many legendary warriors made names for themselves through raids and not necessarily through war. As consistent as his articulated views appear to be with his devastating attack on colonial accounts of headhunting culture of the Nagas, I hold a different view. I argue that the headhunting culture is deeply rooted in our ethos and values whether or not we approve of it today, and that it is almost indissoluble for our identity construction. The task is to reinterpret it and, if necessary, reinterpret it in a way that the contemporary world would understand as well.

Though headhunting was part of warring practices, it is not to be misinterpreted as the reason or the cause of wars originally or generally. In other words, wars were not fought just for the sake of human heads. Heads were collected in wars and

---

[16]He has identified and briefly discussed all the popular colonial views, 10 in all, on the explanatory account of headhunting. See p. 385. Similar accounts have also been mentioned by J.P. Mills in his article (Mills 1935: 418-428).

[17]In his book, Shimray classifies and describes 5 different forms of Naga war, including raids (Shimray 1985: 79-93)

raids for a more fundamental reason, a point which will be explored in more detail below. A common myth on the origin of headhunting culture echoes the point I am making here:

> One day, a warrior was resting by the road on his way home. He noticed that the spot where he was sitting was swarmed with ants and they seemed to be engaged in a frantic affair. He watched them keenly and discovered that in fact the ant groups were having a fight. After some time, the activities of the ants became less frantic and he could see only a few of them. As he continued watching these few, he discovered, to his amazement, that these few were engaged in a peculiar activity. They were beheading the slain ants and were carrying off their heads! (Ao 2012: 101-2).

Having noted the above points, it is still not clear as to how one ought to make sense of the culture of headhunting in the context of the Nagas. Just assuming that headhunting culture was widespread in different parts of the world in the pre-modern time is hardly sufficient. As suggestive as the above myth is, it leaves many things unexplained, especially from a modern rational perspective. However to claim a single reason that can be considered as the correct or absolute explanation is unlikely to be possible for the simple reason that there is no objective or commonly acceptable criterion to settle on for the diverse Naga tribal groups. As such, the next best thing would be to ask the purpose it had served and its significance to our ancestors. Through a consideration of its significance, one can perhaps try to retrospectively deduce the most plausible explanation. It is this direction that I will try to develop in the pages that follow.

LOCATING THE PRACTICE OF HEADHUNTING WITHIN THE NORMATIVE STRUCTURE OF NAGA SOCIETY

As pointed out earlier, headhunting was not outside the normative structure of Naga society. In other words, its origin cannot be explained in terms of a culture of lawlessness as in 'every man becomes a law only unto himself.' It was not the result of political anarchy as has been believed by some colonial writers, shown for instance in the following quote: 'A quarrel, however, between two villages, or even between two families of the same village, leads to miserable results – blood for blood, treacherous surprises, cruel punishments.' (Latham 1969: 97). Our ancestors strongly believed in the primacy of norms and customs over the interests of individuals or groups within the society. Unwarranted disturbances or violence in the community was seriously dealt with. Headhunting took place between warring villages and never deliberately between citizens of the same village or between friendship-villages or allied villages.[18] In other words, headhunting was a socio-religio-political activity that operated within a well demarcated political jurisdiction. It had the mandate and sanction of the village authority. For instance, before going for war/raid, warriors needed to observe certain rituals and abstain from sexual intercourse and after returning from war/raid, they could not return to their home directly but they had to stay in the *morung* (male dormitory) to undergo the rituals associated to the custom of headhunting.[19] In short, the culture of headhunting among the Nagas was well regulated by socio-religio-political norms.

The fact that headhunting happened within the normative structure of the society did not entail that all adult males were expected to become headhunters. Though the headhunting culture has been essentialised as the defining identity of the Nagas, in actual practice headhunting was not the *vocation* of most adult males. Put differently, not all the adult males would naturally become warriors though no one was restricted from becoming one. In holding this view, I disagree with the popular view which holds that headhunting culture is a kind of rite of passage from boyhood to manhood, and that a man without taking a head would find great difficulty in winning a wife (Smith 1925: 70; Shimray 1985: 75). Only when the village had to be defended against enemy attacks or when it invaded another village,[20] then and only then was every abled bodied male expected to participate in war. As far as the Chakhesang tribe is concerned, only some would be recognized as (full time) village-warriors. These warriors would guard the village as a full-time duty. When others were busy in the fields, they would be guarding and scouting the area. Each morning before anyone would cross the village gate, they scouted the areas commonly used by the villagers for cultivation or for fetching drinking water. Only after performing this duty, the villagers would usually go out of the village. For this service, that of warriors, each household gave a portion of their harvest to them. Village warriors themselves would usually not cultivate land. Even if they had land, others would work for them. When a warrior would successfully bring

[18]Traditional friendships between villages were established with great seriousness and solemnity involving rituals and feasts. Such friendship and alliance is very important for the peace, prosperity and security of the village. As a rule, every village would have some friendship-villages. A village can also make alliance or friendship with some individual warrior or some clan from another village. The existence of such practices negates the stereotype that Naga villages were isolated from each other. On the contrary, it shows that vibrant diplomacy was the order of the day.

[19]The details relating to headhunting rituals are meticulously described by both Thong in his article (Thong, 2012b: p.376) and Thong in his book (Thong, 2012a: pp.17-18).

[20]Under normal condition, no full-fledged war would be declared between villages though raids would continue between warring or enemy villages. Full scale war would happen generally when a village openly challenged another village to decide who was more powerful or when a territorial dispute could not be resolved amicably.

home a head from another village, the villagers offered him grains and other food items in addition to giving him a hero's welcome with war cries and dances. It is said that if a warrior would successfully take three heads in a year, the contribution from the villagers would enrich him significantly.

Another important role of the warriors was that of the founding of a new village. From a different angle, it may be argued that to establish a new village was one of the biggest tests of a warrior's courage and skill. Without a warrior, no new village could be established as it was thought it would not survive without one. Though headhunting was not as widespread as is often imagined, there could be no village without a warrior to provide protection. When a village lacked one, normally some good warrior(s) from another village would be invited by offering incentives, such as offering the best settlement area. For instance, when one village was facing security problems due to the lack of skilled warriors, the people of that village approached my village (Kikruma) with a request to let some warrior settle in their village. One noted warrior from our village, by the name Yosu, agreed to settle in that village. When he settled there, the village was named after him and called Yosuba, whose literal meaning is 'Yosu is here' or 'Yosu's settlement.'[21] Usually the largest or best shares of the land would go to the warriors. However, since they defended the land, they often also occupied lands in the village borders, especially in 'grey' or disputed areas.

Given the important roles they played in the village, headhunters were highly respected and honoured by all. It is said that some mighty warriors would go to different villages and collect 'taxes'[22]. For instance, a warrior from Khezakeno village by the name Azo, who was believed to be 8 feet tall, used to ride a buffalo to collect 'tax' from the neighbouring villages (Zehol and Zehol 2009: 29-30). Sometimes, the collection of 'tax' in neighbouring villages by warriors were done rather randomly. They could walk into a neighbouring village and pick a chicken or piglet of their choice without being questioned. Some of them would do the same even within their own village. Apart from such unpleasant practices by some of them, warriors in general would be given special privileges. Among the Chakhesang, only a warrior had the privilege of standing on the monolith stone when it was being pulled in honour of the couple performing the *Feast of Merit*.[23] Other than the economic benefits mentioned above (i.e., land and wealth), songs were sung in warriors' honour. They also earned the right to decorate their attires with curved images

[21]After a lot of issues and with the final consent of our village, Yosuba village has been renamed as Enhulumi in the present time.

[22] Tax in the sense may be understood as a protection tax or even a tribute.

[23]The Feast of Merit was the most important feast among many Naga tribes, the performance of which would earn the hosting couple (only married couple could host it) the right to wear special shawls and decorate their house with specific items including horn-shaped wooden structure.

of human heads or the hair of women whom they killed. Among the Konyak tribe, warriors would wear necklaces with curved images (normally of metal) of human head to indicate the number of human heads they had taken. For the Aos, a specific shawl (called *tsungkotepsu*) was designed originally only for the warriors (called *nokinketers*, meaning 'those whose daos have power or magic') but later on it was permitted to be worn by the village rich who had performed the *Feast of Merit* as well (Ao 2014: 16-17). In this way, rewards were instituted by the community to celebrate the life and achievement of a warrior.

REINTERPRETING THE HEADHUNTING CULTURE

To argue that the headhunting culture of the Nagas was not due to a culture of lawlessness is not the sole focus of this paper however. This misconception has been dealt with by several writers including some colonial writers. Rather my interest here is to suggest that the practice has a deep-rooted connection with some of the fundamental values of life, namely, equality, justice and freedom. This is not to say that headhunting was instituted to promote these values, but that it reflected these values from the vantage of modern interpretation. It is from the analysis of these and related concepts with special reference to headhunting that I will now attempt to interpret the practice of headhunting among Nagas. Let me begin with the observation of H.B. Rowney: 'The Nagas have no kind of internal government, and acknowledge *no supreme authority*. If spoken to on the subject they plant their javelin on the ground and declare that to be their Rajah, and that they will have none other' (Rowney 1969: 102; emphasis mine).

In the process of writing this article, I realized that, for Chakhesang Nagas, there is no historical record or narratives of one village surrendering or submitting to another village, and through which a relation of ruler-subject was established between villages. Interestingly we even lack the term 'surrender' in our languages.[24] It is true that a powerful or 'mother village'[25] would be recognized in terms of certain tax or tribute. This was especially common among those Naga tribes

---

[24]I have been trying without result lately to find this term 'surrender' in other Naga languages as well. My initial inquiries of Naga tribes include Angami, Ao, Chakhesang, Lotha, Mao, Rengma, Rongmei, Sema, Tangkhul, Zeliang, This is not to say that Naga people of have no idea of surrender. As a matter of fact, there were established ways by which a person can save his/her life when pursued by warriors. In his book, Shimray describes those circumstances and forms of 'surrendering' to warriors in order to save one's life (Shimray 1985: 93-97).

[25]By 'mother village' I simply mean a village from where members came out of it to form new villages and to which they depend for performing one or more religious rites and rituals during important occasions.

which practiced hereditary chieftainship. But this was more a customary practice of recognizing village's leadership role or religious role rather than the act of submission or surrender of one's autonomy.

The right to live with dignity and freedom as a sovereign or autonomous village was the unquestioned belief of the Chakhesang Nagas and I infer that this is true for Nagas in general, despite varied forms of government, ranging from the hereditary chieftainship among the Naga tribes in the eastern side to republican forms of democracy among western tribes. One of the reasons for holding such a view is that there was a total absence of imperialistic ambition among the Nagas. Wars or raids were not known to have been carried out to enslave or oppress others. There was no record of a powerful village trying to impose their custom or religion or language on a weaker or defeated village. A defeated village would not give up its right of self-governance, nor would it be demanded from her. The internal affairs of any village would not be disturbed by an outside force unless invited so for specific reasons. If a village was too weak to defend herself, then diplomacy would often take over and war or rivalry between the two parties would come to an end. Shimray, for instance, narrates the common practice among the Mao tribe as follows: 'The weaker village would to the enemy village with a wine-pot, a spear and a spade. When such presents were brought, the war ended without raising the question of surrender and payment' (Shimray 1985: 96). As such, the right of every village, weak or strong, to remain as a sovereign political institution was upheld almost like a sacred belief.

The basic inclination of human nature for harming one another in the form of revenge is one way of asserting equality. In the Hobbesian view, the nature of humans is such that even the weakest by treachery and cunningness can kill the strongest of man, and that this serves as a natural indicator that humans are equal to one another. It may be pointed out that between unequal relations such as masters and slaves or conquerors and the conquered, or even between some kind of hierarchical relations in a society like parents and children, the term 'revenge' is normally not applied to action or violence involving the two parties. Rather the (re)actions of the former group are better read respectively as acts of punishment or discipline in relation to the latter and the latter in relation to the former are better read as acts of rebellion. Within this type of relationships, neither threatened the other with the 'language' of revenge. Even if, for instance, a son kills his father out of some grudge, we may not typically look upon his action as a revengeful act. At best, his action may be regarded either as appropriate or inappropriate, justified or unjustified. In other words, revenge is peculiarly the language of the equals.

Imagine the following scenario in the pre-modern Naga context. Someone from village-A kills someone from village-B over, say, a land dispute. It would then be natural for Village B to seek justice. But the obvious question would be this: 'How can one seek justice when there is no higher authority over both the villages to which one can appeal for justice?' The natural desire for justice was made more difficult by the absence of independent judiciary and regular police. In the absence of such an arrangement, one can only think of taking revenge - *life for life*. But how can one ensure that the dead of someone has been avenged? For that, some evidence would be needed. We can ask further – 'what is the best evidence to claim victory or success in such a vengeful mission?' The most likely choice in the context of the Nagas was to bring back a head. A head has been considered as a symbolic mark of respect and identity among the Nagas. The head of an animal would be offered during important occasions to only some people such as the village chief or headman, or the eldest person in the clan, or the eldest among the siblings. As a symbol, the practice of giving and receiving a head of an animal has been well institutionalized. Certainly, it was not given to any. Ao (2014: 13) observes:

> in villages when animals are slaughtered for community feasts, the head of the biggest animal is *always* (mine) given to the chief or the headman as a token of recognition of his status in the community.... The heads of chickens or even fish heads cannot be eaten by anyone else except the head of the family, i.e., the father [among the Sangtam Naga tribe].

The heads of animals butchered or hunted would normally be displayed at the house of the rich and powerful. A traditional house of a rich man (performer of the Feast of Merit) in the context of the Chakhesang tribe would be decorated by the curving of mithun heads on special planks that form part of the frontal wall at the veranda. A head, in this sense, was a symbolic marker of status and identity. Accordingly, it is possible to infer that a human head not only served as an evidence of a kill but more fundamentally that the honor of that person or village had been restored by taking away a head from the enemy village. Interpreted thus, the symbolic act of restoring honor through the culture of headhunting serves the function of delivering justice as well.[26]

Seen from this perspective, headhunting as a form of justice vis-à-vis revenge is not directed towards some specific individual. It can be arbitrary. If the slain is from the same village, that by itself would be sufficient. The dead is avenged and justice is considered achieved. To an outsider, especially from a modern liberal perspective, the act or custom of killing someone for no crime of his or her would be to distort the very concept of justice itself. However, the Nagas' sense of identity was not individualistic but communitarian in nature. For Nagas, the identity of an individual is primarily understood in relation to one's community. Collective identity was more fundamental than individual identity. Hence if a crime was related to headhunting, it was treated as a direct, deliberate and open challenge to

---

[26]Apart from its symbolic function, the culture of headhunting suggests that the historiography of Nagas need to be approached from the perspective of embodied and performative history.

the honor of the village in question.[27]

In the absence of a larger political organization beyond the village authority to deal with questions of justice in terms of inter-village feuds, revenge cannot be simply dismissed as immoral and savage. The reason is that the community expects revenge whenever a wrong is done to one party by another party (both within and outside the village). However, revenge between members of the same village never involved the practice of headhunting though in extreme cases, revenge may become violent including murder. However even in such extreme case, a person's head was never decapitated. It may be worth mentioning that killing a person from the same village was considered 'murder' while the killing of a person from another was headhunting. If someone took revenge within or outside the village in order to defend the honor of a person or a village, it would never be interpreted as unlawful or morally wrong. Rather it was looked upon as a virtuous or rightful act. This was perhaps due to a very strong sense of equality rooted in our culture.[28]

It may be noted here that revenge in the sense I am using the concept here has both personal and non-personal elements. It is personal in that it is an act initiated by the wronged person and justice was sought to be achieved personally. Revenge of this sort normally happens within the community. Revenge in the context of headhunting is also impersonal in that revenge needed not happen directly between the two (or more) persons involved. Anyone from the village of the afflicted clan or community can take revenge on anyone from the village of the perpetrator. The impersonal element of revenge is consistent with the word 'ga', the suffix for head taking, which has no moral connotation and has no element of personal offence. Compared to modern forms of warfare, this way of seeking justice between two sovereign political entities is less violent and economic in that the question of justice is taken care of without having to declare war on the entire village for the action or activities of some individuals.

It follows from the above that revenge was primarily seen as a form of delivering justice and, as such, it was justified by the society (Tinyi 2017: p. 57). Conversely, failure to rise to the social expectation of taking revenge created imbalances to the justice system given that Nagas had no regular police or courts to enforce justice. The implication is that without first rejecting the system of traditional justice as practiced by the Nagas, it is difficult to demonize or write off the culture of headhunting itself. To put it within the framework of my argument,

---

[27]A similar observation on the notion of revenge is being noted by Jelle Wouters in Chapter 6 of this volume. In the same chapter, Wouters has also provided a detailed and interesting account of identity and identification.

[28]It may interest some to know that from my village there is a person by the name 'Khupo' which literally means 'revenge' and he even named his first son as 'Khasuho', meaning 'never give up'. If taken positively, it means that injustice should be avenged by all means.

headhunting reflected the Nagas' belief in the inherent principle of equality.[29] The larger implication is that headhunting is indispensable for understanding the ancestral philosophy of Naga life, their beliefs, values and practices. Accordingly, the foregoing account on headhunting and its relation to the basic value systems of the Nagas may be taken as a proto-type model through which we can understand, explain and (re)interpret ourselves as Nagas.

CONCLUSION

To sum up, let me reiterate my central points. I explored and examined the concept of headhunting from an insider's perspective. I have done this by analysing the term 'headhunting' in the Chokri language of Chakhesang tribe on the one hand, and in relation to the elitist culture of trophy hunting during the colonial time on the other. However, my basic attempt has been to locate and interpret the practice of headhunting within the larger framework of the values and normative structures of traditional Naga society. In doing so, I am suggesting the possibility of rediscovering and reinterpreting our value systems and traditional practices in order to understand ourselves better. Such an exercise is likely to affect the ways we see ourselves – seeing each other as equals – and this in turn may significantly change the way we see and relate with each other as Nagas. Not only that, this may also provide us with interesting insights as to why we not only constantly question the superiority of others, and the right of others to subjugate us, but also struggle passionately to reclaim our rights to live as free and equal people.

[29]This type of equality is however not the same as modern liberal principle of equality which is grounded in individualism but rather it may be considered as collective or group equality.

08

CHRISTIAN CONVERSION, THE RISE OF NAGA NATIONAL CONSCIOUSNESS, AND NAGA NATIONALIST POLITICS

Shonreiphy Longvah

Naga is a term of foreign origination that classes together a heterogeneous group of people. Each Naga tribe follows its own socio-cultural, political, agricultural and other practices. Nonetheless, as pointed out by Owen (1844: 7), 'the similarity of features, habits, language, and practices, undoubtedly bespeaks them to be of one common origin', and this common origin, fostered by massive Christian conversions, led to a desire for a common political future. Mao commented that in the remote past Nagas did not apply the term 'Naga' to refer to themselves. Rather, in ancient days, Nagas described themselves in reference to their habitat, i.e., their village (cited in The Morung Express 31-6-2013). The history of those communities who came to identify themselves, or were thus identified by others, with the term 'Naga' also remains obscure. This obscurity fascinated western anthropologists who started tracing the origins of the Naga people based on their physical appearance, political and cultural practices, traditions, languages and religion. But while they came up with various hypotheses, including faraway origins in China and Mongolia, till today no anthropologist or historian has been able to trace the exact place of origin of these 'enigmatic' warrior tribes. Such enigmatic origins are not unique to Naga tribes alone. Several other tribal communities in Northeast India display a similar mysteriousness in their origins. Many argue that the absence of written records and a 'clear and consistent oral history' as factors for this enigma. For instance, Burling (2007: 4) pointed out that various tribes in Northeast India 'talk as if their ancestors once lived somewhere else, but migrated at some point in order to reach the previously uninhabited territory where they made their final home'.

Having briefly introduced the 'Naga', this chapter proceeds by discussing the impacts of Christianity on Naga national politics. As illustrated earlier by Angelova in this volume, Christianity forms an 'intrinsic part' of the 'contemporary identity' of the Sumi Naga. This however is true for all the Nagas. Christianity indeed has become the clearest if not the most readily accepted factor Nagas today are identified with. This chapter particularly argues that massive Christian conversions, while not the sole reason, was a major catalyst behind the rise of Naga nationalism. By the 1940s, a majority of the Naga population was Christianized (although a meager percentage still followed the ancient religion, or the *Hao* religion as Tangkhul Nagas call it). By the mid-1950s, Nagas were embroiled in a national movement for their freedom, and in this, Christian religion acted as the 'backbone' (Lorin & Spees, 1990: 355-363). I indeed argue that religious conversions to Christianity resonated with changes in the political and socio-cultural sentiments of Nagas.

From the 1830s, several efforts were made by Christian missionaries to spread the Gospel of Christ in what is now referred to as Nagalim.[1] In 1838, Miles Bronson visited the Naga Hills inhabited by the Konyak Nagas, but 'his mission was an unsuccessful one' (Mawon 2015: 157). Roughly three decades later, the missionary E.W. Clark visited the Naga Hills and, in 1876, settled with his wife Mary Clark in the area inhabited by the Ao Nagas (Henningsen 2007: 77). In other words, the 'Christian Missionaries began their work first in the Ao Naga area' (Sema 2013: 59). From that moment onward, Christianity gradually spread across Nagalim, although slow at first and not without setbacks. It was recorded that Nagas found it hard to abandon the traditions of their ancestors, and they were therefore deemed 'conservative' with little interest for change (Allen 1905: 40, 45). It must, indeed, have been with great difficulty that Nagas gradually abandoned their traditional religion and practices.

Allen (1905: 39) remarked that 'nothing less than a strong desire for social advancement would induce a Naga to adopt a religion which would impose on him so many troublesome restrictions.' Christianity seemingly offered this social

[1]The term 'Nagalim' and 'Nagaland' means the same literally, i.e., both refer to the land of the Naga people. In this manuscript, the former will be used because the latter often applies to the State of Nagaland created within the Union of India in December 1963. Nagalim means all the land of the Nagas both in India and Myanmar. With an exception of the Nagaland state, in India, Nagas are a minority in the states of Manipur, Arunachal Pradesh and Assam. In Myanmar, the Nagas are found in the Kachin state and Sagaing sub-division.

advancement, and, over time, Christianity took a firm hold across the Naga country. If Christianity was first introduced in the northern hills of Nagalim, it also spread to its extreme south, inhabited by the Tangkhul Naga tribe. Here, the gospel of Christ was introduced by the American missionary couple, William Pettigrew and his wife Alice Pettigrew from 1896 onward. If, in the history of Nagas' conversion to Christianity, the Ao Nagas were the first to convert in present-day Nagaland, the Tangkhuls were the first to do so in the state of Manipur. Amongst other things, the advent of Christianity integrated the hitherto 'unorganized Naga tribes' (Shimray 2005:45), as I will discuss in more detail below. The introduction of Christianity also came with western education, medicine, and way of life. Education opened the eyes of the Nagas to the modern world and made them realize that the term Naga though foreign in origin, was a term that could connect them under a single political rubric.

This, indeed, was the time in which Nagas' political consciousness was on the rise, and with British withdrawal becoming imminent Nagas came to reject the idea that their land, which was under a special dispensation during the British rule,[2] should pass into Indian hands (Baruah 2003: 321). This rejection was due to the germination of Naga nationalism, which, in turn, was largely shaped by the introduction and advent of Christianity. That said, Christianity was not the single factor that triggered the onset of Naga nationalism. Other factors such as introduction of western education and the involvement of the Nagas in the two World Wars also worked to cultivate the ideas of belonging to one distinct national group (Longvah 2015: 68). In addition, the growth of Naga nationalism was also based on the desire to preserve and protect their identity and culture, and to free themselves from any foreign occupation, whose rulers and inhabitants looked down upon them as 'backward' and 'primitive'. Thomas (2016: 2) discusses at length how disparate Naga tribes, therefore, came together and demanded an independent nation to 'reconstitute their identity, demarcate their national space and defend it from further incursions'. This consciousness of a common identity paved the way for aspirations of self-determination, which means that Nagas themselves would

---

[2]Under the British administration, Nagas experienced a special treatment such as the enactment of the 'Inner Line Regulation of 1873' that prohibited British subjects from going beyond a certain line towards the Naga areas without a pass or license issued by the Deputy Commissioner (Horam 1975:13, cited in Shimray 2005:38-39). This regulation, modified as per the needs of the time, is still active in the state of Nagaland. In 1880, moreover, legislation was enacted that classified the Naga tribes as 'excluded' and their areas as 'excluded areas', with the aim of protecting the Naga areas from possible economic exploitation by the peoples of the plains, thus indicating that the Naga Hills were always separate from the rest of Assam. Throughout British rule, Nagas lived by and large on their own and continued their social and political activities as the British hardly interfered with the traditions, customs and village administration of the Nagas (Shimray 2005: 39-41).

determine their own political, administrative, cultural and socio-economic affairs. Based on the historical given of Nagas being distinct from the Indian nation, the Naga commonly termed their movement as a national movement. They considered India as a foreign country, a colonial master who, akin to the British earlier, had trespassed into their land. This led to a warlike situation between the Nagas and the Indian Government.

In this chapter, I will first highlight some colonial writings on Naga traditional religion and critique their accounts based on data accumulated through participant observation, interviews, and the reading of secondary sources. Next, I will focus on Christian conversions of the Nagas and discuss how such conversions advanced the rise of Naga nationalism. This will be followed by examining the relationship between the Naga Movement and Christianity as well as the recent complications to the Movement caused by factionalism within the broader Naga family. Relatedly, the role of the Church and Christianity in mitigating the complications and volatilities of factionalism will be discussed. I conclude by arguing that Christianity propelled manifold changes in the Naga society, of which, the most important change was the rise of Naga political consciousness.

A CRITIQUE ON THE COLONIAL CLASSIFICATION OF NAGAS AS 'ANIMISTS'

The Naga people and their culture intrigued western anthropologists since the 19th century. As discussed by Wouters and Heneise in this volume, it became 'a cradle of British social anthropology'. When British troops first encountered some Naga tribes in 1832, they were resisted violently by, what they saw as, 'ferocious hill-people'. Nagas resisted them because they encroached into their homeland without permission. Prior to the arrival of the Britishers into some parts of the Naga country, western education and way of life were completely alien to Nagas who transmitted their ancestral knowledge and wisdom through oral traditions. The Nagas, a conglomeration of many tribes (some listing it to more than 60 tribes), had no script of their own. Therefore, they had no written record of the way of life they led in ancient days. Their ancestral practices, knowledge, warfare, agriculture, matrimony, hunting, burial, art, ideas, and other cultural practices was imbibed, preserved and transmitted from one generation to the next through oral traditions, mostly in the forms of folktales and folksongs.

In the colonial era, the relationship between the British and the Nagas was mostly limited to those Nagas inhabiting the Naga Hills District, which was created in 1866 with an area of 9,446 square kilometers. By the late 19th century, 30 per cent of the Naga areas - of an approximate total of 100,000 to 120,000 square kilometers - were conquered and ruled by the British (Shimray 2005: 31; Iralu 2005: 190). The British left the Indian sub-continent in 1947, well before they succeeded in subduing the entire Naga country. Many of the British officials in the

19th century combined their duties as colonial administrators with the perusal of ethnological inquiries. These two duties were nevertheless related, as it was thought that ethnographic information on Naga tribes would help the colonial government administer and control them more effectively.

The British colonial policy towards the Nagas in the 19th century was principally based on punitive expeditions to stop the Naga raids against British subjects in the plains of Assam. Later on, such expeditions were carried out to protect the conquered Naga villages from attacks of then still independent Naga villages. Through punitive expeditions, some Naga villages adjoining Assam were controlled 'on and off' by the British from Assam. Allen (1905: 2) referred to this as the 'period of control from without, by a system of expeditions or promenades'. The end of the 19th century saw a firm establishment of British headquarters within the Naga territories of Samaguting (present day Chumukedima) in 1866 and Kohima in 1878. Operating from these headquarters, British punitive influences became more effective, and brought many Naga villages within the fold of colonial administration. Initially, minimal or 'absolute non-interference' vis-à-vis Naga traditional systems of authority, their customary laws and practices was upheld, that is, as long as it did not challenge British authority. This period was known as the 'period of control from within, the period of absolute non-interference' (Allen 1905: 2). However, the 'non-interference' policy could not contain the independent spirited Nagas from raiding other villages (both Naga and non-Naga), and of practicing 'head-hunting' warfare amongst themselves. This, the colonial government, found not desirable and therefore it decided to directly interfere, pacify the area, and introduce minimal forms of administration. Head-hunting was thus abolished although its practice reportedly continued until the 1960s in unadministered areas of Nagalim (Das 2013: 97). This direct interference was known as the 'period of control from within, merging into gradual absorption into British territory' (Allen 1905: 2).

After the British effectuated control over the Nagas, much became written about Nagas by colonial officers posted there. Many of these views ought to be critiqued, but here I confine myself to critically interrogating colonial views on Naga religion.

Chidester (2009: 52) posits that the 'fear of the unknown, belief in spirits, or submission to the authority of a higher power' constitute the basic features of religion. Darwin (cited in Chidester 2009: 62, 68), in an attempt to explain the origin of religion, argued that 'belief in God or a Supreme Being' was not the universal characteristics of religion, rather, 'belief in unseen or spiritual agencies' seemed to be universal. Thus, broadly speaking, all religion in some way or another believed in the existence of 'unseen' entities or spirits. They simply differ roughly in their expressions of that belief. Since the 19th century, traditional Naga religion was commonly identified with the term 'animism'. This perhaps was due to the presence of strong animistic beliefs and practices, their everyday lives being influenced by spirits, and by their attempts to appease these spirits to ward off calamities. Sitton (1998: 69-70) argued that this indeed formed the basic tenets of animism, which was generally defined as the 'belief that non-living objects have souls (life) and that natural phenomena possess supernatural or magical power.' The proclivity of the Nagas to offer sacrifices in order to keep the evil spirits satisfied might have prompted Michell (1883: 206) to remark that Naga religion was a 'species of devil-worship' and of them not believing in a 'supreme being'. Various colonialists, however, argued to the contrary and forwarded the view that Naga traditional religion believed in the existence of both a supreme being and various other spirits, and therefore defined their religious practices as 'animistic' (Allen 1905: 88; Elwin 1961: 10).

Prior to the advent of Christianity, Nagas nevertheless had a clear conscience of their religion. The writing of Mawon in this volume clearly indicates that Nagas were a highly religious group of people; all their social, cultural, agricultural practices, and celebration of festivals, were undertaken with utmost reverence and appeasement of their god and other spirits (good and bad). For that matter, Owen (1844: 8-9) disagreed with the generally held notion by those in Assam that Nagas had no religion. He narrated:

> The existence of a singular practice amongst them negates the idea of them being without religious feelings, for to what can we ascribe the following observance if it be not intended as devotional. At every cross-path they meet on a march, each, whether man, woman, or child, breaks off a branch or leaf of a tree which is thrown on a heap whilst passing – and these continue accumulating until an eclipse takes place, when the whole are removed by fire. The motive for so strange a practice I could never ascertain, with any nearer approach to correctness than my interpreter's knowledge could afford me, viz. that their Supreme One might see their observance, and reward them accordingly.

Read thus, Nagas have been wrongly essentialized as 'animists'. Today, this notion is indeed subjected to debate. Empirical study and not *a priori* assumptions on traditional Naga religious beliefs indicate that Nagas cannot be considered as full-fledged 'animists'. Most Naga tribes had a clear idea of the Supreme Creator[3] and of the afterlife or a second world. They worshipped the Supreme Creator ('the

---

[3]The Supreme Creator has been accorded with different names by different Naga tribes. For instance, the Semas called it Alhou; Angamis, Terhuomia or Ukepenuopfu; Konyaks, Kahwang; Aos, Tsungrem; Moas, Ora, and Tangkhuls called it Varivara, a derivative from the term Uri Ura indicating things that had been in existence since ancient times (Shikhu 2007:12-13). Nagas in Myanmar refer to the Supreme Creator as Thishaw, Maitai, Atengpu, Khenung Thongpu, etc. (http://www.nagasinmyanmar-burma.com/p/religious-condition.html)

Lord of all spirits', 'the benevolent God') as the last resort when appeasing various spirits on earth failed (Shikhu 2007: 13). But while Nagas believed in the existence of the Supreme Creator, they hardly worshipped Him and the supposed reason behind this was:

> Because He was believed to have lived in the sky, too far away that He did not interfere in human affairs and struggles. The Nagas did not worship or offer sacrifices to the Supreme Being on a daily basis because He was considered to be a benevolent God and not requiring propitiation. It was only when all their sacrifices to the malevolent spirits of lakes, rocks, trees, hills, and caves failed and resulted in constant harassment, sickness and natural calamities, that they resorted to the worship of the Supreme God who was believed to be the Lord of all spirits. (Shikhu 2007: 13)

Such ancestral practices indicate that Nagas also believed in the existence of spirits residing in inanimate objects. However, upholding the latter by omitting the former seems to have been the predominant reason why Nagas were considered as 'animists'. Mention may be made here that such a co-existence of belief systems is not the characteristics of Nagas alone. In fact, many major religions like Hinduism, Buddhism, Jainism and Islam also contain animistic beliefs and practices and yet these religions were never considered as a form of 'animism'.

In the world of ancient Naga religion, 'shamans', or *Khunong* in the Tangkhul language, who were believed to possess the ability of travelling the realm of the dead people, or *Kazeiram*, those who communicated with the dead people, could heal diseases, drive out evil spirits, and interpret dreams and signs, occupied a highly revered social position. The well-established concept of *Khunong* strongly indicates that most Naga tribes believed in life after death, insisting that the soul does not perish at death, but would continue to live in the land of the dead. Therefore, things such as utensils, domestic animals, cloths, food, and weapons, that might be necessary for setting up a new life in the land of the dead, were arranged for the deceased in the burial ceremony (Shikhu 2007: 15). Even after converting to Christianity for more than a century, the Tangkhuls are still found to uphold the notion of *Kazeiram*. For instance, in February 2017, 94 years old Ramyaola Mawon, presuming she would not survive for another year, was making arrangements by gathering those stuffs which she would require on meeting her ancestors in *Kazeiram*. This belief is a common phenomenon among the elderly Tangkhul population.

It may further be mentioned that the practice of shamanism is still in vogue although today they have added the prefix Christian, making them 'Christian-shamans' or 'visionaries' famously known as *Vareshi Khunong* by the Tangkhuls. As a result of the existence of such a strong and organized belief system (which was argued to be absent in animism), a kind of doctrine for the Tangkhuls and many other Naga tribes, it can be hypothesized that Naga belief systems were more 'advanced' or 'complex' than animism and that, therefore, traditional Naga religion cannot be classified as simply 'animistic'. Indeed, the strong doctrine of the afterlife also negates the 19th century colonial accounts which argue that at the most Nagas had a vague concept of the soul or life after death (Allen 1905: 89; Elwin 1961: 10).

By the 19th century, Nagas were exposed not only to Christian religion but also to Hinduism, Buddhism, Jainism and Islam although the latter failed to appeal to the Nagas (Allen 1905: 40, 89). Only Christianity could influence the Nagas to forsake their traditional religion. However, and irrespectively of what form traditional Naga religion took, what it did not provide Nagas with was a common platform to come together politically, in the way Christianity achieved, as I will now argue.

NAGA NATIONALISM AND CHRISTIANITY

Nationalism is, above all, 'political'; it can be seen as an attempt of a culturally distinct people to attain political self-determination (Hechter 2004: 6-7). Kohn opined that nationalism is first and foremost 'a state of mind', 'an act of consciousness' (cited in Shimray 2005: 52). It is an 'ideological movement to attain and to maintain the autonomy, unity and identity of the existing or potential nation' (Smith 2001: 335). Across the globe, nationalism is a factor that stimulates a strong feeling of dislike of other people, which sometimes leads to communal violence, ethnic cleansing, even genocide.[4] Barrington (1997: 174) defines nationalism as 'the pursuit – through argument or other activity – of a set of rights for the self-defined members of the nation, including at a minimum, territorial autonomy or sovereignty' and concludes that every form of nationalism involves the 'setting of membership and territorial boundaries'. For Upreti (2006: 536) 'nationalism is a process whose ultimate objective is to draw a distinction between peoples on the basis of ethno-cultural identities in order to claim sovereign rights over a particular territory'.

Along the lines of these definitions, Naga nationalism can be defined as Nagas' desire for political freedom and independence across a contiguously inhabited area currently bifurcated between India and Myanmar. Nagas' articulation of a 'distinct identity' is fanned by beliefs in common origins, history, religion and political destiny. Based on this, Nagas emphatically assert that they have every right to be independent from both India and Myanmar, whom they see as 'occupying forces'.

---

[4]Some examples of such instances are the Jewish holocaust, ethno-national related violent conflicts in Bosnia, Kosovo, Sri Lanka, East Timor, Rwanda, Somalia, Northern Ireland and Israel-Palestine, among many others.

Besides a common denominator offered by Christianity, Naga nationalism - a movement based on the 'constructed', 'imagined', or 'invented' idea of Naga nation - is also a response and reaction to colonialism (Wouters 2016:101-102). Simply put, Naga nationalism, as 'an act of consciousness', is a movement searching for political recognition of Nagas' right to self-determination' (Shimray 2005: 52-53).

Nag (1999:14) enunciates that in the colonial period, the sole objective of India's national movement was to rally Indians together in opposition to British colonialism and establish itself as a 'nation' based on 'pan-Indian identity' and 'regional linguistic-cultural identity'. The point made by the Nagas was that they were never a part of the 'pan-Indian' project or for that matter the constructed Indian nation. They therefore aspired independence from any foreign domination, particularly from the dominance of the newly Independent Indian State. However, the Indian State was not willing to recognize Naga aspirations for freedom. Terming it as the first 'secessionist' problem of the newly Independent Indian State, Naga aspirations were met with ruthless military techniques. Galtung (2000: 57-58) indicates that the loss of 'freedom' or independence – 'to be the master of a house one can call one's own, not to be lorded over by some other nation' – often forms the basis of 'deep conflicts that threaten deeply rooted needs'. Indeed, the desire for 'freedom' is the basic point upon which the consciousness of Naga nationalism has been constructed. Memories of the past freedom that lingered in the minds of the Nagas prompted them to struggle for their present freedom, which manifested itself in the form of a direct violent conflict with the Indian Government.

Naga nationalist sentiment, however, remains a young concept whose origins date back roughly to the early 20th century. Mawon and Longvah (2014: 338-339) postulated that the spread of Christianity along with the establishments of modern political and administrative systems by the British, modern education, and participation of thousands of Nagas in the two World Wars led to the birth of educated middle class and 'modern thinking citizens' among the Nagas. They rose above their village and tribal loyalties and dreamt of uniting all Nagas. Ultimately, this led to the birth of Naga nationalism.

Prior to the arrival of the British and the subsequent domination of one-third of the entire Naga areas, each Naga identified themselves with their village and each and every Naga village existed more or less independently of each other (on the Naga 'village republic' see Wouters, this volume). Back then, 'security' meant fortifying their village in defense of attacks from other villages. In fact, for effective village security, brave men with the ability to hunt heads and protect the village were considered valued assets (see Tinyi, this volume). Thus, the feeling of collectiveness or belonging to a single Naga family was largely absent. At this juncture, during the First World War, around 2000 Nagas were sent to France as part of the Labour Corps. After returning from France, some of them along with few Naga government officials, educated men, and several village headmen established the Naga Club in 1918 (Shimray 2005: 60). The formation of the Club laid the groundwork for Naga nationalism. The Club, which was the first of its kind in Nagalim, drew its members from various Naga tribes, and was both social and political in nature (Vashum 2000: 65). Later, the Club became more fixated with the promotion of a sense of understanding and fraternity among the Nagas, to unite them, and to discuss the important affairs of the Naga society at large (Singh 2004: 37). On 10 January 1929, the Club submitted a memorandum to the Simon Commission asking the British to leave the Nagas alone to decide their own future if and when they would leave the Indian Subcontinent. Thence on, there has been no turning back in Nagas' asserting their aspiration for independence, though the bearer of the torch has over time changed from one political organization to the other.

Across the globe, in various political movements generated by the consciousness of nationalism, religion played a significant role. In Africa, the Middle East, South America, Central Asia, the Indian Subcontinent and South East Asia, religion harnessed many nationalist causes (Percy 2001, cited in Mawon & Longvah 2014: 337). In Nagalim, it was Christianity that undoubtedly triggered the wave of Naga nationalism. Nakhro (cited in The Morung Express 22-2-2017) opined that by the 1940s and 50s, Christianity had induced Nagas to belief that 'God has a special geo-political plan' for them and it was likely because of this belief that, Nagas refused to consider themselves as a part of 'Hindu India'.

Thus, the Naga national movement for independence was Christcentric from the very beginning. The *Yehzabo* (Constitution) of the Federal Government of Nagaland (FGN), the political organ of the Naga National Council (NNC), succinctly acknowledged the sovereignty of the Christian God over all affairs of the Naga people. The Christian God was believed and worshipped as the Almighty God who sustained and will sustain the Nagas in times of trial and hardship (Lasuh 2002: 77). In fact, in 1956, there was an order from the NNC that the Christian God 'ought to be included in every practical field of Nagas and, therefore, as many pastors as possible should be appointed to prepare the war affairs' (Elwin 1961: 63). Later, in the 1980s, the National Socialist Council of Nagaland (NSCN) - accused at one point by Naga Churches for leaning towards the ideology of 'anti-religious' Communism - propagated the ideology of 'Christian Socialism' with the aim of 'strengthening the ethnic unity of the Naga tribes'. Towards this cause, they subsequently succeeded in the large scale conversion of Naga tribes in Eastern Nagaland and Myanmar, which had hitherto been largely untouched by evangelical activities (Shimray 2005: 54). Even in the 21st century, the generally accepted adage 'Nagaland for Christ'[5] remains as a connecting link between the church and the Naga movement.

---

[5]The concept 'Nagaland for Christ' propagandized that Nagaland was to be the first completely Christian State in Asia and therefore, it was the duty of Christians to fight the 'Hindu Government' in order to preserve their religion (Elwin 1961: 63).

The concept of Naga nationalism was also strongly related with the biblical accounts of Israel's deliverance from the hand of its enemies whenever they sought the presence of God in their lives. In fostering this concept, the Bible acted as the guidebook from which the Naga movement drew its strength. By equating their plight with that of the Israelites, the Naga nationalists firmly established the belief that walking and working according to the decree of God would enable them to accomplish their political goals. Indeed, there exist overwhelming stories on how Naga nationalists miraculously survived difficult situations because of God's powerful protection. Such stories boosted the morale of Naga nationalists, and induced them into the belief that in order to attain independence they must trust in God. For them, to be a good nationalist was also to be a good Christian and vice-versa. Thus, there was a strong nexus between the Naga movement and Christianity. In fact, the Naga nation was believed to be bestowed by God and therefore protecting it became the utmost duty of the Naga nationalists (Sakha cited in Eastern Mirror 17-11-2015). Sangtam (cited in The Morung Express 13-12-2016) also argued that among Nagas, nationalism was a 'divine calling' and thus it was strongly supported and advocated by tribal churches, various church councils and associations.

Till the late 1950s, the Naga national movement under the aegis of the NNC, while certainly inspired by Christianity, did not have a singular position on matters of religion, and granted its followers the freedom to practice the religion of their choosing (Thomas 2016: 4-5). The *Yehzabo*, in fact, recognized both Christianity and Naga traditional religion (Lasuh 2002: 90). However, in the subsequent decades, the NNC's stance was transformed and Christianity became more publicly infused with the national movement. The defense of the Naga nation was coalesced with the defense of Christianity (Thomas 2016: 4-5). This linkage between Christianity and the consciousness of Naga nationalism became so strong that the Indian leaders considered the Naga political movement as a 'religious movement' inspired and mediated by foreign missionaries and Christianity (Thomas 2016: 3-4). This conviction made the Indian Government sensitive to the presence of Christian missionaries in Nagalim. As a result, in 1954, American missionaries were accused of instigating an independent state movement against India, and were forced to leave Nagalim (Lasuh 2002: 550).

Among other things, the local entry of Christianity opened vistas to modernity through modern education and through which the idea of modern nation-state came to be more firmly established in the minds of the educated Nagas. It helped them realize that historically, culturally, politically, socially and religiously the Nagas were different from the rest of the Indian population. Hence, of all the factors mentioned, the role of Christianity in fostering Naga national consciousness was certainly remarkable. Had Christianity not been introduced to the Nagas, the opportunity provided by missionary schools and other educational institutions would have been missed out as well, and this would likely have prevented most Nagas from thinking outside the realms of their clans, villages, and tribes. Thus, Shimray (2005: 42) notes that in Naga history, the conversion of the Nagas to Christianity was a revolution and more significant compared to British colonialism. Sanyu (cited in Shimray 2005: 42) stated that the message of the Gospel was the beginning of all things in Naga modern history. Further, the Government of People's Republic of Nagaland (GPRN), the political organ of the Isak-Muivah led NSCN, also declared that the propagation of Christianity, along with the imparting of education by opening missionary schools, made the greatest contribution to the political uprising of the Naga society (nationalism) (cited in Shimray 2005: 42). Similarly, Das (2013: 95-98) commented that the 'political construct' of Naga nationalism was largely influenced by Western education and Christianity and that the 'most educated tribes were also the most Christianized group'.

With the advent of Christianity, inter-village warfare was replaced by inter-village relationships and the placement of Christ at the epicenter of that relationship. Along with the promotion of Christianity, the term Naga was also popularised, assimilating once diverse villages and tribes into an evolving notion of a Naga nation. This unified Naga political identity could materialize because of mass conversions to Christianity, which, in turn, was inextricably linked with the consciousness of Naga nationalism as the converted masses became the harbingers of the national movement. Along with the gospel of Christ, the doctrine of Naga nationalism was preached by local evangelists in all the nooks and corners of Naga territory, including those places where missionaries had not yet reached. The Church role in disseminating Naga nationalism as an 'unquestionable truth' continues today. For instance, the Tangkhul Naga churches across India dedicate at least one Sunday in a single calendar year as the prayer cum fasting day for the Naga political movement.

CURRENT STATUS OF NAGA NATIONALISM

Since the late 1990s, a new twist of event seems to have captured Nagalim and especially the Naga national movement. Initially, and for a long time, the Nagas projected the Indian Government as their sole enemy, the one that prevented their freedom. The Central Government, in response, resorted to cruel and ruthless methods to subdue Naga aspirations for self-determination. This nourished a strong anti-Indian sentiment among many Nagas. They vocally declared that 'Nagas are not Indian in any sense'. Moreover, the trend was that Naga civilians were victimized after every armed conflict between Naga nationalists and the Indian Army. The latter often made no distinction between Naga civilians and Naga nationalists in exerting their revenge. For them, since most Naga civilians had some level of sympathy for the nationalists, all, including women and children, were considered hostiles. The Army subsequently resorted to all forms of human rights violations such as ransacking property, burning down villages and granaries, deliberate starvation, torture, rape, murder, village grouping and moving people into, what were de facto, concentration camps (Shimray 2005: 68-72; Luithui & Haksar 1984: 26-37). All along, the Nagas suffered for guarding their national identity. There was little to no media to cover their side of the stories, while no outside observers were allowed to report the grave situation at hand. The Nagas, therefore, had no one with whom to confide their miseries and sufferings. Despite untold suffering, this was also the time when the Nagas were 'solidly' united for their political cause (Luithui & Haksar 1984: 26). However, today, the scenario has changed due to the rise of factionalism within the Naga movement, and which has fragmented the Naga nation.

The struggle for independence of Nagalim is an enduring story that still evades a solution. Therefore, in an effort to come up with an honourable and acceptable solution, the Naga peace process had been undertaken since August 1997 when a ceasefire was declared and a political dialogue started between Naga underground leaders and the Indian Government. In 2015, the 'Naga Peace Framework Agreement' was signed between the two conflicting parties. The outcome of this Agreement however, is yet to be known.

Apart from the ongoing Naga peace process, there had been two earlier peace processes. However, the failures of the first two peace processes were followed by the intensification of infightings within the Naga movement. For instance, the failure of the 1964 peace process plunged the Nagas into a phase of violent internal bloodshed alongside the violence afflicted by Indian armed forces. The 'moderate Nagas', who were willing to find a solution within the Constitution of India, were targeted by the so-called 'extremist Nagas', who sought for a solution outside the framework of the Indian Constitution. Consequently, there was a clear split between the two, each with its set of followers.

In their effort to deliver the Naga people from the cruel inhuman treatment of the Indian Army, some Naga nationalist leaders made a pact with the Central Government in 1975, which came to be popularly known as the Shillong Accord. However, this only further divided the Naga people. A section of the non-accordists, that is, those who considered the Accord as 'the most ignominious sell-out made in the history of the Naga people' (Shimray 2005: 104), formed the National Socialist Council of Nagaland (NSCN) in the year 1980 and continued fighting for political independence. In 1988, the NSCN was divided into two factions largely because of an internal leadership crisis. One faction, under the leadership of Isak and Muivah came to be known as NSCN (IM), while the other, under the leadership of Khaplang, as the NSCN (K). Ever since, the two parties have been at loggerheads, while, at the same time continuing their armed struggle against the Central Government, though at different levels. Over time, the NSCN (IM) turned more powerful and gained the support of a sizeable section of the Naga masses. In 2007, the NSCN (IM), however, suffered an internal division when Azetho Chophy formed the NSCN (Unification). Likewise, on June 7, 2011, the NSCN (K) suffered a similar fate when Kitovi Zhimomi (General Secretary of NSCN (K)) and Khole

Konyak[6] (Chief-in-Command of the NSCN (K)) defected and instituted the NSCN (KK). Within a span of a year or two, the NSCN (U) was merged with the NSCN (KK). Further, in March 2015, after Khaplang decided to pull out of the cease-fire agreement with the Centre, a group from within the NSCN (K) and in favour of the continuation of the cease-fire, formed the NSCN (Reformation) under the leadership of Y Wangtin Naga. The present political scenario in Nagaland is that, on one hand, the Naga nationalist groups are fighting against the Central Government for their political independence, while on the other, they are fighting amongst themselves for power and territorial domination in the name of Naga nationalism.

Factionalism, which is the root cause of all internal fighting among Nagas, has led to the situation of 'peacelessness' in Nagalim, despite the ongoing 'Indo-Naga' ceasefire. Today, factionalism seems often based on the issues of tribe-ism, leadership crisis, and the tussle for power, and has proven to be a menace that can destroy the hope of a common destiny preciously forged under the banner of Naga nationalism. It also empowered New Delhi to degrade the credibility of Naga nationalists to a state of opprobrium. Right from the days of Jawaharlal Nehru, New Delhi adopted the policy of 'divide and rule' in order to denigrate the Naga national movement and, provided inordinate attention to the 'loyalist' moderate Nagas. This policy succeeded in splitting asunder the once united Nagas interwoven by the spirit of nationalism and Christianity. Most destructively, the rise of factionalism befuddled the Naga national struggle prompting one to ask as to what exactly are the Nagas aspiring for today. This query brings us to the roadside dhaba sign in Assam, cited by Wouters (2016: 98), and which reads: 'Before you place your order, please decide what you want to eat', and which can be translated into 'Before the Naga places their order they first need to decide what they want to eat.' Vociferously, Nagas continue to assert 'sovereignty as their birthright and unchangeable objective', yet the display of factionalism has also been equally loud, inducing one to remark that perhaps factionalism has obscured the proclaimed political objective of the Nagas.

Factionalism, thus, had wide ramifications for the Naga political movement. Towards this end, various Naga civil society organizations but specifically the Forum for Naga Reconciliation (FNR) and Nagaland Baptist Churches Council (NBCC) are presently playing an important role in urging the various Naga outfits to reconcile and to stop bloodshed among Naga brethren. These organizations function under the motto 'forgive and forget', invoking the ethics of Christianity on the ground that all Naga nationalists are Christians (Longvah 2015: 105).

Because of the belief that religion unites the Naga people, the FNR, headed by respected church elders and leaders, are endeavoring to reconcile the feuding Naga nationalist factions since the year 2008. However, Naga reconciliation efforts

[6]In March 2016, Khole Konyak joined NSCM (IM).

did not begin with the FNR. It was the Council of Naga Baptist Churches (CNBC), later changed to NBCC, that laid the foundation of the Naga unity move as early as 1991, when it articulated a vision to organize a Naga High Level Summit with the intent of providing a joint platform where various Naga factions could meet 'without any strings attached' (Lasuh 2002: 393). To make this possible, the CNBC constituted the Peace Commission and this committee organized a second Naga High Level Summit in 1992. After this, the CNBC urged the Baptist Peace Fellowship of North America (BPFNA) to help in addressing the anguish of the Naga people. The efforts of the CNBC to collaborate with the BPFNA in order to further the Naga unity move bore some fruit when in 1997 the BPFNA, along with the CNBC, convened the so-called Atlanta Meeting from 28th July to 3rd August, in Georgia, America. The Atlanta Meeting was a call for Naga Reconciliation, one rooted in the biblical claim that lasting peace can only be achieved on the basis of 'confession, forgiveness and restoration' (Lasuh 2002: 443).

Evidently, the Church played a significant role in the Naga reconciliation process. Reconciliation, here, simply means 're-establishment of fractured relationship' among the various Naga factions. It is the process of uniting the different Naga nationalist groups in order to pave the way for a final resolution of the long drawn Naga political movement. However, despite relentless efforts by the Church, achieving unity among Nagas remains a herculean task as certain nationalist groups remain reluctant to trust the Church because of past bitter experiences.

Certainly, in the initial stage, the Church role in disseminating the sentiment of Naga nationalism was beyond doubt. Subsequently, however, in order to stop the inhuman treatment meted out to Nagas, the Church started the work of securing peace and stability in Nagalim, even at the cost of Naga freedom. In the late 1950s, then prominent church leaders along with other Naga leaders formed the Naga People's Convention (NPC) that subsequently negotiated the creation of Nagaland state inside the Indian Union. The creation of Nagaland state was however vehemently objected to by the Naga nationalists. For its role in the making of Nagaland, the Church was accused of changing its political stance by Naga nationalists, for leaning towards moderate ideologies, and for agreeing to a 'compromised peace'. Furthermore, in the past, the Church was also severely criticized for its dubious role in signing the Shillong Accord; and in circulating negative thoughts about the NNC and Thuingaleng Muivah, the General Secretary of NSCN (IM) as well who they alleged had embraced communism after spending time in China (Shimray 2005: 89-91). Because of this role, the Church was accused, in some nationalist circles, of working against the spirit of Naga nationalism and for being 'instruments' of the Indian State (Shimray 2005: 89). Since the Church was unable to gain confidence of the nationalist groups, therefore, the onus of Naga reconciliation was subsequently handed over to the FNR.

CONCLUDING REMARKS

Even in the 21st century, there are still many things yet to be researched about the Nagas and their ways of life. There is more than that meets the eye when one talks about the Nagas and their political movement. What is clear, however, is that Christianity propelled manifold changes in Naga society - changes in religious, social, cultural, moral outlook, customary laws and political practices and aspirations. These changes have both negative and positive connotations. For instance, when viewed from a political dimension especially the nationalism that it awaked, the changes that occurred can be considered as a boon. However, when viewed from socio-cultural and other dimensions, the changes were often more of a bane.[7]

Christianity integrated the otherwise independently existing Naga tribes and gave political meaning to their realization of a common identity. Influenced by the common idiom Christianity offered them, the Nagas for the first time replaced their village identity with a wider Naga national identity. Based on the Christian values of love, mercy and forgiveness, the Nagas shed their 'head-hunting' culture and forged a relationship of brotherhood which contributed significantly to the rise of Naga nationalism. Christianity, undoubtedly, played a significant role in the consciousness of Naga nationalism, although, in the longer run, it also failed to 'negate tribal identities' (Sangtam, cited in The Morung Express 13-12-2016). In fact, ancient Naga tribal, clan and village solidarities still remain very strong and are not a forgone story. Such parochial solidarities have also fueled infighting among Nagas.

What seems remarkable, in conclusion, is that while Christianity gave rise to the Naga Movement, the same Christian principles and values are today invoked by the FNR to protect the Naga movement from disintegration. In both ways, Christianity and Naga nationalist politics remain closely related.

---

[7]Elwin pointed out that Christianity and Christian missionaries followed a culturally destructive policy, and robbed the Nagas of many of the things which gave vitality to their lives. He further accounted that the missionaries insisted on a convert becoming a teetotaller; and that they restrict themselves to one wife. At some point Naga converts were not even allowed to eat the flesh of mithun since this animal was associated with sacrifices at 'heathen' festivals. Moreover, the great 'Feasts of Merit' were stopped; boys (youths) were forbidden to attend the Morung. Naga converts at times even often stopped dancing, while the art of weaving suffered since generally converts adopted European mill-made dress (1961: 78). Thus, Christianity came at a cultural cost, leading to the discontinuation of many ancestral cultural practices among Nagas.

ACKNOWLEDGEMENTS

I would like to thank Jelle J.P. Wouters for his expert review and editing of this paper, as well as Michael Heneise and the anonymous reviewer for thoughtful comments and assessment.

▪ ▪▪ ▪▪

09

MASCULINITY IN THE MARGINS: MEN AND IDENTITY IN 21ST CENTURY NAGALAND

Matthew Wilkinson

Although there is no singular 'Naga masculinity', there are common themes that cut through ideas of manhood and the assumed roles of Naga men in Nagaland. These include the realities and perceptions of tribalism, the experience of living in an environment of conflict and an exceptional space, and the status of being a marginal community in India. In this chapter, I discuss how these themes shape the construction of masculinity and masculine norms in Nagaland today. I explore the perceptions that surround 'tribe', not only as a network of relations, but also as a construct of identity that, from the outside, is often associated with ideas of temporal distinction and primitivism. I consider the ways insurgency and exceptional state violence have shaped local ideas of manhood and masculinity, reifying ideas of men's roles as cultural guardians, ones that often romanticize a culturally 'pure' past that marginalizes women and excludes non-Naga communities. I discuss how this discourse of cultural guardians frames discussions of migrants and experiences of marginality. In so doing, I build on earlier work by Longkumer (2015) that sheds light on how Naga identity is actively engaged with, and in whose process communities are not simply 'passive onlookers' but are active participants in the making and remaking of identity. In agreement with Longkumer's (2015) focus, that identity is actively engaged with and not simply ascribed or received, I consider how this active engagement with identity shapes local debates of identity and marginality.

This research focuses on masculinity, and hence it is important to link 'masculinity' to the subjects of the research, men. Masculinity has become a referential term for thoughts and actions associated with 'being a man', the everyday experiences of men, and the unequal relationships between men and women (Thompson 2012). Hearn and Pringle (2006: 7) acknowledge that the term 'masculinity' is convenient shorthand to refer to how men act, think, believe and appear, or are made apparent. Likewise, Smith (2010) defines masculinity as 'the trait of behaving in ways considered typical for men' (Smith 2010:1). Considering masculinity requires a naturalization of the biological - sex, and a focus on the cultural - gender (Connell & Messerschmidt 2005). That is not to say that masculine considerations marginalize or ignore the physical aspects of sex and gender altogether, but that the focus of masculine theory and research is the cultural, social and political aspects of gender - its construction, reception, performance, and attitudes and thoughts surrounding gender. This overall ethic is aptly summed up by Fausto-Sterling, 'men are made, not born' (1997: 219), an adaptation of De Beauvoir's 'one is not born, but rather becomes, a woman' (De Beauvoir 1949: 330). In light of this, this chapter focuses on the experiences of men in Nagaland, but not in the quotidian sense. Rather, I focus on the themes and constructs that surround, frame, and shape ideas associated with men and manhood.

Young men in particular are the focus of this discussion. Youth is notoriously difficult to define, being a culturally elastic concept, and while defining youth is not the focus of this chapter[1], this chapter cautiously frames "youth" as individuals born in Nagaland from the mid-1980s to the mid-2000s. There are three reasons for this focus. Firstly, Nagaland has experienced significant changes that affect young people in particular since the mid-1980s. The peace processes beginning in the early 1990s, along with the 1997 NSCN(IM) the 2001 NSCN(K) ceasefires have reconfigured, but not completely ended violent conflict between Naga insurgent groups and the government, and also between each other. Secondly, Nagaland has 'opened up' in this time, with the relaxation of the Inner Line Permit system in Nagaland and several neighbouring states in 2011, and an expanding tourism industry aimed at Indian and international markets. This has increased interactions with 'mainland' India and occurs alongside the ongoing process of Northeast India's transition from a 'frontier' to a 'corridor', changing the way many young Nagas and Northeast Indians relate to India, to each other, and how identity operates at different levels (McDuie-Ra 2016). In other words, people growing up in this era are presented with, in many ways, a wholly different Nagaland from that of their parents and grandparents. Finally, Nagaland is a young persons' state.

---

[1]It has been discussed in depth by Cole & Durham (2008).

It is amongst the five Indian states with the highest percentage of persons aged between 10-14 years (12.6%). Nagaland also has the second highest population of adolescents in India aged 10-19 (24.2%), the fourth highest percentage of people aged 15-24 (21.9%), and the lowest percentage of elderly people in India (5.2%) (Government of India 2011).

Young people are also at the centre of the community. They are often more dependent than older demographics, with the exception of the very elderly, on existing networks (Mcdowell 2001). These networks include the family networks they rely on, the peer groups they conform to, the clubs and organizations that represent and protect them, and the wider ethnic and national community they identify with. At the same time, however, young people exist in a 'liminal legal and political space' (Gergan 2014: 70), where they are often seen as 'adults in waiting' (Skelton 2010). This puts young people, and in particular young men, at risk for pursuing status and recognition through alternative means, often through violence, drugs and alcohol (see Nilan et al. 2011). Young people also experience higher rates of domestic violence (Holt et al. 2008) and outside-of-the-home violence (Hagedorn 2008), higher risks of imprisonment (Cox 2011), homicide (Farrington et al. 2012) and suicide (Canetto & Cleary 2012). Young people shoulder the greatest burdens of unemployment (Kieselbach 2003) and lack of opportunity (Jeffrey 2010). In essence, the insecurities and challenges faced by young people exist in layered ways that are related to their centrality in the community but also their marginal status within it. The agency of young people needs to be understood as operating at these multiple scales (Gergan 2014). In other words, young people need to be understood as not simply a liminal population, but as living with various forms of vulnerability and opportunity simultaneously in relation to this liminal status. I aim to shed light on the factors that shape this agency and identity in a changing Nagaland.

'NAGA'

A distinct 'Naga' identity is a relatively new construction. Although designations of a 'Naga' group in the hills east of Assam and north of Manipur were not a new or exclusive construction of colonial anthropologists, communities in the Naga Hills appear to have had little sense of commonality or unity in the past. As stated by Hutton:

> It is generally assumed in a vague sort of way that those tribes which are spoken of as Nagas have something in common with each other that distinguishes them from the many other tribes found in Assam and entitles them to be regarded as a racial unit in themselves... the truth is that if not impossible it is exceedingly difficult to propound any tests by which a Naga tribe can be distinguished from other Assam and Burma tribes which are not Nagas (Hutton in Mills, 1922:xvi)

Similarly, Woodthorpe states:

> Various deviations have been given for the name *Naga*, some supposing it to come from the Bengali word *Nangta*, in Hindustani 'Nanga' = Naked. Others think that the *Kachari* word *Naga* = a young man = a warrior, supplies the name; While others again derive it from '*Nag*' = 'a snake'... the name is quite foreign and unrecognized by the Nagas themselves" (1882: 56).

Less than a century after Hutton's statement, and just over a century since Woodthorpe's, the phrase "we are Nagas by birth, Indians by accident" has become commonplace in political speech and protest language in Nagaland (Hussain 2009:100). This articulation of Naga identity is the result of a myriad of local and imported ideas, and is continually developing and changing (Wettstein 2016). Simultaneously, new adjacent forms of identity exist and are gaining relevance alongside clan and tribal identities in Nagaland and wider Northeast India (McDuie-Ra 2016). These identities are not exclusive, but inclusive, and are indicative of the fluid nature of identity, and of how new constructions of identity are engaged with without necessarily replacing older constructions. This fluidity does not suggest that identity is fleeting or flexible to the point of being ephemeral. Rather it suggests that identity is shaped by many factors that may have roots in history, but are also continuously evolving, recreated, and re-interpreted.

Identity in Nagaland and its gendered aspects have deep roots in the colonial experience, and these roots, I argue, are reified in renegotiations and reconfigurations of identity today. As stated by West (1994: 55), "The use of the term Naga, as personal and political identity today, stems from the aspirations of hill peoples toward self-determination, but its construction as a viable entity is very much part of that colonial past". Understanding this historical influence is therefore important for understanding its contemporary manifestations.

'HEADHUNTERS AND SAVAGES': CONSTRUCTING A FRONTIER IDENTITY IN COLONIAL INDIA

> The idea of violent savagery was part of the script that legitimated conquest, but that violence was then supposed to be tempered by a new Christian conscience and Protestant work ethic... The headhunter is a stubborn image of violence threatening from the outside... Most Europeans thought he would vanish from the stage of history by the middle of this century, but his time has not passed, and indigenous peoples will not let us forget it
> Hoskins 1996: 43

Hoskins (1996) argues that in the postcolonial era, these ascriptions have been appropriated by indigenous communities; "indigenous people have stolen the script and rewritten it" (ibid). The framing of men and masculinity in Nagaland has proceeded along similar lines. In the Naga Hills, colonial administrators and anthropologists focused on ideas of temporal distinction, violence, and primitiveness. In the post-colonial era, constructions of manhood and masculinity in Nagaland, though not directly a reflection of this colonial discourse, are nevertheless informed by it.

At first glance, this argument appears to make two controversial claims. One, that all discussion of India's Northeastern Frontiers and the Naga Hills involved negative stereotyping and ascriptions of savagery and violence. This is not the case. Wouters (2012) argues that these stereotypes were only half of the picture, that colonial discussions of the Northeast were not homogenous and uniformly negative. Negative stereotypes involving temporal ascriptions were rife, especially during the consolidation of the Naga Hills and other Northeast Indian highlands, but positive ascriptions existed as well (ibid). These ascriptions, violence and primitiveness, continued to serve the needs of colonial administrators, albeit differently in two ways. First, they tended to contrast highland communities with Hindu Indian communities, justifying continued special treatment of the North-Eastern Frontier. For example, discussing Kachari festivals, Endle (1911: 53) states

> These Kachari festivals are almost always attended by an immoderate consumption of the national rice beer... On the other hand, they have their good side in that they help to keep the people to some extend beyond the influence of the destructive vortex of Hinduism, in which their simple primitive virtues might otherwise be so readily engulfed, and the adoption of which in whole or in part is invariably accompanied by a grave and deep-seated deterioration in conduct and character.

Second, they emphasized the acceptance of Western norms in Northeastern communities in a manner that contrasted those members that had adopted Western lifestyles from those that had not. Gurdon's (1914: 6) description of Khasis in Meghalaya, offers a telling example:

> Khasis of the interior who have adopted Christianity are generally cleaner in their persons than the non-Christians, and their women dress better than the latter and have an air of self-respect about them. The houses in a Christian village are far superior, especially where there are resident European missionaries... It is a pleasure to hear the sound of the distant church bell on the hill-side on a Sunday evening, soon to be succeeded by the beautiful Welsh hymn tuned which, when

> wafted across the valleys, carry one's thoughts far away. The
> Welsh missionaries have done, and continue to do, an immense
> amount of good amongst these people.

While there certainly is a heterogeneity of descriptions, some positive and some negative, the problem of agency and identity remains pertinent. Colonial officer-anthropologists constructed an understanding of the Northeastern Frontier based on their positions as producers and as products of the Empire. New ideas, lifestyles, political and social organizations found at the Frontier were not only different, but were seen as uncivilized and in need of civilizing. Whether this was framed as violence and savagery in need of being tamed, or as noble savages in need of the protection of colonial administrators, understandings of the Northeast were, with very few exceptions, a means to a civilizing mission.

The other apparent claim this argument suggests, related to the above, is that Naga men have no agency over their own identities, that "Naga" is merely a colonial construct. This too is not the case. There is growing debate on the roots and Orientalist underpinnings of identity in India. Dirks' (2001; 1992) seminal work on caste and identity argues that the colonial discourse transformed institutions in India, including caste and tribe. In other words, the colonial experience shaped identities. This has been mistaken in some cases as arguing that colonialism created caste and tribe (Fuller 2016: 458). Piliavsky (2015), on the other hand, argues that colonial stereotypes drew from tribe and caste stereotypes that were already well established. While this chapter does not engage directly in this debate, it does focus on two issues of identity formation that touch on this debate and are relevant in Nagaland.

To begin with, the majority of anthropological information produced in Northeast India, and wider South Asia, are colonial accounts, which are rarely separable from colonial state-making and society-shaping missions (Wettstein 2016; Ngully 2014; West 1994). Because of this, colonial anthropology is a field as valuable to understanding the role of state-making in the framing of identities in line with Dirks'(2001; 1992) focus, as it is to understanding how identities shaped the state-making mission, Piliavsky's (2015) focus.

Furthermore, oral histories, as are those of many Naga communities, have been prone to reinterpretation according to colonial understandings, a phenomenon that is already well discussed by Tezenlo Thong and is revisited below (Thong 2014; 2011; 2010). Rather than discussing the normative quality of ascriptions or their veracity, this section focuses on how these ascriptions are understood in contemporary Nagaland and the role they continue to play in framing ideas of masculinity.

Two themes in particular are recurrent in post-colonial readings of colonial discussions of men in the Naga Hills: head-hunting and primitiveness. These themes have dominated contemporary understandings of colonial and pre-colonial Naga society. Nagas as headhunters appear in most histories of the Naga Hills. Today this discourse is employed as a means of presenting Nagas as cut from a primitive and savage stock, as still holding to a supposedly ancient culture of savagery and ritual violence but in new materializations such as insurgency and organized crime (Patil 2011:1000).

At the time of the earliest reports of groups in the Naga Hills, Europeans had not yet directly contacted Naga communities. McCosh wrote: "[the Nagas] are the wildest and most barbarous of all the hill tribes, and looked upon with dread and horror by the neighbours of the plains, who consider them as ruthless robbers and murderers"(1837:p.156). Colonial imaginings and reproductions of Nagas continued to employ this perspective in writing a history and forming a discourse of the Naga Hills.[2] Colonel James Johnstone (1896:27) described Angami Nagas as "a strong built, hardy, active race... they have a mainly independent bearing, and are bred up to war from their earliest years". Likewise is Woodthorpe's description: "bloodthirsty, treacherous, and revengeful all Nagas, even the best are" (1882:65). Butler described Nagas as "savages" (1875: 313), "warlike" (ibid: 320), having a "thirst for blood" (ibid), and coming from "long generations of anarchy and bloodshed" (ibid: 313). Johnstone (1896), regarding his own intervention in an uprising at Kohima speculated that "the result would have been no one who knows the Nagas can doubt; five-hundred and forty-five headless and naked bodies would have been lying outside the blockade" (159).

Indeed, head-hunting and other violent acts did occur in the Naga Hills and the Northeastern Frontier, and there are confirmed instances of beheadings (Reed 1942: 178). Colonial officers bore witness to human skulls on display in Morungs and dangling from trees at significant sites (ibid: 189). The true source of these heads, whether hunted by rivals, dug after a burial, or kept as a traditional memorial, forms a debate of its own (Zou 2005; Thong 2012; West 1985; West 1994). Reports of widespread and common head-hunting, however, were seldom confirmed, and much of the discussion of head-hunting appearing in the diaries and letters of colonial administrators such as Butler, Woodthorpe and Johnstone, and missionaries such as Lorrain, were informed by rumour, speculation, and a growing conviction that the Frontier *must be* a space rife with chaos and head-hunting, despite few actual recorded instances of beheadings (see Thong 2012). These descriptions of the Naga Hills drew heavily on a few early accounts. Woodthorpe's (1882) notes are lifted directly from Butler's expedition memoirs, some several paragraphs in length. Lorrain (1915: 85), who described his own experience as "I found myself in the midst of a wild head-hunting tribe of savages, traversing through dense jungles" later clarified that he had not met with any head-hunters directly, or witnessed a beheading, but that his interactions were limited to "sons of head-hunters" (Ibid.: 235). Gait (1906: 312) notes that "blood feuds and head-hunting now survive only

---

[2]Venusa Tinyi offers a thorough and nuanced discussion of headhunting as a practice and a cultural identifier in chapter five of this volume.

in the memory of the older generation which is rapidly passing away." American army personnel encountering Naga communities during WWII made claims that "there was no doubt that the Nagas were still taking heads when we were in their country". This was followed by the clarification that "I did not personally see any collections of heads in the Naga country… my only contact with the Nagas was the visit several of them made to our marching line and demonstrated the use of their crossbows" (Randle & Hughes 2003:44, 45).

The Naga Hills always represented more than a geographical delineation from the plains and foothills of Assam. They were a divider between the legible and controllable Empire, and an illegible, untaxable, region beyond the reach of colonial administration. The space was framed as untamable and in need of harsher and different treatment compared to many other Indian territories in the form of an excessively violent campaign of subjugation and control. Notions of the 'tribal man' were central to this civilizing mission. By necessity, this 'tribal man' was seen as violent, resistant, and unpredictable. Tribal man in colonial South Asia was a construction of temporally and Social-Darwinist oriented notions of primitivity and violence, a construction that served the needs of colonial administrators, and the curiosities of colonial anthropologists and audiences. Correspondence by Deputy Commissioner of the Naga Hills, Hutton, illustrates this civilizing logic well:

> In these circumstances we cannot hope to civilize our own half-savage peoples so long as they see raiding and head-hunting practiced by their brothers and cousins just across the border. In order to complete our mission of civilization within our own borders we must gradually extend the area which we control (Reed 1942: 155).

Likewise, the Governor of Assam's Secretary stated in April 1937 that 'there is little doubt that any considerable relaxation of our control would inevitably lead to head-hunting and tribal warfare' (Reed 1942: 88).

This was not a phenomenon unique to the Naga Hills. Primitiveness and savagery were paradigms that applied to the much of the lower Himalayan region, from the Chittagong Hill Tracts of Bengal (now Bangladesh), to the highlands of Sikkim and Tibet, and encompassing highlands and hinterlands in Indochina as well (Scott 2009). Arguably though, the construction of temporal distinction and savageness in the Naga Hills was louder, more anthropologically invested, and certainly has maintained relevance in ways different to many other highland communities. Headhunting and the related cult of the primitive have become integral parts of identity in Nagaland, an identity that is constantly evolving. Discussed below, these colonially informed ascriptions have taken on new meaning, coexisting with, and complementing other aspects and shades of identity.

INTERNALIZING THE SAVAGE: HEADHUNTING IN THE MODERN CONTEXT

> We are still very confused about ourselves. From a society of head-hunters, we directly shifted into a modern, Western society. We are in the middle of an identity crisis
> Anen Molungnenla, quoted in Ghoshal 2012

Earlier constructions of savages and primitive spaces have ramifications for identity extending into the post-colonial era. Colonial structures that were used to define and regulate populations have been co-opted and adopted by the formerly colonized themselves when identifying themselves as a distinct group (Said 1978: 24). Essentially ascriptions applied to populations often turn into cultural identifiers of those populations. Thong (2012) discusses two ramifications of this process: self-primitivisation and self-alienation.

Self-primitivisation involves the appropriation of colonial ascriptions by subjects. The image of the 'savage', 'primitive', 'headhunter' or 'cannibal' is assumed to be an accurate depiction, and becomes a feature of identity of that community or group, a process not unlike Bourdieu's framing of self-structuring structures - *habitus* (1984; 170). In New Zealand, European notions of a 'cannibalistic' Maori have been subsumed into modern notions of Maori identity (Tempesta 2005: 120). In Papua New Guinea, Brison (1996) notes the adoption of savagery, aggression and notions of perpetual violence into Kwanga identities based on the colonial portrait of them (Brison 1996). Likewise, ideas of Nagas as 'headhunters' have become embedded into Naga identity. Singh (2006: 1) notes a Naga interviewee as saying 'your head would be decorating this drawing room had you met my forefathers a hundred years ago'. The actuality of these claims is of little concern, as they have *become* social truths.

The second phenomenon identified is one of self-alienation. The relationship between a community or individual and their history is defined by the colonial experience. Old customs become taboo, or shamed. Introduced customs such as Christian ceremonies and holidays became the new norm. Through this, history is divided between the time before Christianity and civilization and the time after. Pre-colonial histories are thought of as savage, timeless and ancient. Christian developments are considered enlightened and a time of cultural rebirth. In Nagaland, the expression 'from darkness to light' has been popularly employed to refer to this change (Kiranshankar 2011).

However accurate colonial headhunting reports may be, the contemporary myth of widespread and pervasive headhunting nonetheless has become embedded in popular understandings of Nagaland, as well as Naga people's understandings of themselves and their past. The legacy of the violent, savage, Naga man, the headhunter, is one part of masculine identity in Nagaland today. This construction seems especially salient in tourism narratives.

TOURISM AND IDENTITY

Tourism operates through the creation of spatial and temporal narratives (Henderson & Weisgrau 2007: 64–65). These narratives bind a space to a time, portraying the past in the present for an audience, the tourist, to experience and escape into (ibid).Tourists are presented with a space advertised as 'traditional', 'authentic', pure, and exotic (Tucker 2003: 2-3, 30-34). This has been described as the 'cult of the primitive' (Mumford 1934: 237).The tourist is presented with a 'timeless society', a romanticized step back in time to a pre-modern world (Wang 2000: 87). Tourism is the business of linking sites and experiences with these expectations (Henderson & Weisgrau 2007, p.65).

Picard (1990: 198) argues that the outcomes of these narratives cannot be compartmentalized, that the host community cannot perpetuate and exploit narratives constructed for and by tourism without these narratives overlapping into the larger cultural discourse. The lines between the invented and embellished cultures that are sold to tourists, and the lived and identified cultures that belong to a community become blurred (ibid). In other words, culture, among other things, is bent and changed to suit the demands and expectations of tourists and this process shapes identity itself.

This phenomenon is not limited to expressions of culture alone. The geographic space itself and control of who can and cannot enter this space is shaped by the presence and demands of tourists. Mendis (1981) describes the spatial outcomes of the surge in tourism to Sri Lanka from the mid-1960s:

> We are compelled to create these tourist enclaves since we are obliged to fulfill the expectations of our visitors who come here to sample a taste of paradise... Hence the strenuous efforts at window-dressing, camouflaging the hell-holes of squalor that blot the landscape, and sweeping the dirt under the carpet, take the form of rounding up beggars, keeping the cities clean, and planting colourful flowers on our roundabouts. We cover up the festering sores with bright raiment and present our visitors a cheerful, smiling Lanka who in reality is nothing but a sick and anaemic old lady with a painted face'
>
> (Mendis 1981: 90–91)

In Sri Lanka, the onset of tourism brought with it changes to the physical constitution of Colombo, its capital. 'Tourist spaces' were isolated from the poverty of the city, beggars were expelled from these spaces, priority was given to keeping these spaces clean and beautiful. The city as a narrative packaged and marketed to tourists was separated from the city as a reality lived by its residents.

This is similarly the case in Nagaland today. State tourism promotions involve selective histories that omit as much post-independence violence as possible. Where necessary or unavoidable, discussions of violence are contextualized within a larger picture of 'warriors' with a historical resistance to outside influence (Patil 2011). State promotions are also highly gendered, using male imageries of warriors, headmen, chiefs and headhunting and featuring women as passive subjects engaged in traditional women's activities and wearing traditional shawls. Tourism companies present moderated histories of the Northeast, while occasionally mentioning the politically contested nature of the region, a marketable Naga identity is the focal point, with a common and exotic theme continually appearing – 'headhunters' (Lonely Planet 2015), 'former headhunters' (Brahmaputra Tours n.d.), 'fierce tattooed headhunters' (Greener Pastures 2012), 'state of the headhunters' (GO Travelling Ltd 2015). This fascination with headhunting and the ideas of primitivism portrayed in colonial texts is the cultural export the Naga tourism industry is based on. A timeless, pre-modern space is the pull that brings in tourists and attracts global interest. This tourism narrative is perhaps most loudly promoted in Nagaland's annual Hornbill Festival.

HORNBILL

> The 20-lakh [2,000,000] strong Naga people, by nature, are fun lovers, and life in Nagaland is one long festival
>
> Hornbillfestival.com

The Hornbill festival is organized by the Nagaland State Tourism Department and Nagaland Art and Culture Department (on the Hornbill festival see also Longkumer, this volume). The annual festival was established in Kohima District in 2000 with aims to revive, protect and preserve Naga heritage and attract tourism (Hornbillfestival.com n.d.). The festival involves Naga dancers dressed in traditional clothing, live theatre, morung tours, souvenirs, food and clothes stalls, acrobatics, pig-chasing, wrestling, a motor rally, the Hornbill International Rock Contest, the Miss Nagaland Beauty Pageant, and chili-eating contests (Longkumer, 2015). Young men at the festival are presented in traditional warrior uniforms, holding shields, daos and spears. Officially this cultural extravaganza takes place at Kisama, a 'Naga Heritage Village' 10 kilometers south of Kohima.

The site is designed as a mini-village and was commissioned by the State Government of Nagaland featuring amphitheaters and stages, traditional morung dormitories, and small trade and food stalls. Similar to Mendis' (1981) discussion of Sri Lanka, Kisama village is temporally and spatially oriented towards satisfying the demands of the tourist audience. During the Hornbill season, the space is 'activated'. It is cleaned, structural repairs are made, roads leading to the site and the major arteries of Kohima are hurriedly patched up, and the space is populated by traditionally dressed dancers, guides, wares-sellers and food staff. The site is presented as a traditional village, an enclave where time has frozen and the mythicized headhunter reappears for an international audience. When not 'in season', Kisama reverts to a peri-urban space of the city. Being a 'site' with a specific purpose, there is no thoroughfare traffic and little reason to pass through outside of the tourist season. Young people frequent the site because of this. Here they can drink alcohol with relative privacy, and make noise and mess away from the gaze of their families and gossipy neighbours.

Ao (2006) argues that such globalizing phenomena as Hornbill alters identities in Northeast India into marketable brand names – 'Naga', 'Khasi', 'Mizo' for example. This involves the subsuming of cultures into amorphous masses, marked by often derogatory and widely applied identifiers such as savageness, primitiveness, and headhunting.

Culturally significant practices are transformed into cultural shows. Clothes that often denote complex meanings that are hidden to visiting audiences become loud and vibrant costumes. Icons and items, both practical and culturally significant, become souvenirs, often produced far away from the spaces they are presented as a piece of and attached to. The Hornbill has also become a space of contentious representation of control and authority (Kikon 2005). The ten-day Festival is opened with the Indian National Anthem, and the presence of the Indian Army is highly visible (Longkumer 2013, p. 93).

'Touristification' proceeds from within (Picard 1990: 199). The narratives that are created and embellished to suit the demands and expectations of tourists are also internalized, and become a part of the cultural discourses of the host communities (ibid). This might take the form of emphasizing specific cultural habits and items that interest and attract tourists, and de-emphasizing parts of a culture considered ordinary, banal, or offensive to the tourist. In Nagaland, this process has been informed by the colonial discourse, where issues of primitiveness, savageness and specifically headhunting have been emphasized by state institutions such as the Nagaland State Tourism Department and the Nagaland Art and Culture Department, and by private tourism companies. The narratives constructed emphasize stereotypes of a male Naga warrior. Promotions link violence today and in recent decades with this warrior typology. For young men in Nagaland, the tourism discourse and its products, such as the Hornbill festival, reify ideas and expectations of men as dominant, violent, and anti-modern. The issue is not that the Hornbill festival itself is the source of this cultural interpretation. Rather, the festival is both an expression of this interpretation, and plays a role in informing the interpretation as well.

Longkumer (2015) considers four layers of meaning of the festival for contemporary Nagas. The festival educates young Nagas and is a form of Naga cultural revival. Second, the festival reinforces a sense of Naga community. Third, the festival attempts to supersede local variants of identity and to encourage a state-wide Naga identity. Finally, the festival is a reconfiguration of the Naga identity to rewrite Naga history on its own terms, rather than being spoken for by colonial sources and distant academics. Overall though, Hornbill and the wider tourism discourse is a part of what Longkumer describes as cultural hybridity. That is, the melding of an often highly idealized, and in the case of Nagaland often externally directed 'traditional' identity, with aspects of modernity that relate to contemporary issues and values. This dichotomy between 'traditional' and 'modern' is problematic in a temporal sense - what is 'traditional' often finds ways of being more relevant in 'modern' contexts and issues than it was even in the 'traditional' context it is claimed to emerge from. The melding of traditional and contemporary themes nonetheless is complimentary. "Imagery of exoticism portrays an idea of Naga culture through the performance of identity" (Longkumer 2015: 61). I argue that these themes are even co-constitutive. Interpretations of 'traditional' values and identity are framed by a myriad of contemporary social and political issues. These issues, however, are also shaped by interpretations of tradition and identity.

INSURGENCY, AFSPA, IMPUNITY

Demands for independence in the Naga Hills has been a pervasive issue since before Independence. As early as 1929 the Naga Club expressed its desire for an independent and separate Naga nation. Other ethnic groups in the Northeast including the Kukis, Garos, Bodos, Assamese, and Mizo communities have also made demands for independent ethnic spaces of various degrees, from absolute separation and independence as is the case with Nagaland, to autonomy and recognition as a federal state of their own as with Garos in Achik-land. Within these space-making projects are dozens of insurgent outfits demanding recognition and competing for legitimacy and overlapping claims to land, governance, and resources.

These calls for separatism have been met with a militarized response from Delhi. The Armed Forces Special Powers Act (AFSPA) 1958 allows the government far-reaching powers in 'disturbed areas' in Northeast India, effective since 1959 in parts of Assam, Manipur, Meghalaya, Mizoram, Arunachal Pradesh and Nagaland. Under the Act, the region has been heavily militarized, with broad, sweeping powers handed to the military executive, and an effective impunity for transgressions from the law. In essence, the AFSPA creates a state of exception in nominated disturbed areas (McDuie-Ra 2009a; Kikon 2009). The military presence has been associated with human rights abuses and abuses of power, with regular searches of people and homes, road closures, curfews, arbitrary arrests and violent and sexual attacks committed by soldiers (Farrelly 2009; McDuie-Ra 2009b; Gaikwad 2009).

This state of exception has complex outcomes in Nagaland. On the one hand, the Indian army has legal impunity throughout the state. Military bases dominate town and city spaces, with checkpoints at or near most entries to large towns, and regular searches of vehicles. These interactions, due to the army's impunity, are fraught with tension as it is clear to many that arrest, harassment and even death are not unrealistic possibilities. The impunity claimed by the Indian army in the state and in other 'disturbed areas' puts young men at especially high risk of arbitrary arrest, searches, assault and summary executions, commonly under the guise of being 'killed in crossfire' between insurgents and security personnel. Although the risk of this has reduced since the 1997 and 2001 ceasefires[3]*, discussion of the risks posed by the army and abusive soldiers continues to be common.

On the other hand, insurgent groups justify their presence as a response to the Indian army. These groups exploit a waning but still substantial degree of popular support, and related to this, a degree of impunity for their own abuses and transgressions. Insurgency affects young men in a number of ways in Nagaland. Young men are targeted by insurgent groups as potential recruits. Groups such as the NSCN(IM) and NSCN(K) have offices dedicated to recruiting and enlisting young men. This can be an attractive option for unemployed and bored men, especially as insurgency offers an income, a sense of adventure and a purpose for many disaffected young men. Although women are also involved in these groups, the groups are predominantly male. From my own experiences spending time with members of groups in Dimapur, Phek District and Mon District, joining a group brings with it a sense of camaraderie, a way of actively defending vaguely framed Naga interests, offers access to drugs and alcohol and is associated with ideas of manliness and adulthood. However, interviews by the author in 2016 with former members of two Naga insurgent outfits bring to light violence employed in the everyday management of groups. New recruits are in some cases beaten, sleep deprived and forced to take part in repetitive manual exercises to break down egos on entry, and maintain the superiority of officers. There is also ongoing and widely discussed violence between groups, especially the NSCN(IM) and NSCN(K) (Lacina 2009).

For Nagas outside of these groups, regular 'taxes' are enforced with the threat of violence, a practice that is increasingly resisted, but nonetheless is still a regular occurrence in both urban and rural contexts (Anonymous 2013). Although arrests of extortionist members are more common, in many cases these abuses continue to be tolerated and acceded to rather than go through the risks, frustrations and dead-ends of pursuing justice through the state police and courts. My own interviews with businesses owners in one large Naga town brought to light both a disdain for the practice and for extortionists' violent behaviour, but also an understanding that the funds extorted went to a shared interest in resisting an Indian hegemon and maintaining the Naga resistance, one which many business owners continue to support, despite the violent means employed to reach that end.

Where the AFSPA (1958) creates a state of exception empowering and giving

[3]*The NSCN-K ceasefire has been discontinued following an attack on a military convoy in the state of Manipur in June 2015.

impunity to the Indian Army, that power and impunity itself grants a degree of responsive impunity to violent groups opposing the occupation. Young men, and indeed the wider population as well, experience fear and apprehension from outside of their communities through the AFSPA – from Indian soldiers, but also from within – from insurgent members and extortionists.

MARGINALITY AT OUTSIDE AND AT HOME: NAGAS AS MARGINAL CITIZENS

Outside of Nagaland, perceptions of Nagas held by many 'mainland' Indians, a term I employ recognizing its problematic breadth, reflect those produced by the colonial and tourist discourses, especially in gendered terms. Stereotypes of backward, head-hunting men and sexualized stereotypes of women abound (McDuie-Ra 2012a; McDuie-Ra 2013; Smith & Gergan 2015). Women are seen as immoral and 'loose' and are often the targets of sexual attacks and sexual discrimination, men are often also viewed as alcoholic, unpredictable, and violent (McDuie-Ra 2012: 48). Recent developments such as the success of Mary Kom in the 2012 London Olympics have encouraged a greater awareness and acceptance of Northeast Indians in mainland India. There is a growing acceptance of Northeasterners as 'Indian', rather than as a peripheral community. Furthermore, fluent English in many Northeastern communities has opened job opportunities for many Nagas outside of Nagaland, especially in major Indian cities, for Naga women in particular (ibid).

Despite these inclusive developments, racism continues to be a dominant theme in interactions between men from the Northeast and Nagaland, and 'mainland Indians' (Smith & Gergan 2015, p.127; McDuie-Ra 2012b). This discrimination is one aspect of the 'anxious belonging' experienced by Northeast Indians (Middleton 2013). Nagas and other Northeast Indian communities live within the borders and are confined by the laws of India, but are also not Indian in the traditional sense, being considered different in terms of race, language and appearance, and are subjected to alienation and discrimination both within their home communities, through the AFSPA, and in mainland India through everyday experiences of racism and discrimination.

In Nagaland, the discourse of 'outsiders' and invaders is one of the strongest points of support utilized by politicians and insurgent groups. The presence of outsiders, especially of Bangladeshi migrants in the state, has been a focal point for the insecurities of young Naga men. Immigrants are seen as suspicious, as illegal migrants or more commonly "IBIs" (illegal Bangladeshi immigrants), and as a threat to Naga representation in the state. Popular resistance to migrants, especially to Bangladeshi migrants, has become a part of masculinity for many Naga men. Bangladeshi migrants are seen as threatening due to their overwhelming numbers, Bangladesh's close proximity to Nagaland, a popular sentiment that Bangladeshis take jobs away from Nagas, and stereotypes of Bangladeshi migrants as uneducated, dim-witted, dirty, and as rapists. In this environment, Naga men are self-styled as protectors and guardians of Naga territory and culture from an oncoming wave of migrants who look different, hold different values, and are perceived as capable of numerically overwhelming the Naga population in Nagaland (Kotwal 2008).

This discourse was displayed in the 'Dimapur lynching' of March 5 2015. Although, both men and women took part in the attack, men were the overwhelming majority, and references to 'our women' suggested that many young men assumed a place as primary social guardians, and exercised ownership and guardianship of Naga society and women through violence (Laskar 2015). Dolly Kikon (2015) argues that the international focus on xenophobia and men's violence in reporting on the lynching obscures the contentious cultural and political issues of representation in Nagaland and that Nagas were portrayed as a xenophobic and reactive collective. This chapter doesn't disagree. What I argue, though, is that the Dimapur lynching was many things. It was an expression of frustration and impatience with a widely percieved inefficient and ineffective legal system. It was a violent outburst aimed at a group that is unpopular in Nagaland, especially so in Dimapur, where Bangladeshi migrants are more numerous. It was also multifaceted, with few media accounts highlighting the role of the Naga Mothers Association in opposing the mob, and little international recognition of criticisms of the lynching by Naga activists, journalists, academics, and politicians in the aftermath. However, the rhetoric that surrounded the lynching, of xenophobia, hostility towards Bangladeshi migrants, and the perception of Nagas as under threat from IBIs is one part of a larger discourse that is popular with many young men in Nagaland, that Nagaland is under threat of being overwhelmed by (mostly) Bangladeshi migrants, that Nagas are at risk of becoming a minority population in Nagaland.

Discussions of the perception of Nagas becoming a minority in Nagaland have evaded wide academic discussion, but remain a predominant issue at the local level (Sandham 2016; Johari 2015; Kashyap 2015; Eastern Mirror Nagaland 2015). Differing from neighbouring Assam, where a substantial attention has been given to the issues surrounding Bangladeshi migration (Mahanta 2013; Baruah 1999), attention has been given to Bangladeshi migration in Nagaland only recently. The ways that a perceived and often embellished risk of marginalization of Nagas in Nagaland through demographic shifting shapes the way Naga men place themselves and their role in the community remains understudied. One focus of the migration issue that has been given attention, though, is unemployment.

Young Nagas find it hard to find work in Nagaland, and increasingly leave the state to find gainful employment in other Indian cities (McDuie-Ra 2012b). With few opportunities to find work and a growing culture of tertiary education, whether that comes from recognized Universities and training centres, or from dubious providers; young men find themselves 'waiting' for employment after school for longer periods (Government of Nagaland 2007). This phenomenon is not unique to Nagaland, but is a growing issue among young men in India, colloquially termed 'timepass' (Jeffrey 2010). Although not strictly a gendered issue, timepass in South

Asia seems to largely an issue faced by educated and unemployed men. Men are unable to meet the demands made on them to find work, or get married, and are "dogged by a sense of not having achieved locally salient norms of masculine success" (ibid: 11). In contrast, Bangladeshi and Bihari migrants have a visible presence in construction and manual labour jobs due to their lower labour costs and a general unwillingness among many young Nagas to engage in these forms of labour. This visible ease with finding work has become a focal point for local political agitators and has contributed to anti Bangladeshi and Bihari sentiment. It has led to Bangladeshi migrants in particular becoming scapegoats for employment woes in Nagaland (Karmakar 2015).

CONCLUSION: MANIFOLD MASCULINITY

There is no prototype 'Naga man' as many earlier colonial accounts attempted to construct. Earlier ascriptions portray pre-modern, mythologized, savage ideal, one that satisfied the curiosities and social Darwinist leanings of early Western researchers and audiences, while also serving the needs of and being conveniently in need of saving by colonial administrators. Contemporary understandings need to be placed in a context that has re-appropriated these often highly mythicized characterizations. Naga men in the twenty-first century navigate systems of colonial ascriptions and stereotyping; a context of exceptionalism, violence and impunity; and an identity perceived by many to be marginal in wider India and under threat at home. Greater connectivity and increased movement between Naga communities, heartland India, and Asia has brought new possibilities for young people exploring and expressing identity, challenging traditional norms and on some levels placing 'Naga' into a wider 'Northeastern' identity. At the same time, though, older ideas of social guardianship and cultural ownership continue to shape social relationships and loudly proclaim "Naga" as a distinct identity, albeit for new reasons and in new ways - new opportunities to re-appropriate colonial narratives for employment and a burgeoning tourism industry, and fears of an oncoming wave of outsiders. Despite the fluid and changing nature of identity, and masculinity for Naga men, a distinct Naga identity continues to frame political and social debate, especially of issues such as migration and marginality.

■ ■■ ■■

10

CONTINUITY AND CHANGE IN HAO NAGA FESTIVALS

Somingam Mawon

In Manipur, festivals have become focal sites for performing identity and fostering unity among ethnic Nagas. State planners have found ways to capitalise on such events as they have sought to recast Manipur's typically fraught reputation, as a place immersed with violence and unrest, to one more appealing for tourists. The *Lui-Ngai-Ni* festival, for example, is observed annually on 15 February under the aegis of the United Naga Council (UNC), an apex civil body representing about twenty Naga communities in Manipur[1]. Among the many aims of *Lui-Ngai-Ni*, the celebrations articulate sometimes very distinct traditions, which are understood as expressions of a common Naga heritage. This celebration, however, invariably carries broader political overtones as the Naga hill areas in Manipur remain underdeveloped, and many see this as the result of irreconcilable differences with the Imphal valley Meitei communities that dominate state politics. The celebration

---

[1]These include the Anal, Chiru, Chothe, Kharam, Koireng, Lamkang, Liangmai, Mao, Maram, Maring, Moyon, Monsang, Poumai, Rongmei, Tangkhul, Tarao, Thangal, and Zeme Naga communities, among others.

of the festival, then, is also an act of articulating difference as well as disagreement with the political status-quo. The first ever *Lui-Ngai-Ni* was celebrated in 1987, and the government of Manipur soon moved in and recognised the festival, declaring 15 February a state holiday. A decade later, India's Ministry of Tourism listed *Lui-Ngai-Ni* as one of the great tourist festivals of India. No longer an indigenous 'micro-event', the *Lui-Ngai-Ni*, akin to the Hornbill festival in Nagaland state, today links up 'to larger economic, cultural, religious and political processes that have wider consequences for the future of the Nagas' of Manipur (Longkumer 2013: 95-6).

However, the origins of this festival lie largely in the *Luira* festival of the Hao (Tangkhul) Nagas[2], and this chapter is concerned with describing the continuities of this traditional Hao festival, the changes that can be observed, and the reasons underpinning those changes. Importantly, the word 'Lui' in the *Lui-Ngai-Ni*, derives from the Hao *Luira* ('to sow'). The assimilation of Hao cultural traditions into the larger cultural and political space in the state is not insignificant, and this chapter is a preliminary examination of these themes, while focused on how the *Luira* is remembered, how it is variously celebrated, and how the 200,000 Hao Nagas that mostly self-identify as Christians negotiate traditions in light of modernity.

HAO FESTIVALS

Hao festivals broadly fall into three categories: religious, agricultural, and those more-or-less of a non-religious social nature. In all, there are fourteen festivals celebrated by the Hao Naga, and these include:

> *Luira* – seed sowing festival
> *Zingkāng Phanit* – rain invoking festival
> *Manei Phanit* – lit. 'a festival signifying that busy season is at hand'
> *Yarra* – youth festival

[2]The term Hao is the traditional nomenclature of the Tangkhul Nagas (see Mawon 2014). With a population of more than 200,000, the Hao are among the largest of all the Naga tribes in India and Myanmar, and are settled in the borderlands of Manipur and Northwest Myanmar, with a significant diaspora also living in Imphal, Delhi and Shillong. Today, there are 261 Hao villages, with 232 in India and 29 in Myanmar. The lingua franca Tangkhul, a Tibeto-Burman language derived from some Hao dialects, was largely developed and encouraged by early Christian missionary William Pettigrew, along with his earliest converts. Prior to carrying out his missionary work among the Hao in 1896 (with British government permission), he surveyed the Hao villages of Hunphun, Hungpung, Shirui, Khangkhui and Peh in October 1895 (Luikham 2002: 83).

Mangkhap – post-paddy transplantation festival
Kashong Kahao Phanit – festival of 'warding off dangers to the standing crops'
Yampāt – a Peh village festival
Dharshāt or Dharreo – pre-harvest festival
Chumpha – festival related to granary (also known as 'post-harvest festival')
Nāsut Phanit – 'ear piercing festival'
Longra Kashak – festival related to youth dormitory
Thishām – festival related to death
Zaiham Makhum – festival related to weaving
Hamrui Phanit – a clan festival related to pottery

While most Hao festivals last little more than a day, with no great feasts, music, folk games or sporting activities, and thus are not costly to the community, major festivals such as the *Luira*, *Yarra*, *Mangkhap*, *Chumpha* and *Thishām* can be very expensive, and participation of the whole community is more or less obligatory. Generally, festivals follow the agricultural cycle, and thus both signal and prepare the community for the year's various seasons of work.

Luira (also pronounced *Luitā*), in particular, provides a rich set of practices and performances, including different forms of Hao music[3] accompanied by traditional Hao musical instruments, and *Pheichak* (folk dance), that in many ways stand out from the other festivals. The word *Luira* is derived from two Hao words namely, *Lui* (field) and *Ra* (to till or to dig), and thus means 'to till or to dig the paddy field', literally. *Luira* is celebrated for anywhere between 9 and 13 days, depending on the climatic condition of the Hao villages. The colder the village climatic condition, the earlier the observance is scheduled, and therefore the fixation, duration, date and month, of *Luira*, varies from village to village. Hao villages such as Longpi, Lunghar and Kuirei, for instance, observe this festival during the last week of *Tharao* (January). Some other Hao villages like Hunphun celebrate *Luira* generally in the month of *Marun* (February). Hao villages like Hungpung, T. Chanhong, Tashar, Ramva, Ringui and Shokvao, in turn, observe the annual seed sowing

[3]Hao Music can be broadly categorised into Hao Laa (Hao folk songs) and Hohoing (a form of Naga vocal music). Hao Laa are of various types based on themes. Hohoing can be broadly categorised into three viz. Khamahon (a melodious vocal sound with overlapping musical tones), Hokharai (a combination of recitation and the production of vocal sound in musical tunes) and Kakahang (howling).

festival in the month of *Mayo* (March). In the pre-Christian period, *Luira* marked the beginning of the year, which is why some considered this festival the New Year festival of the Hao people. The festive order of events greatly depends on the village concerned, and the number of days scheduled for the celebration varies from one village to another. However, most of the customary practices related to *Luira* among the Hao villages remain more or less consistent.

On the eve of the *Luira* festival, rituals such as the *Kapā Khayang* ('a ritual performed through the process of bamboo splitting') and *Harkho Khayang* ('a ritual performed by throttling a fowl') are performed by the *Shimkhur Sharva*, a family priest. These are done in order to portend the future of the family. The performances of these rituals help them foresee the living conditions of a family including the agricultural activities in that year. On notification of any bad omen during the ritual performances, the family priest will seek the assistance of the village shaman to rid himself and the family of such a bad omen. *Khanong* – a village shaman – communicates with the god of Hao religion called *Ameowo* (as argued by Longvah, in this volume, Naga ancestral religion such as Hao religion is not 'animism', but a traditional religion focused on a supreme God), through the sacrificial ritual performance of *Harnao Vāreikathā*, namely divination through sacrificing a fowl at the village gate to ward off evil. This is to say that through propitiation *Ameowo* has the power to take away bad omens that may affect the community. Thus, before *Kumdhar* (the Hao New Year), the community appeals to *Ameowo* to keep disturbances throughout that year at bay. *Kha Sit* is also performed on the eve of the *Luira* festival. A form of collective work in the village, and usually undertaken before or on the eve of *Luira*, *Kha Sit* entails washing utensils, cleaning agricultural implements and weapons, as well as footpaths, houses, and public areas. It is also a day to ward off 'evil elements that bring ill luck, diseases, evil spirits, etc., from the village'. During these days, visitors are neither allowed to enter the village nor are the villagers allowed to leave the village for fear of disrupting the 'prosperity of the village' (Shimray 2000: 136). One customary practice performed on the day of *Kha Sit* is *Kapā eina Mei Khalap*. It is a traditional way of making fire with dried bamboo, firewood and some pieces of thatch or straw. Since the Hao New Year starts with this festival, they remove ashes, charcoal from the hearth, and prepare a new (fresh) fire. In other words, it is a tradition to make a fresh fire during the seed sowing festival among the Hao people.

The *Luira* is considered the 'festival of festivals' of the Hao Naga 'during which continuous festivities, traditional and cultural swing and sway take place adorning themselves with colourful costumes and ornaments. It is a time of mirth and gaiety, altogether forgetting the impending hard work at hand' (Luikham 2009: 89). The festival involves feasting, folk games, and sports activities on days where the performance of religious rituals is not already scheduled. Further, the festival cannot be celebrated without *Hohoing* – a form of Naga vocal music, and *Hao Laa* (Hao folk songs). Musical instruments like *Talla*, a type of trumpet, and *Tingteilā*, a fiddle-like instrument, are also used. The order of events[4] during the *Luira* depends on the village, though as previously mentioned most of the customary practices related to the seed sowing festival among the Hao villages are more or less similar.

Some important practices and events that take place during the seed sowing festival include the already mentioned *Kha Sit*, the *Sāthithang* ('animal slaughtering day'), *Shangrei Rukthang* ('a day of ritual performance by the village chief'), *Luikathui* ('seed sowing ritual'), *Yarui Rukthang* ('a day of ritual performance by the villagers'), *Laa Khanganui* (maiden dance), *Thingneira Khangakhun* (tug-of-war), singing *Hao Laa* and *Hohoing*, *Pheichak Kachak* (folk dance performance), *Kha Sho* ('opening of the village gate'), *Kha Ung* ('leaving the village') and *Kha Leinganong* ('village market day'). Of all the events, *Laa Khanganui* is considered as the most important festive event of the seed sowing festival. I now present a brief discussion on some important customary practices and events of this festival.

Shangrei Kharuk is another ritual involving the invocation of *Ameowo* by the *Awunga* or village chief, and *Awungva*, the wife of village chief. It is also known as *Wungrei Rukthang* or *Shangrei Rukthang*. On this day, the village chief and his wife perform the seed sowing ritual *Luikathui*. After the invocation, they sprinkle the blood of a fowl on the seeds, and then sow the seeds on the ground. During the ritual performance, the village chief and his wife also use *Kapaiwon* (flower of wild berry tree), *Sahārwon* (flower of cherry tree) and *Nāpawon* or *Mayāngwon* (flower of peach). It is believed that when these flowers bloom exuberantly it signifies prosperity, while their beauty is taken as symbolic of divine promise. Before the performance of this ritual, it is a taboo for any villager to sow seeds in the ground (Luikham 1961: 47). It is also taboo to touch or cut down any plants on this day. Decoration of the above-mentioned flowers at the house of the village chief marks the end of *Shangrei Kharuk*. The two main reasons for the performance of this religious ritual are (i) to seek *Ameowo's* blessing over the cultivation; and (ii) to give the privilege to the village chief and his wife of sowing the first seed in the ground as a sign of respect and honour by the village community.

Yarui Kharuk - *yarui* meaning 'public', and *kharuk* meaning 'the process of propitiation or invocation' - refers to the process of ritual performance and propitiation to the *Ameowo* by the village community as a whole. It is also known as *Yarui Rukthang*. As with *Shangrei Kharuk*, the blood of a fowl or chicken is sprinkled on the seeds and then sown on the ground on the day of *Yarui Kharuk*. For the propitiation of the paddy field, flowers like *Kapaiwon*, *Sahārwon* and *Nāpawon* are used. Here, the ritual performers are the villagers. On this day, every household in the village decorated their houses with the above-mentioned flowers. Unlike in *Shangrei Kharuk*, there is no taboo to touch or to cut down plants on the *Yarui*

---

[4]See Luikham (1961: 46-47), Shimray (2000: 135-143), Luikham (2009: 88-94), Pheirei (2010: 63-67), and the order of events narrated by Mw. Ramyaola and Mw. Yangyirla (cited in Mawon 2015: 85-86).

Rukthang. One of the main reasons for the observance of this religious ritual was to seek protection and blessing for their agricultural farming from the *Ameowo* so that the villagers would harvest in abundance later that year.

Kha Sho – *kha* meaning village, and *sho* meaning 'to open' – means to open the village gate. The *Kha Sho* is signalled by the burning of dried twigs and leaves, purposeful leftovers, of the jhum cultivation (Shimray 2000: 143). Before the *Kha Sho* is signalled, the villagers are not allowed to leave the village, nor are guests allowed to enter the village. On this day the *Yorlā* (a married woman), relatives, visitors and travellers flock to the village in order to participate in the *Luira* festival. According to their tradition, the most important guests of the seed sowing festival are the *Yorlā*[5]. One of the traditional values pertaining to the seed sowing festival is the observance of *Yorlā li Rayar Kahei* or *Yorlā Sā Khami*, which is a gifting of a large portion of meat to a married woman by her natal parents and uncles, as well as by her brothers. Apart from these practices and events, feasting is one important feature of the *Luira* festival. Luikham (2009: 91) wrote, 'by tradition, all who happen to come into the home (in any house of the hosting village) are offered meat and drinks (rice beer) known as '*Rashā Khangaphang*' as per established custom of hospitality. Nobody is allowed to go away without certain amount of refreshment.' Longvah (2001: 54) also points out that the best rice beer, rice wine and meat are served to the relatives, visitors, travellers and neighbours during this festival. In short, everyone is welcomed to enjoy food and drinks during this festival. Lunghar (1987: 39) wrote: 'it is during this festival that they would find out the most generous man of the village through his offering of rice beer, rice wine and meat to the visitors, relatives and other guests of the festival.'

Kha Ung – *ung* ('to leave' or 'to part') – means the departure of the relatives, visitors and travellers from the host village. The pronouncement of *Kha Ung* is usually made towards the end of the *Luira* festival. It is taboo for any guest to remain back in the host village after this pronouncement. In a sense, it is therefore necessary for any guest to leave the village on this day. However, such a strict code of conduct or taboo is not applicable to the *Yorlā*. The observance of *Kha Ung* marks the end of the seed sowing festival for many Hao villages.

Laa Khanganui is known as the maiden dance which is considered the most important festive event of the *Luira* festival. The performers, wearing a uniform dress code[6], are the *Laa Khanganui bing*, or unmarried girls of the village, and

[5]The custom of meat gifting to *Yorlā* (a married woman) is not only performed during the festivals of the Hao Nagas, it is also done on some solemn occasions like marriage ceremonies, 'feasts of merit', and Christian celebrations such as Jubilee and new church building dedications. The culture of 'meat gifting' to *Yorlā* symbolises the relation and bond maintained by the Hao men and women.

[6]Shimray (2000: 142) describes the dress code of the performers: 'The dancers wear a uniform of Phangyai Kashan (a sort of wraparound) down to the knee, a pair of brass

some consider this performance a 'virgin dance'. These performers, however, are chaperoned by some married women to help them in singing the Hao folk songs related to the *Laa Khanganui* performance. Apart from married women, the performers are also accompanied by the men of the village. The men sing *Hohoing* at the beginning and at the end of the *Laa Khanganui*. This performance is usually organised in the village chief's courtyard or in the open space of the village playground.

While performing the maiden dance, the performers move in a circular motion, singing and dancing the Hao folk songs, which praise the brave and the rich men of the village, as well as the 'feasts of merit'. During the performance, the performers use no musical instruments, but the rhythmic striking of the *Kazao* or *Zaokui* (brass bangles) produces a melodious sound. The movement of the legs and hands of the performers are simple, but uniform. The 'dance is soft and slow in uniform movement of hands and legs rocking the body gracefully according to the tune of their songs' (Shimray 2001: 138). It is pointed out that if any girl 'joins the dance after defiling her body for fear of public reprobation, some prodigy happen viz. either her *Kongsīng* (necklace) broke or become loose amid the dance or domestic animals like dog, fowl, etc., enter the dancing semicircle and went out by her side' (Shimray 2000: 142). Chastity of the unmarried girls is strictly observed among this group of people. Thus, the Hao people allow only the unmarried virgin girls to take part in the *Laa Khanganui* performance. Apart from this most exciting and fascinating event, *Thingneira Khangakhun* (tug-of-war), *Khamahon* (a melodious vocal sound with overlapping musical tones) and *Pheichak-Pheishon Kasī* (folk dance performance) occupy an integral part in the *Luira* festival of the Hao Nagas.

Thingneira Khangakhun – *Thingneira* means 'a creeper rope', and *Khangakhun* 'to pull' – is a tug-of-war contest in which two teams or groups pull opposite ends of the rope. The team or group dragged across the central line loses. During the *Luira* festival, it is a must to play *Thingneira Khangakhun* (Longvah 2001: 55). The collection of a creeper rope from the forest is done by the men, especially by village youth. Those who collect creeper ropes usually sing *Hohoing* on their way home, and before the beginning of the game, two elderly men of the village perform the *Thingneira Makhuntā Khami* (an inauguration to the game). During this performance, the elderly men sing *Hao Laa* related to the *Luira* festival and pull

---

bangles called Zaokui, one on each hand; two sets of bead necklace of missed colours called Kongsāng, one worn around the neck and the other dangling down from the head, both covering the breast; a set of a sort of ornamental belt around the waist on top of the skirt covering the buttock called Khom Mashim. It is against the social etiquette to clip or tie the hair as such all the maidens hair are let loose nicely hanging down at the back... These practices are very much vogue in the past and the same though not common is still prevalent today.'

the creeper rope from opposite ends.[7] All the villagers, young and old take part in the game, asking for *Masi-L̠ngyai* or *Mawon*[8] ('to seek wealth and prosperity') from *Ameowo* (Luikham 1961: 46). It is generally held that if the creeper rope is torn into two after the hard struggle between the two equally matched groups, it will lead to an abundant harvest. Apart from this game, they also play other games such as the *Khangatuk* (wrestling), *Rai Kathat* (mock war), *Zeip̠ Khangatam* (javelin throw) and *Sikui Kaphung* (a game of 'carrying wooden pestle').

The interrelation between festival and agriculture activities may be observed, as due consideration to their seasonal agricultural activities is given while fixing the schedule of any Hao festivals. The fixation of date and duration of the festivals is the prerogative of the *Awunga* (village chief) and *Hangv̠a* (village councillors). Another observation is that it seems clear that there exist a variation of duration and date, ritual performances and the sequences of events from one village to another, and more so from one region to another.[9] However, the meaning of the festival and the purpose for the observance of the festival remains the same in all the Hao villages. They perform rituals during the festival for two main reasons: (i) to seek blessings and (ii) to ward off bad luck and evil spirits. The generosity and hospitality of the Hao people during the festive seasons is also everywhere observable.

CHANGING ASPECTS

Recently, in the Hao hills, the Hungpung Awungshi Organisation (HAO) of Hungpung village erected a wooden monument which is called *Tarung Kashun* in 2004, Shokvao village did so in 2012, Tashar in 2013, Lamlai Hanjamphung in 2014, Shangshak in 2015 to revive their culture of *Mar̠n Kas̠* (Mawon 2016: 193) and Lungshang village in 2017. Today, the once individual affair called *Mar̠n Kas̠* or 'feast of merit'[10] has become a community affair, rather than being hosted

---

[7]In the words of Shimray (2000: 140): '...every villager young and old touched the rope at the village ground... This touching of Thingneira is called Seichang Khamei Khamayok, meaning invoking prosperity or good luck.'

[8]Hao word Mawon is derived from two words viz. Ma (rice) and Won (flower). Literally, the word Mawon means the flowers of the paddy rice in the field. Symbolically, the word Mawon refers to wealth and prosperity.

[9]Traditionally, the Hao villages can broadly be divided into 9 (nine) regions viz. Raphei (North), Somra (Northeast), Rem (East), Veikhang (Southeast), Kamo (South), Kharao (West), Khaorui (Southwest), Kharao-Raora (Northwest) and Kathur (Centre) [Ruivah 1993: 18].

[10]According to Jelle J P Wouters (2014: 8-9): the feast of merit 'was not just a wealthy ambitious villager's gesture to host a feast, or indeed feasts, but it was morally and socially

individually as was the case in the past, because of many reasons. The three main reasons are (i) economic constraint as the culture of *Marān Kasā* is an expensive affair; (ii) unavailability of a wooden post of a desirable size for the feast largely because of deforestation; and (iii) many Hao people may no longer find 'honour and merit' as much as they did in the pre-Christian days.

While the contemporary celebration of *Marān Kasā* constitutes a change, what remains similar is that, generally, the *Awunga* (village chief) and *Hangva* (village councillors) continue to fix the date and duration of village festivals. Further, it is observed that there is a continual usage of Hao music and musical instruments in some of the performances. Despite modern changes in the festivals, there are elements that cannot be done away with. These include the role of *Awunga* in conducting the festivals, practice of meat gifting to *Yorlā* (a married woman), singing *Hao Laa* (Hao folk songs) and *Hohoing* (a form of Naga vocal music), performing *Pheichak* (folk dance) and *Laa Khanganui* (maiden dance), and playing tug-of-war, among others, during the festivals. In short, in many aspects of the festivals, there are no major changes, at least not in principle.

Hao music also continues to occupy an integral part of Hao festivals as well as during agricultural activities and on other occasions. In the absence of teaching-learning process between the older generation and the younger generation today, Hao folk song experienced a reduced popularity in the present day. Many Hao people hold that they are witnessing the loss of their music and musical instruments in the face of western songs and the electronic musical instruments of the western world. Hao artistes like Rewben Mashangva have modified and have refined some of their musical instruments such as *Tingteilā* (Hao fiddle), *Yangkahui* (bamboo flute) and *Seikongthei* (cowbell), which enabled them to play these instruments along with other electrical musical instruments. One prevailing trend in the Hao society is the 'remixing' of Hao folk songs with western songs. For instance, a song entitled 'Ngashan' (2015) composed by one Hao artist by the name of Ngathingpam Tangvah is a mixture of different genres such as folk song, *Hohoing,* and rock song. It is a song about *Luira* festival, in which the artist sought for the revival of the Hao culture associated with this festival.

A major change, however, is that in the recent past, *Luira* is seemingly used as a platform to 'bridge' the hill-valley divide in Manipur. For many years, Manipur witnessed ethnic conflict particularly between the Nagas and the Meiteis, often seemingly fostered by the state government. One myth asserts that the Hao Naga and Meitei shared the 'same progenitor' in a distant past; stating that the village chief of Hungpung (one of the Hao villages) was the older brother of Meitei Maharaja. This myth of origin has been 'contested' in many writings, however.

---

expected of him to do so, as intrinsic to a wider moral economy and order of social stratification in which the less prosperous could count on the village rich to now and then showcase their largesse.'

Figure 14. Womenfolk playing *Thingneira Khangakhun*.(Photo by Arkotong Longkumer.)

In the writings of T.C. Hodson (1975), A.S.W. Shimray (2001), and Sothing W.A. Shimray (2000), among others, it is explained that a 'loose relationship' was maintained in the past between the Hao Naga and the Meitei. But the question of domination or suzerainty over each other did not arise, as far as recorded in history and oral traditions. In 2010, Okram Ibobi Singh (then Chief Minister of Manipur), though he had hardly visited the Hao hills throughout his political life, unveiled the monument erected at the residence of Hungpung village chief on the occasion of Hungpung *Luira* (Mawon 2014: 39). This was viewed as a political move wherein the government of Manipur attempted to 'relive' the myth of 'brotherhood' of the Hao Naga and Meitei. But to replace the earlier 'trust deficit' with projections of 'oneness' between the hill and valley is unlikely to realize in the near future, as the present relation between them seems to be on the basis of 'verification' and not on the principle of 'trust'.

With the turn of the century, sections of Hao villages began to observe some other festivals such as the Kachai Lemon festival, *Hāthei Phanit* ('chili festival') and *Shuri Kaso Phanat* ('garlic festival'). Since the Hao people began to observe these festivals only during the last few years, the question whether should be termed as indigenous festivals arises. However, since a festival is a themed celebration concentrated in time and delivered with a clear purpose, the new festivals of the Hao people can be termed as festival. All the three new festivals have its clear purpose, theme and celebrate on a specific time. They are home-grown festivals and are evolving gradually, and are also celebrated with the support of some of the governmental institutions and NGOs. These new Hao festivals have the objective of creating awareness on the importance of lemon, chili and garlic cultivations among the Hao people, and on the potential economic outcome that would profit the cultivators who mostly belong to the poorer section of the society. The celebration of these new festivals constitute another dimension of change.

The advent of Christianity[11] and the introduction of formal education in the Naga Hills by Christian missionaries played a significant role in moulding the attitudes and outlook of the Nagas towards the outside world. Many Naga writers argue that Christian missionaries took a poor view on the Naga culture. Horam (1977: 73-74) remarks, 'the missionaries sought to plant a replica of the western concept of norms and standards of life, and these were conveniently introduced as part of Christianity.' Sema (2013: 60) remarks that the American Baptist missionaries were the first who considered 'all the Naga culture and heritage as evil and anti-Christian like feast of merit, singing folk songs and folk dance, etc.' He continues: 'the introduction of formal education by the missionaries was also responsible for western culture and way of life to creep in' (ibid). For some, Christianity in the Naga Hills is an 'imported one' (Lotha 2013: 77). Lotha suggests that Christianity was 'transplanted from America and Europe. If the Protestants are too American, the Catholics are too Greco-Roman...The whole implications seen to be that if the Nagas cannot be white in skin, they should be white in their way of worship' (ibid). To this day, many church leaders continue to subscribe to ideas of implanting western norms and standards into the life of the Nagas.

The question of continuities in Hao festivals with the now longstanding influence of Christianity is one that preoccupies community leaders and scholars alike. No doubt, culture is never static, and simply observing the changing durations, costumes, levels of participation, the order of events, as well as the kinds of music and musical instruments already gives one a sense of significant changes. Christianisation, since 1896, and the introduction of modern education, closer association with other communities, economic constraints, and a whole host of other factors have contributed to change. Most Hao people hold that Christianisation by the foreign missionaries and Christian conversion, such as that of Ruichumhao Rungsung,[12] is the single most important factor that brought cultural change in Hao community. For example, for many years, the Hao Christian converts were not

[11]Solo (2006: 4) and Zeliang (2005: 28) wrote that for the first time 12 (twelve) students were converted to Christianity (Baptist denomination) on September 29, 1901. In the same year, the first Baptist Church in Manipur was built at Hunphun village (Sangma 1987: 275). In this hill, the Roman Catholic began their missionary works in 1946 and the Adventist Church in 1951 (Shimray 2000: 181).

[12]Ruichumhao Rungsung of Songran (Somdal) village was one early Hao Christian convert who played an integral role in the Christianisation of the Hao people.

allowed to organize their indigenous festivals by the early Christian leaders,[13] and this is one major reason why the Christian festival particularly Christmas is given 'more important' place in the Hao areas today.[14] If Christianity is today an intrinsic part of Sumi Naga 'contemporary identity' (Angelova, this volume), Christianity is similarly deeply embedded and implanted, and has revolutionised and transformed the Hao people. Christianisation and assimilation with the western culture are major factors responsible for the discontinuation of the observation of many festivals and also for the many changes in the festivals of Hao Naga.

Many Hao festivals are no longer observed, some are dying, while some are reviving or are being revived in modified forms. Hao festivals that are no longer observed include *Zingkāng Phanit, Manei Phanit, Kashong Kahao Phanit, Yampāt, Nāsut Phanit, Chumphạ, Longrạ Kashak, Thishām, Zaiham Makhum Phanit* and *Hamrui Phanit. Yarrạ* festival is dying, *Mangkhap* is reviving and *Luirạ* is revived in modified form. Today, a section of the Hao villages like T. Chanhong (since 1993) observe *Chumkhot*, which is a modified and Christianized form of *Chumphạ* festival. *Khamui Phanit*, a modified form of the rain invoking festival, is observed by a section of the northern Hao villages, including Chingjaroi. All the surviving Hao festivals are observed for shorter duration compared to their pre-Christian period. In some cases, however, customary practices in modified forms are still being observed, although today the Christian God is invoked rather than *Ameowo*. For instance, while performing *Hokharai* (a combination of recitation and the production of vocal sound in musical tunes) during the seed sowing festival, the Hao people are now addressing and invoking the Christian God for blessing. Here, the Hao communities celebrate their festivals to seek blessing for protection over their agricultural farming, and give thanks to the Christian God, whose power, they now believe, can help them yield more production from their agricultural activities.

Today, the seed sowing festival is observed for 3 to 5 days, and the oldest sequences of festive events are no longer maintained. In principle, the customs of *Khạ Sit* ('village social work'), *Khạ Sho* ('opening of the village gate'), *Khạ Ung* ('leaving the village'), *Shangrei Kharuk* ('ritual performed by village chief'), *Luikathui* ('seed sowing ritual'), and *Yarui Kharuk* ('ritual performed by villagers') continue to exist. In practice, the above-mentioned customs are not observed as strict as they were prior to Christianity. This is not to say that the *Luirạ* festival, and *Laa Khanganui* (maiden dance) do not occupy an important place in community life today. Further, the singing of *Hohoing* (a form of Naga vocal music) associated with the maiden dance continues to be performed by village men. Some Hao villages like

---

[13]Personal interview with Benjamin Rungsung (85 years of age in 2012) of Sinakeithei village, Tuimayang Chahongnao (84 years of age in 2012) of T. Chanhong village, and Sw. Kayangnam (91 years of age in 2012) of Tashar village.

[14]Personal interview with A.S. Haora Zimik (76 years of age in 2011) and A.S. Kazaching Zimik (79 years of age in 2011) of Ramva village.

Hungpung and Hunphun continue to give special importance to this event. One informant, but reflecting common sentiment, said: 'we have to value our cultural heritage, without which we are no less than people with no cultural identity of our own.'[15]

Ritual performances during the *Shangrei Kharuk* and *Yarui Kharuk* are no longer performed as the rituals are seen to violate the Ten Commandments of the Old Testament, particularly: 'You shall have no other gods before Me' (NKJV 1988: 65). In other words, the ritual performances and the invocation to any gods including *Ameowo* violates the new faith. The seed sowing ritual called *Luikathui* is performed in some pockets among the Hao such as in Hungpung village before the observation of the festival. However, such performances are not made known to all the villagers, and are no longer addressed to *Ameowo*. It is now commonplace to invoke the Christian God where it was once customary to invoke *Ameowo*. In the pre-Christian period, it was taboo for any villager to sow seeds before the performance of the *Luikathui*. However, such taboos are no longer observed today. Further, the performance of *Luikathui* is now one of the cultural items competed between groups or localities of the village like Hungpung during the seed sowing festival.

Rice beer and rice wine have been in use among the Hao people for centuries, yet the advent of Christianity, primarily the Baptist denomination,[16] discontinued its consumption in most Hao villages as its uses were considered 'un-Christian'[17]. Contrary to the teachings of Baptist missionaries, the Catholic priests and evangelists condone the use of rice beer and rice wine, and adjudge its intake is not 'unchristian', provided it is consumed moderately. Till today, the use of rice beer and rice wine during the *Luira* festival is found in some sections of the Hao Catholic populations like Hungpung and Longpi Kajui. They continue to sip rice beer in public gatherings, while singing *Hao Laa* and during the leisure hours of the *Luira* festival.

Hao people continue to use the flowers like *Kapaiwon*, *Sahārwon* and *Nāpawon* or *Mayāngwon* especially for decoration during the seed sowing festival. For the Hao Nagas, the beauty of these flowers symbolises the promising days ahead in their

---

[15]Personal interview with A.S. Barnabas Hungshi (62 years of age in 2012) and Y.R. Phamila (93 years of age in 2012) of Hungpung village, Tuingapam Seipainao (87 years of age in 2011) of Tashar village, Haopa Layam (94 years of age in 2012) of Longpi Kajui village, Khashung Mawonao (92 years of age in 2011) of T. Chanhong village, and Zingthan Zingkhai (91 years of age in 2012) and Ruichumshai Rumthao (70 years of age in 2010) of Hunphun village.

[16]Today, more than 90% of the Hao populations are Christians, of which more than 80% are Baptist denomination.

[17]Personal interview with Mw. Ramyaola (87 years of age in 2010) and Mw. Yangyirla (84 years of age in 2010) of T. Chanhong village.

lives. The use of these flowers in the *Luira* festival is itself a traditional aspect which they continue to find relevant in the present context.

Not much change in the costumes and attires worn by the performers during the festival is observed. The two changes in the costumes and attires worn by the performers during *Luira* are (i) the performers wear bodice called *Sihup* usually black or white in colour to cover their body, and (ii) the performers' attires are seen more artistic and also wear other cosmetics during the performance. They continue to use no musical instruments while performing the maiden dance. The rhythmic striking of the performers' brass bangles produces a melodious sound, which is used as the rhythm of the maiden dance performance.

Folk games like *Thingneira Khangakhun*[18] (tug-of-war) during the *Luira* festival are still played, and the *Hohoing* during the collection of a creeper rope are still being sung, though these have been in decline. Further, the beliefs associated with the festival, such as the connection between touching of the *Thingneira* (a creeper rope) and a plentiful harvest, is now a belief of the past. Of late, some Hao villages have started to use ropes sold in the market, citing difficulties locating creeper ropes in the forest.

Unlike in the pre-Christian period, today non-participation of the villagers in the seed sowing festival is not punishable. The absence of such rules, however, does not necessarily cause non-participation. The practices associated with honouring *Yorlü* (a married woman), for instance, continue to occupy an important place in the festivals. In comparison to the pre-Christian period, today the *Yorlā* admittedly receives a smaller portion of meat, and this may be due to economic constraints and substantial population growth in the villages. But such customs, similar perhaps to the modern Mother's Day, are cherished by the community, as they offer an annual occasion, especially for the men, to publically honour the women in the family. As such customs are embedded within the *Luira*, they also contribute to the renewed relevance and continuance of practices that contribute to community cohesion.

[18]With the passing of time, Hao people began to play Thingneira Khangakhun (tug-of-war) on many other occasions organised by the student bodies and the civil organisations of Hao Naga like Tangkhul Katamnao Saklong, Zingtun Longphang, Raphei Katamnao Long, Kathur Long, Aze Katamnao Long, etc., during their conferences and sports meet. Occasionally, some Hao villages like T Chanhong play this game in the Christmas festival. In Hao Naga diaspora, the student organisations organise cultural meet in towns and cities like Imphal, Dimapur, Shillong and Delhi, wherein Thingneira-Khangakhun is played occasionally.

Figure 15. Stone monoliths erected at Hungpung village chief'sresidence.
(Photo by Arkotong Longkumer.)

CONCLUSION

The revival of some Hao festivals can be seen not only in the Hao villages, but also in the Hao diaspora. For instance, Hao people living in the Indian metropolitan cities such as Delhi, Guwahati, Bangalore, and Shillong, among others, began celebrating their own Luira in modified forms. The revival of festivals and other cultural practices among the Hao people seems to have initiated in their quest for protecting and asserting their identity as well as preserving and promoting cultural heritage in a time of rapid social change.

Reviving old festivals is certainly replete with challenges, especially when evaluating rituals traditionally devoted to old Hao gods. This is exacerbated by the fact that Hao community are now more invested in Christian festivals such as Christmas, which they hold in common with broader Naga society, including in neighbouring Nagaland state. The old ways, when they are reaffirmed, are 'Christianized', in the sense of reorienting rituals toward the Christian God, employing Christian prayers and singing hymns during the festivals.

The scale, as noted, of feasting and joyous merrymaking of the festival has dwindled considerably, posing challenges for the survival of the old festivals. These festivals are still considered 'traditional' however, even though in practice there are considerable 'modern' changes seen in their performances, costumes, participation, duration of the festivals, order of events and in the use of Hao music. The surviving Hao festivals are more inclined towards Hobsbawm's concept of 'custom' or 'invented tradition', than to his concept of 'tradition' that is 'invariant' (Hobsbawm 2000).

Finally, this chapter suggests that, though Christianity is now all-pervasive and has brought significant changes in the lives and customs of the Hao people, this does not entail a major incompatibility with the old ways. Shimray (2000: 183) suggests, for instance, that 'one can be a true Christian at the same time a good Tangkhul.' For instance, in Hao villages, churches provide invaluable public spaces to the villagers to come together. Christian principles are also seen as a positive influence in village affairs, such as governance. In many ways, Christian institutions today seem well positioned to be the agents to resuscitate 'degraded' Hao culture. This is especially relevant in relation to old community-strengthening customs that safeguarded social cohesion and were deeply embedded in Hao culture, and these are not incompatible with the values of the new faith.

ACKNOWLEDGEMENTS

I acknowledge the valuable guidance of Lapynshai Syiem throughout my doctoral studies, as this article forms part of the thesis. I also wish to thank Michael Heneise, Jelle J P Wouters and reviewers for reading and commenting on this work.

■ ■■ ■■

11

TRADITIONAL GOVERNANCE IN TRANSITION AMONG THE YIMCHUNGER NAGAS

Francis Cheerangal

The Yimchunger Nagas are among the sixteen 'official tribes' of Nagaland state, and largely inhabit the remote Tuensang and Kiphire districts bordering Myanmar. Yimchunger village governance, as with many of their Naga neighbours, has been noted for its democratic nature, with village elders - or *kiulongthsürü* - traditionally performing what constitutes the legislative, executive and judicial functions of administration. Among the Yimchunger, the village, as the prime political entity in relation to its neighbours, is a unit mediated through patrilineal clan membership, genealogies and social institutions. The close-knit administrative structure, underpinned by unwritten clan laws, contributes to community stability, and this older system remains largely in place and active. Modernising processes, as in minority societies across Asia, introduced significant change, initially under the aegis of British 'non-interference', and subsequently under the policies of the Indian state. More recently, initiatives such as the Nagaland Communitisation Act of 2001, have sought to incentivise local governance structures to accommodate development goals by transferring ownership and management of education, health, and infrastructure responsibilities to village committees. This chapter serves as a brief overview of Yimchunger social polity, and addresses these shifts in brief, with attention to continuities and discontinuities in traditional practices.

The Yimchunger are generally settled in the hilly areas west of Mount Saramati, which sits on the Indo-Myanmar border, and in Helüppong in the west.[1] Their lands share borders with Longleng district in the north, Phek district in the south, Mokokchung and Zunheboto districts in the west, and Myanmar in the east. Neighbours include the easterly Khiamniungan Nagas, with whom they share a common ancestry, the Changs in the north, and Sumi, Sangtam and Pochury communities in the west. Shamator town serves as a centre and, per the 2011 census, the Yimchunger population numbers 66,972[2], spread over 92 villages in six ranges, namely, Pungro, Thsorunto, Shamator, Mango, Kewung and Showubah. Although they have much in common with their Naga neighbours, they self-identify as a distinct cultural-linguistic group, and as a distinct 'tribe' among the Nagas.

Many Yimchunger historians suggest that their ancestors migrated from the east, crossed the Chindwin River (Myanmar), and established a village at Mekong valley. After some time, they left and journeyed to Aruru, following the course of the Tizu River. From there, they migrated to Juri in Myanmar. Later, following the Tizu and Zunki rivers, they searched for a place to establish a permanent settlement. They travelled in two groups: the first followed the river, while the second searched over-ground, the aim being to find the safest and most defensible location. The two groups remained apart for some time, although they eventually came together and settled in one place. This is the reason why they are known as Yimkhiunger[3] (later written as 'Yimchungrü'): 'yim,' meaning 'search or look for' and 'khiungrü' meaning 'those who reached or found'. Other oral accounts suggest that the migration route of the Yimchunger was more closely associated with that of other Naga tribes. Generally held to be mongoloid in origin[4], they belong linguistically to the Tibeto-Burman family like other Naga tribes.[5] The Roman script is used with the addition of a letter ü vowel common in Naga transliteration.

TRADITIONAL GOVERNANCE

Traditional governance among the Yimchunger is centred around the dynamic relationship between the *Kuilongthsüpu*, or village chief, and *kiulongthsürü*, or 'those

[1]Hokishe Sema, p.7

[2]Census 2011, Kohima: Government of Nagaland.

[3]The syllable, 'khiu' was spelled out 'chu' later causing a change in the pronunciation over the time. Although Yimchunger is the most common and 'official' name, they are known by their closest neighbours by other names, namely Yachumi by the Sumi, Yansongr by the Ao, Yanchonger by Sangtam, and Yansung by Chang.

[4]S.C Sardeshpande, p.8 (Not in end-references)

[5]M. Alemchiba (1970), A Brief Historical Account of Nagaland, p.3

who make the village' or 'those responsible for the village', a collegial body that consists of the village founders or their descendants. The *kiulongthsürü* exercise jural, executive and legislative powers, and share responsibility with the *Kiulongthsüpu* in managing the general affairs of the village. They speak on behalf of the people and their wisdom is relied upon to solve community problems as they arise. As married men, deemed sufficiently capable and responsible to lead, they bring together and represent the six Yimchunger clans, namely *Jankhiungrü, Jangrü, Khiungrü, Khiphurü, Küsünkhiungrü and Limkhiungkhiungrü*. Clans are clustered into agnate clan families or *kheang*[6] (often referred to as khels). Put simply, the co-founders represent the constituent Yimchunger clans, and make up the representative body of *kiulongthsürü*, of which *Kiulongthsüpu* is the head.

Kiulongthsüpu or Kiulongpütongpuh (lit. 'village owner') is the title of the chief founder of the village, coming always from the *Khiungrü* or 'founder's clan'. As with many of the neighbouring Naga tribes, chieftainship is hereditary and encompasses secular as well as sacred duties. Indeed, when a new village is founded, it is the 'sacred founder's kin'[7] that must be present. The *Kiulongthsüpu* is then assisted by the other clan representatives in making the final selection of the place, along with decisions about demarcation and boundaries.

One of the chief's sacred duties when founding a new village is to offer an animal in sacrifice to the spiritual owners of the land (see von Fürer-Haimendorf 1936). For a first village, this typically entails a large animal such as a cow or *Mithun*. Upon founding a second village, a pig would be offered, and for a third and fourth, a dog. Finally, a chicken would be offered for a fifth and any subsequent villages founded by the same chief. These days his role is mostly ceremonial but, in the past, he was expected to institute laws and regulations to maintain order among the clans and to regulate aspects of village life in such a way as to keep the peace and to balance human needs with the requirements set out by the land's spiritual owners, as interpreted by the founder. Bad harvests and food scarcity, or other problems that might afflict the village, were a constant concern, and often attributed to human violations of important rules and ritual practices. Depending on the severity of a violation, punishments included anything from fines and customary lock-up, to banishment from the village in extreme cases. The status of the village headman is a 'once and for all' position, and restricted solely to the lineage of the *Khiungrü* clan's founder's kin. This pattern, however, also governs each clan's founder's kin represented in the *kiulongtshsürü*. If the immediate descendent of a clan founder is unable to perform his hereditary duties, usually because of age or infirmity, the clan selects a temporary representative. The rightful heir takes over on the death

---

[6]Kheang means the subdivision of the village. It is cluster of families with their houses within a geographical portion of the village mostly belonging to the same clan.

[7]See von Fürer-Haimendorf "The Sacred Founder's Kin Among the Eastern Angami Nagas" (1936)

of the clan chief or when he, the heir, is deemed fit to assume the responsibility.

There is no rule on age, or specified qualification for the representative, but it is the general rule that the person temporarily holding the post would be of noble quality and responsible enough to lead the clan or village, and settle disputes when required. The appointment is a recognition of the person's moral uprightness and personal capacity for management.

In the past, the preferred sites for settlements were hilltops because they offered commanding and ultimately the best defensive positions against unwelcome visitors or intruders.[8] Aside from the *Kiulongthsüpuh* or kiulongthsürü, the *limberü*, or 'those who show the way' or 'those who walk the way" (*lim* meaning 'way,' and *rü* meaning 'people'), were men holding non-hereditary positions in the village. Generally, the Yimchunger have a variety of offices regarded as indispensable for the security and smooth running of each village. Some have remained important institutions despite the many changes brought about by colonialism, Christianity and modernisation. In the following sections, I list the offices that were traditionally involved in the administration of Yimchunger villages, but which are now largely ceremonial.

The *cho-cho-rü* is a messenger or secretary who assists the *Kuilongthsüpu* in passing information to others in the village. A trusted, generally married male, he also works as the headman's main informant. Often a hereditary institution, the *cho-cho-rü* is a physically fit individual, usually from the chief's own clan. If the position is not hereditary, then the *cho-cho-rü* is chosen by the chief in consultation with his colleagues in the *kiulongthsürü*. Another important office is that of *ayangrü*, or clan watchman, one for each *kheang*. Prior to colonial forms of administration, safety and security were a major concern in Yimchunger villages. While the village was under the care of the headman and his assistants, there were further security measures taken through the appointment of a number of *ayangrü*. Their duties were to keep watch and secure the village when others were at work in the fields or asleep during the night. Each *kheang* nominated a person, usually a male, for pre-set days to keep watch over the properties of the *kheang* members. There was no fixed remuneration for services rendered by the *ayangrü*, although the community would, in turns, care for their fields, and assist them with food grains and other maintenance. The *limpurü*, on the other hand, was a 'peacemaker', and each village would select a *limpurü* from among the general village population to settle disputes and conflicts with other villages, whether through negotiation or through official truces. This role was of great importance in pre-colonial times when heated territorial disputes, inter-village raids, and head-taking among warring villages were common. The *limpurü* carried a symbolic green branch during the day and a pine-branch torch during the night to indicate his presence. There was a mutual understanding among neighbours, including other tribes, that the *limpurü* and his

[8]N. Chuba Yimchungrü, p 3.

neighbouring counterparts must be respected and given safe passage. These officers were allowed to walk into any village unharmed and violations of their protected status were considered acts of cowardice, disrespect and great shame. Whenever safe-passage was violated it was considered an act of war, endangering the entire community.

As alluded to earlier, offerings and sacrifices to the spirits were understood as necessary and important ritual practices among the Yimchungers. While the hereditary chief embodied important sacred aspects associated with the well-being of the village, the *amükiamrü*, or priest, performed regular religious rites and functions throughout the village. The priest was selected by the village elders and it was a life-long position. Customary law did not dictate that the office of the *amükiamrü* should be hereditary but, in practice, it often was. The *amükiamrü*'s presence in all important life-stage events was generally expected. He enjoyed great respect and obedience from villagers. While he performed ceremonies of importance to the whole village, a father or clan elder would perform religious ceremonies at the family level, for example in times of sickness, death, marriage, and the start of work in the fields. Finally, the *mahtsahrü*, or 'reconciler', is in some sense peculiar to the Yimchunger Nagas. This is an office of peace and reconciliation. While the role of the *limpurü* is intended to broker peace between the villages or tribes, the role of *mahtsahrü* is intended to maintain peace within the village. He is expected to bring into unity and understanding individuals and groups who are feuding with each other. The *mahtsahrü* is chosen by the elders of the village, who carefully seek out persons gifted in their capacity to sympathise with grieving parties, and to bring about their reconciliation.

BRITISH ADMINISTRATION

The British in many respects sought to maintain these institutions of traditional governance, while at the same time introducing a three-layered system consisting of *gaonburas* (headmen), *dobashis* (interpreters) and district administrators that enabled them to exert control where necessary and communicate. Heads of the clans (referred to as 'headmen') were given the position of *gaonbura*. While they continued to be leaders of their clans, they became an important link between Yimchunger clans and the British government. They received direction and supervision from the district officers though they had little say in formulating the policies affecting their own affairs. The second layer, the '*dobashis*'[9], assisted the British government in establishing successful relations with the tribes as distinct cultural-linguistic communities. They were the interpreters that would mediate between British and

[9]Dobashis originally meant people who knew two languages. (Dui = two, bhasha = language).

village administrators. They were later appointed as judges to settle disputes basing on the customary laws of each Naga tribe. Over time *dobashis* became the judicial personnel. The power of headmen or *gaonburas* was limited to keeping law and order in each village, while district officers supervised the overall administration of the villages, framing and following up all the policies of Government. Thus, the supreme authority was gradually transferred away from the sacred founder's kin. The loss of autonomous governance, even at the lowest levels, eventually limited the chief's role to dealing with petty local matters. In the following section, I discuss more recent developments in terms of village governance that ostensibly seek to re-establish the autonomy of villages in self-governance and decision-making.

MODERN ADMINISTRATIVE POLICIES

The Village Councils Act (1978), The Nagaland Village Councils Rules (1979) and the Village Development Boards Model Rules (1980), although framed largely in relation to state and centrally administered development funds, are relatively recent pieces of legislation through which village councils and Village Development Boards have seen a return to a degree of self-governance. There are strict rules and regulations, for example, concerning the formation and functioning of the Village Council. The Village Councils Act 1978, states for example, that

> a village council shall consist of members chosen by the villagers in accordance with the prevailing customary practices and usages, the same being approved by the State Government, provided that hereditary village Chiefs, GBs, and Anghs shall be ex-officio members of such councils and shall have voting rights.

While the number of council members and the process by which they are chosen have not been imposed by the Act (thus allowing traditional practices to continue), certain structures to facilitate developmental activities have been undertaken. The Village Council includes all traditional leaders like the gaonburas and other representatives from all the 'khels' of the village. The Village Council's tenure is five years, after which its members must be replaced or re-nominated. Further, Village Development Boards have been constituted with all permanent residents of the village as members, and the Village Council must select the Village Development Board Management Committee (VDBMC) for a three-year period, including a secretary who is paid an honorarium for assisting the Village Development Board and the Village Council. The Village Development Board structure was created to facilitate the institutionalisation of a participative process for the implementation of development programmes by benefiting from the strengths of the traditional institutions in the village. Each of the villages in the state, approximately 1000 in number, has formed Village Councils fusing traditional formations with the regulations set out by the State Government. The Council enjoys an autonomous status, and the Councils are federal units of larger tribal bodies called 'Hohos' (the apex body of the tribe). In principle, attention is thus given to preserving the traditional governing system, while adjusting to the needs of the present day. At the same time, the new model is not without its critics. It is, for example, a matter of greater concern that traditional forms of governance are being re-shaped to suit the larger organisational network of state and nationally organised programmes. A village is no longer seen as capable of maintaining old forms of autonomy and self-governance. What is deemed necessary by the state is the readjustment and rehabilitation of antiquated indigenous modes and traditions of governance, so that they align with state developmental policies at all levels.

COMMUNITISATION POLICY

The latest efforts by the State Government to organize village polities, especially the management of resources, has been termed the policy of 'communitisation' (see also Wouters, this volume). Having noted the poor management of resources both material and human in the state, it was R.S. Pandey, then Chief Secretary of the state, who developed this concept of governance. The policy suggested leveraging state funds, expertise, and the regulatory powers of the government, with the social capital of the user community; and combining the best of the public and the private sector systems (Pandey 2010: 15). A key component is the privatisation of resources in user communities, thus leading to a way out of problems of governance, and availing opportunity to the private sector. It would be for the user community to discharge day-to-day management of the responsibilities. In this process, it is not the state moving away from its responsibility but it is a shift of paradigm in which the state would perform the role of a partner, assistant, monitor and supervisor. It is a path towards empowerment, delegation, decentralisation and privatisation at the same time. It is based on the philosophy of Triple T: a) Trust the community, b) Train the community and 3) Transfer power and resources in respect of day-to-day management to the user community (Ibid.:15). It builds up the community from being mere recipients to responsible managers of resources. Being consumer and beneficiaries, the user community has the intent, the desire and the intrinsic motivation to see the institution performing well. Along with trust and training, however, the most important part of communitisation is to transfer requisite power and resources from the government to the community so that it can discharge the expectations of day-to-day management of the institution. This act of transferring the power and resources is called to be the true empowerment in the words of Pandey, "the more the share of power and financial resources from the government to the user community, the more is the empowerment" (Ibid.: 17). The communitisation program was mooted in the middle of 2001 and it was soon the process of implementation after due consultation and studies. The ordinance was promulgated by the Governor in January 2002 to enact the Nagaland communitisation of Public Institutions and Services Act, 2002. In March, 2002 the state Legislative Assembly ratified and passed the legislation which is the first of its kind in India and perhaps in the world.

AN ANALYTICAL VIEW

Naga villages have been spoken of as 'village-republics' based on their independence of external forces and autonomous management of their own internal affairs (Hutton 1921). This makes them a distinct class. Ganguli (1984: 54) asserts that 'every village is an independent, self-contained administrative unit.' This is considered as the basis of the ancient political system of the Naga people and they organized the sovereign village state with their own unique forms of government (Singh 2004). The Semas, Konyaks and Maos practiced hereditary monarchy. The Sema chief had absolute power. Among the Konyaks the chief, known as *Angh*, was highly autocratic. The *Angh* is the head of the administration and political affairs among them. Among the Ao, the village assembly alone is the apex body (J.P. Mills, 1922). Yonuo (1974: 189) goes to the extent of suggesting that the 'Nagas are normally governed by the kings or chieftains of their respective villages, chosen for their bravery in war skilful diplomacy richness in the farm of cattle and land or power of oratory in contrast to the hereditary system in which the office of a king passes to the eldest son on the death of his father', which may be, in a sense, indicative of shifts toward secular rule prior British arrival. Among Nagas more broadly, the village is the highest form of the organization that represents political, social and religious bonds. Naga polities, then and now, are largely based on the representation of its constituents, large or small. Decision-making in most of these polities is based on consensus-making, not elections. The latter are seen to promulgate conflict and power-struggles to the detriment of the community. Almost all the Naga organisations, though certainly imperfect, are motivated by the self-governing democratic principle, motivated to limit as much as possible the politically and economically powerful sections to dominate decision-making.

As argued above, the social organisation of Yimchunger society is built around the *kiulongthsürü*, the centre of all governing authority. The establishment and maintenance of *kiulongthsürü* is built on a complimentary dual structure of patriarchy on the one hand, and participatory democracy on the other. The former ensures that the organising principle of clan lineage structures decision-making, thus patterning the present-day village authority on that set by the founder of the village. The lineage of the founder of the village is continued through the office of *kiulongthsüpuh*, and the co-founders through *kiulongthsürü*. The second principle, that of bottom-up democratic participation, also ensures a delegation of responsibilities in the running the affairs in the village. When fully enacted, the dual system allows every member an opportunity to express themselves on matters affecting them and their constituencies. Discussions, meetings, and the settlement of cases in this structure, are conducted with the concern and participation of those affected. Therefore, participation by the entire community in decision-making processes is considered vital and a key principle in the Yimchunger way of life. This traditional self-ruled government in practice, as it is a form of direct democracy, contrasts significantly with the present forms of state-sponsored electoral politics. Here the traditional emphasis is on participation, consensus and cooperation. Though only a few held offices, the freedom to express one's opinion and to participate in the decision-making process is possible for all villagers. *Kiulongthsüpuh*, though holding the final word on matters, and representing the genealogical wisdom of the founder's lineage, would none-the-less generally follow the wisdom of group consensus. He is not an autocrat but in a very real sense the 'first among equals'. It is his responsibility to discern the best route for the community based on accumulated experience, tradition and customary laws. In this perspective, we can say that Yimchunger governing system holds high the principle of direct democracy, while upholding the primacy of patri-lineage. Though the members of *kiulongthsürü* are inducted based on descent, the freedom of choice, effected by the clan, ensures the selection of the best in a direct democratic manner. Among the many traditional values, the spirit of equality and belongingness to the clan/tribe is very dear to every Yimchunger. It is also assured that any authority, be it religious or social, is primarily to foster community's well-being. Thus, we find various mechanisms, democratic in application, at work in order to usher and maintain peace, justice, understanding and resolution for all within the community, inclusive of the structure and functioning of the governing system.

CONCLUSION

Yimchunger communities have undergone significant change over the past century, experiencing colonial expansion, Christian missions and education, and processes of modernisation. Changes in Yimchunger governance came largely during British times, though the traditional institutions have not entirely disappeared. The premier body of village governance underlines the principle of democratic participation in all phases of life. While the primacy of the chief has slowly faded, the importance of individual participation, which was key in the decision-making processes, has been carried over. The collective decision of the village elders often proved mightier and more effective than a system run on a code of written laws. They are rarely referred to in the early writings of the historians and other writers like the British historians making us to assume that there was very limited interaction of the Yimchunger communities with the outside world. This has perhaps positively helped them in maintaining the old traditions in many ways. The early writers on Nagas, like Hutton and Mills, observed that the elders of the villages, even older than the chief, contributed to the welfare of the village with their wisdom of experience. The unique feature of Naga village administration is the dynamic involved in the decision making that assured democracy and healthy involvement of the public in decision making processes. Shimray (1986: 63) suggests, 'what was important and unique was the participation of the general public in the deliberations on any public issue, giving a chance to everyone to have a say.' This was direct democracy, the true and pure democracy in principle and in practice. Modernisation of the village management has switched over the decision making to 'political power', making villagers mere pawns. This fragments the continuity of the traditional organisation of the village, and consequently causes a breakdown in the decision-making ethos of the people as a whole. The modern agencies of governance tend to limit functioning into mere management of economic projects through village bodies. Thus, the value system tends to deteriorate, and unique ways of governing pass into history.

■ ■ ■ ■ ■

12

MAKING DREAMS,MAKING RELATIONS: DREAMING IN ANGAMI NAGA SOCIETY

Michael Heneise

What then, is this soul or life...which goes and comes in sleep, trance and death?

E. B. Tylor 1960 [1881], 203

Introduction

In his seminal text *The Angami Nagas*, J. H. Hutton noted that 'of all forms of second sight, dreaming is the favourite and the best. The Angamis have almost a science of dreaming' (1921a, 246). He noted that unmarried women, for instance, consulted their dreams while deciding on a marriage partner. Her dream was called *mhonyü* (dream of betrothal), and upon waking, her close relatives would wait expectantly to hear her narration. Grandparents also consulted their dreams in choosing the name of a new grandchild; and daily reflection on dreams could convince a person to abstain from going to the fields, from traveling, or from conducting any number of activities. Ignoring the dream was believed foolish, and could lead to illness or even calamity for the wider community. In addition to these everyday ordinary dreaming experiences, Hutton noted that various specialist practitioners used dreaming as a primary medium of divination. Professional 'dream-women', for example, used dreams to divine the outcome of hunting expeditions, business ventures, or other concerns proposed by a villager (1921a, 246). *Themumia*, or shamanic healers, used dreams as a medium when consulted for more serious matters such as in the case of drought, or a serious illness: '[The *Themumia's*] powers' Hutton wrote, 'vary from merely dreaming dreams to the practice of genuine black magic' (1921a, 242). Others included *terhuope*, or women who in a dream-like trance channelled the voices of the dead. Finally, *tekhumiavi* (lit. 'persons in the shape of a tiger') would lie in a dream-like state, projecting their souls into great feline predators in the forest outside of the village. Able to see through a leopard or tiger's eyes, and control its movements, a tekhumiavi could hunt wild game sometimes miles from the village where his or her human body lay asleep (1921a, 244-247; see also Heneise 2016).

However, readers of Hutton's monograph are left to their own devices to make sense of, or indeed imagine, how this 'science of dreaming' works. How might this 'science' be applicable across ordinary and extraordinary dreaming, and how might it relate more broadly to Naga cosmology? Hutton's observations are certainly indicative of a system, although one is obliged to supplement them with those of analogous traditions. In this paper, I explore Naga dream culture by looking at contemporary Angami ideas about what dreams are, and how they are interpreted, as well as the extent to which the dream subject has agency to affect a dream plot's outcome. I supplement Hutton's data with my own ethnography (Hutton's notes date from 1912-1915 and my own are from 2012-2015), conducted among the same communities, thus also elucidating important continuities.

ANTHROPOLOGY OF DREAMING

The literature on dreams in anthropology is extensive if one considers all that has been studied ethnographically on the subject from the discipline's mid-1800s inception. E.B. Tylor, considered 'founder of cultural anthropology', wrote a great deal about dreams in conjunction with his theories about the origins of religion. For example, in his book *Primitive Culture* (1871) – written within the evolutionist mind-set of his time – he states that:

> The evidence of visions corresponds with the evidence of dreams in their bearing on primitive theories of the soul, and the two classes of phenomena substantiate and supplement one another...That this soul should be looked on as surviving beyond death is a matter scarcely needing elaborate argument. Plain experience is there to teach it to every savage; his friend or his enemy is dead, yet still in dream or open vision he sees the spectral form which is to his philosophy a real objective being, carrying personality as it carries likeness.

Tylor's work on dreams has remained largely obscure, although recent studies (especially Bulkeley: 2016), have sought to re-validate Tylor's ideas, particularly as they relate to experiences of the divine in indigenous religion. Tylor cannot be credited with igniting any kind of broad interest in dream research. That credit goes to Sigmund Freud, and particularly his *Interpretation of Dreams* published in 1900, which became very popular throughout Europe, and spurred the first major phase of anthropological research into dreaming (Poirier, 2003; Tedlock, 1987a). Freud's concepts of 'manifest' dream content ('meaningless' imagery and language as narrated by the dreamer) and 'latent' dream content (a dream's 'true' meaning, obtained only through an examination of the dreamer's past) are often used to distinguish raw dream reports from dream reports that have been psychoanalysed. Freud also suggested that certain dream 'types' were universal, in other words, manifest dream content, regardless of social or cultural setting, would have the same latent meanings. This method was tested in a truly cross-cultural way by C.G. Seligman, a disciple of Freud, who sought out Hutton for material on Naga dreams. Testing Freud's 'dream-types' theory in the broadest possible way, Seligman enlisted the help of hundreds of traveling missionaries, traders, and colonial workers, to collect dream reports from across the British colonies (Tedlock, 1987a: 20).

The direction that dream studies took, through most of the 20th century, followed dominant theories on the subject, seated as they were in western epistemological constructs. These were shaped by a long trajectory of historical processes that have gradually pushed dreams from the public into the private sphere, and increasingly demystified them into 'products of the mind' in the Cartesian tradition of collapsing body and mind (Poirier 2003). Mid-century in the United States, for example, wide popular interest in character traits, led some anthropologists to sieve through raw manifest dream content, pulled from large population samples, in search for clues linking dreams to personality (e.g. Sears 1948; Eggan, 1952; Dittmann and Moore, 1957; Griffith, Miyagi and Tago, 1958; O'Nell, 1965; Gregor, 1981). A similar trend took place within psychology (e.g. Hall, 1951; Hall and Van de Castle, 1966; Hall and Nordby, 1972; and Gregor, 1981). But collecting and isolating dreams from their communicative contexts fell under heavy scrutiny in the 'cultural turn' of the 1980s. Dreams apart from the interpretive spaces where they emerge was now acknowledged as problematic. There was, thus, renewed anthropological interest in studying the 'communicative' processes of dream narration (Tedlock et al, 1987). The explosion of ethnographic work, and subsequent publications on dreams in the last three decades[1], points to

---

[1]For example: Bilu, 2000; Descola, 1989; Epstein, 1998; Ewing, 1994; Firth, 1934; Goulet, 1994; Gregor; 1981; Heijnen, 2005; Herr, 1981; Hollan, 1995; Jedrej & Shaw, 1992b; Kilborne, 1981, Kohn, 1995; Kracke, 1979, 1981, 1999, Lattas, 1993; LeVine, 1981; Lohmann, 2000, 2003d, 2007; Mageo, 2003; Stephen 1979, 1982, 1996; Stewart, 1997, 2003, 2004b; Strathern, 1989; Tedlock 1987c; Tumminia, 2002; and Weiner, 1986.

this now more accepted recognition that dreams are social acts, but also that there exists a 'mutual causal interaction' between society, cultural systems, and dreaming (Lohmann, 2007: 38). Turning now to our discussion of Naga dream culture, I will open with a few notes on context, followed by a discussion of Angami terms, ideas, and practices associated with dreams, and follow with an ethnographic discussion which I place in dialogue with Hutton's observations. I then turn to the significance of dreams in social and political life today, particularly as they constitute new forms of knowledge that face clan and church scrutiny. I then conclude by proposing a broader research project into Naga dream traditions, and potentially among analogous traditions in the wider region.

A FEW NOTES ON CONTEXT

As stated above, this paper draws on fieldwork I conducted between 2012 and 2015 in Kohima, the administrative capital of India's Nagaland state, and the centre of Angami cultural, political, and intellectual life. I was based in the village, and interacted mostly with a single clan, which I will call the *Meya* clan. Kohima is in fact two bodies: a five-hundred-year-old village of 15000, and a more recent 'town' of 250,000. The town resembles other Indian hill-stations in its hybridity of colonial planning and more improvisational post-colonial development, though at its centre lies the distinctive and poignant Kohima War Cemetery – a haunting reminder of the clash of world empires that took place here in 1944, over control of the only main route linking the Assam plain and thus the Indian subcontinent, with Burma and Southeast Asia. In the cemetery, 1420 Allied war dead are interred, and the names of a further 917 Sikh and Hindu soldiers, cremated per their traditions, are etched in a memorial wall. The 5000 or so Japanese war dead did not receive the same honour, though Japanese delegations have visited over the decades, seeking repatriation of identifiable remains.

Kohima's living inhabitants compose an equally cosmopolitan populace, with all the Naga tribes and sub-tribes represented, often living there temporarily whilst employed in the services sector, or in the government administration, alongside sizeable non-Naga Indian, Tibetan and Nepali communities, in many cases settled in the region since British times. Kohima is also, of course, the epicentre of the Indo-Naga war - Asia's most protracted conflict. The restrictions on visitors that in many respects isolated the Nagas from the outside world from the 1950s onwards, have been relaxed in recent years due to a de-escalation of the violence. This is largely the result of a ceasefire signed in 1997 between the Indian state and the National Socialist Council of Nagalim – Isaak Muivah (NSCN-IM), the largest of a dozen or so splinter groups that emerged after the breakdown of the original Naga nationalist movement in the 1970s. As the Indo-Naga conflict is discussed at greater length in other articles in this issue, and given the limited scope of his paper,

I will not discuss this further, though I reference the conflict when directly relevant to the discussion. Finally, it is important to note that, although Kohima village and Kohima town are contiguous in most respects, the discerning visitor soon becomes aware of their distinction. This is clearly tangible to non-clan residents, and particularly tenants, living within the traditional village boundary, and subject to often severe clan laws and restrictions.

The importance of context in relation to dreams will become clearer further in the paper. But first, I offer a brief overview of Angami dream culture, define a few important terms, and link this with Hutton's observations.

ANGAMI DREAM CULTURE

Angami dreams (*mho*) are experienced (and remembered) differently depending on levels of practice, interest, alertness (*rho rhü*), and 'giftedness' (*mhaphruo*) of the dreamer, though generally it is believed that dreams are revelatory for everyone. Dreamers can draw truths about the world from a spirit-mediated realm of knowledge. At a first level, dreams reveal signs that may be interpreted in the course of remembering and publicly narrating. It is incumbent upon the dreamer to remember their symbolic arrangement and to consult a memorised lexicon of meanings accrued through personal experience and through the shared experiences of others. In the event of an enigmatic or even disturbing dream, the dreamer will typically consult an elder, usually wise and skilled in dream interpretation. On the other hand, dreams can be doorways into an expansive terrain that the dream-self temporarily cohabitates with a host of other entities – ancestor spirits (*u chie ruopfü*), and powerful deities (*terhuomia*), all of whom are conscious and may or may not chose to make an appearance or share knowledge with the dreamer. Hidden from most, this terrain can be seen by gifted dreamers with an unusual ability to 'wake up' while asleep, and can navigate its contours and interact with its entities. If there is an underpinning general logic to Angami dream experience it is that this realm of spirit-mediated knowledge parallels waking reality and thus is always present and potentially accessible. Traditional shamanic healer-diviners (themumia) operating at the margins of the community communicate with tutelary spirits and thus may access this spirit realm and its knowledge (cf. Joshi 2012, 127). Children and individuals traveling or hunting alone are believed to be susceptible to a form of spirit entrapment or 'forest song' in which, like the Greek sirens, spirits draw unsuspecting persons into the forest through enticing melodies to a point where they cross over into the spirit realm - a central theme in Angami folklore.[2] As spirit entities have foreknowledge of human reality, and dreamers can

---

[2]Here I am drawing on Easterine Kire's term for the phenomenon (cf. 2011, Forest

tap fragments of that foreknowledge, one can anticipate and attempt to affect the 'coming into being of the present' (Kracke 2003, 222).

If word spreads of a person having had a particularly unusual dream, the question is rarely 'is the dream real or true?' but usually 'when will it happen?' or perhaps 'who is the dream about?' Typically, however, dreams are of a more quotidian nature and may or may not yield any surprising information. In my field notes, it was typically married women in the village that shared their dreams, often with their daughters, nieces or other female relatives and close neighbours in the early hours of the morning. Although dreams are commonly shared openly, ominous dreams are shared with discretion. In the distant past, such dreams would only be told under the covering of the kitchen hearth so as not to be heard by spirits who might attempt to manipulate the outcome it portends. An elder skilled in interpretation might be consulted, but typically this would be done also under the elder's hearth covering. This is a practice I have not seen first-hand, though the oldest generation still has memories of it. Nowadays, distressing dreams are brought to a local church to be prayed over. In extreme cases, prayer counsellors are consulted, and prayers of intercession are offered by a small gathering. A well-known prayer counsellor, often referred to as a 'prophetess' at the Baptist Revival Church, was regularly consulted about dreams before she died in 2013 just as I began my field work. Although I did not have an opportunity to meet her, numerous informants spoke of her prophetic dreams being shared publicly in church services (a practice one finds in many charismatic Christian churches throughout the state), with ministries being developed as a result of the messages gleaned in her dreams.

Whilst a spectrum of 'types of dreams' may be drawn up in our attempts at envisioning a system of Angami dreaming, two categories emerge. Most dream narratives highlight the symbolic nature of their experience, and these then require interpretation. The other main category, namely *mhaphruo* dreaming, involves greater self-consciousness while in the dream. In other words, the dreamer is aware of their own agency, and their ability to gain knowledge through interaction with other conscious entities. These categories are also consistent with Hutton's own observations a century ago.

As already mentioned, Hutton corresponded and shared his observations with C.G. Seligman, the first anthropologist to engage in a broad systematic study of manifest dream content. Hutton shared two accounts with Seligman, and by examining them we can identify important continuities with Angami dreaming experience today.[3]

Song, Kohima: Barkweaver Publications.)

[3]The archive is catalogued under Hutton, Ms. Box 3, 26, Pitt Rivers Museum Archive, Oxford, and available online at http://himalaya.socanth.cam.ac.uk/collections/naga/record/r73000.html

HUTTON'S OBSERVATIONS

In 1915 along a newly constructed road about 140 Kilometres northeast of Kohima, Hutton built an inspection bungalow near the village of Baimho. The villagers had warned him not to build on the proposed site, though it was conveniently situated on a mall mound with a good water supply. The Baimho villagers had used the site to perform sacrifices to the spirit of a man that had drowned in the Tizu river.

> A few months after the bungalow was finished I went and stayed in it for some local business. I occupied the west bedroom and my night was spoilt by a horrifying nightmare in the course of which I saw a creature like a human child with a monstrous big head creeping across the floor; the principal feature of the dream was the quite unreasonable fear which I experienced and which caused me to perspire so freely (the weather was quite cool) that my pyjamas and sheets had to be dried in the sun the next day. I thought it was a bad, a very bad dream and put it down to having eaten the roe of some fish they caught and brought me from the river, and thought no more about it. A little later Mr Mills had occasion to come to Kohima, some 70 miles, to consult me about some matter, and in the course of his stay he asked me if I had ever had an unpleasant experience in any of the Mokokchung inspection bungalows. I mentioned a scorpion in the bathroom at Nankam, but he explained that he referred to psychic experiences. I said I thought not. He asked me 'not at Baimho?' To which I replied then that I had experienced the worst nightmare I remembered since my childhood there, but that was all. When I started to recount it he stopped me and went on. The only difference in our accounts seemed to be that whereas the creature with the big head that I had seen had unkempt hair, he had seen it bald – or it may have been the other way round. We agreed that we would tell no-one of this experience but would find excuses to send people to Baimho and find out later if they had such dreams.

Their first 'victim' was a man by the name of Meikeljohn of the Assam Forestry Department who was transferred to the Garo Hills and had stayed in the Baimho bungalow prior to leaving. Hutton asked if he had experienced anything unusual there, and he said he had not. Sometime later a second person, Dr N.L. Bor, also in the Forestry Department, left the Naga Hills to fill in for Meiklejohn in the Garo Hills – though Hutton and Mills had forgotten to ask him about Baimho. When

Bor and Meikeljohn met, however,

> Meiklejohn asked him whether he had been to 'the haunted bungalow' while in the Naga Hills. He replied that he supposed Baimho was meant. He had gone to sleep in a chair on the veranda after he had arrived, having walked some ten miles from his last halting place, but was so frightened by a dream that instead of sleeping at Baimho as planned he had packed up his kit again and walked on another twelve miles to the next bungalow the same afternoon.

In the text accompanying his detailed dream experience and subsequent experiment, Hutton also includes an excerpt detailing the use of Angami dream symbols and interpretations, namely:

> to dream of being bitten by a tic, which cannot be pulled out is an omen of approaching death, while to dream of a man dressed entirely in new clothes is a sure premonition of the death of the man thus seen. A curious instance of this came within the writer's own experience. He left Kohima for a tour in the Kezama villages on September 8th 1913. At the moment of leaving, his own interpreter, Zelucha of Jotsoma, came up to say that he was not feeling very well and would prefer to join later after two or three days, so another interpreter, Vise of Viswema, was taken in his place. Mao was reached on the 10th, Kezakenoma on the 11th, Razama on the 13th. At Razama, Zelucha was expected to arrive, but another interpreter, Solhu of Kezakenoma, came instead, saying that Zelucha was going to die. When asked how he could possibly say this, as Zelucha had been quite well a few days before and had not been really ill when Vise saw him, Vise said that he had dreamt of him on the night of the sleeping at Mao, and had seen him dressed entirely in new clothes. This, he said, left no doubt. The news of Zelucha's death reached camp at Tekhubama on September 16th.

Though Hutton only includes these accounts in the margins of his monograph, he is careful to be as precise as he can with the details of his experience. In other words, he leaves little doubt as to his own puzzlement concerning the agency of spirit entities on the dreamer, and indeed the predictive accuracy of dream-mediated divination. Perhaps more importantly, his accounts are consistent with contemporary observations among the same communities Hutton studied. To substantiate this claim, I now turn to my own observations. Here, I also discuss the importance of context and setting.

THE ANIMATED LANDSCAPES OF DREAMS

The centrality of spirit encounters, their inter-generational character, and the importance of the landscape in dream narratives, were especially impressed upon me in an initial interview with a software developer named Senyü[4]. Senyü often explained aspects of his dreams that many other informants left out, largely I think because he was a mentor in his own work, and accustomed to giving careful, clear explanations. My first interview with Senyü happened nearly a year into fieldwork, and at a critical point when I was exploring whether linkages existed between the many accounts I had recorded that emphasised dream symbols, on the one hand, and on the other hand the kinds of dream experiences that seemed to entail a different level of consciousness - out-of-body experiences, remote viewing, interacting with ancestral spirits, and sometimes traveling at-will across landscapes. Were these fundamentally different modes of experience? In a sense, Senyü's accounts brought these two fields (and my two field notebooks) together. He began with symbols and their often counter-intuitive interpretations (not atypical of dream symbols in cross-cultural dream research), and moved organically toward what seemed like the other extremity along a continuum - where he did not describe symbols as much as conversations and interactions, often with the spirits of his mother and grandmother, who sometimes advised him about actual difficulties he was experiencing in daily life. His interaction with the spirits of the dead had real-life consequences, particularly on his health.

College-educated, single and in his mid-thirties, Senyü practically lived at his office, often sleeping the night while working tight deadlines. Buzzing with activity, the day I visited his work-place, all the computer stations were occupied, with fifteen or so employees from various parts of Nagaland busily shifting through symbols and icons on their screens, entering lines of code, and creating a cacophony of mouse-clicks. Senyü knelt by one of the younger female web developers sitting by the entrance, and in pencil marked out corrections on her printout - 'this line of code is separate so that this command is not obstructed'. A second co-worker waited patiently nearby for his turn. Minutes later as we sat down to talk, I asked him whether he thought codes in dreams had any significance. He seemed pleasantly surprised to hear me ask this, and immediately responded with a big 'yes'! When I asked him to elaborate, he began a conversation that lasted the rest of the day, of which I include only a few examples here. He began, as I said, with symbols:

> If I see dogs it translates to relationships with girls, or something with the opposite sex. Snakes would translate to enemies. If I see meat, or see myself eating it means bad health.

[4]Senyü's real name and profession have been anonymised.

If I see ceilings it means prayer - I need to spend more time in contemplative prayer. If I see walls it has something to do with the future - challenges that will affect my future. If I see schools - schools are very important. When I see myself going back to school and studying or trying to give an exam, for the next one month there will be a test, and I have to be really prepared. If I see the police, these are about events in the next few days I should avoid. It might be a party, but whenever I see police in my dreams, if people call me to a party, I have to avoid it.

'Really? Even presently?' [me]

'Yes, even now'

'What happens if you ignore your dream?' [me again]

I'll go there and get too drunk, or I'll just mess up everything. And if I dream of our underground insurgents, it will be something that comes to me, like some situations that I can't avoid, it will come and hit me. If I see certain people, based on my reading of those people, it may not be exactly about that person, but someone similar. If I see friends that have passed over, it's because they have a warning, they have come to warn me.

Throughout this first meeting, Senyü described how his upbringing had a lot to do with his understanding and appreciation for dreams. He and his brother were raised by his mother in the Dimapur valley, 70 kilometres northwest of Kohima. Senyü recalled spending hours as children listening to their mother and family elders sharing their dreams: 'They were stories to us - like storybook fantasies, we loved to hear them'. Senyü's mother was a keen observer of messages that appeared to her in both her dreams and in waketime reverie. Senyü recalled that his mother enjoyed the companionship of the spirits of her dead mother and grandmother, and often conversed with them while going about her daily routines. They were especially present in anxious times, and Senyü shared one especially poignant account that happened on the day he was born:

My mother never let me out of her sight when I was growing up. She never even allowed me to spend one night in Kohima. Even if we came up to Kohima, we had to go down again. My mother often received instruction in her dreams and visions. When I was born, I was declared stillborn. My mother's grandmother came into the hospital room in a vision, and said that I was not a stillborn and that she had to take care of me properly, and to never let me out of her sight. She then turned around and told the doctors that I was not stillborn.

This kind of intervention involving communication with dead relatives in dreams and reverie, accompanied Senyü and his brother throughout childhood and adolescence. Senyü described an instance in which the spirit of his mother came to his aid in a difficult situation he experienced only two years earlier – one in which he spent time contemplating death:

> At times, I also get troubled, like when a friend passed away about two years back in a tragic accident – he was drowned in a river. His girlfriend came and told me that she was having a problem. I told her to pray and make sure she finds an... In the Catholic tradition, we call it intercession, and someone must intercede on behalf so that the guardian comes and takes you... But at that time, I started getting – not feeling well; as if I'm about to die or something. And then I realised that ... I even started posting on my Facebook updates about life and death at that time, because it was a very strong, overwhelming thing. And then one night my mother came and she was so angry in my dreams. And she said, 'never ever contemplate death and life like this. Your friend was in your house trying to disturb you and he had brought a lot of friends and they were waiting for you, but I chased them all away.'

One significant feature that appeared often in his narratives was the way dreams revealed the location of spiritual activity in the landscape – activity that would have been perhaps quite familiar in older times. In one account, Senyü illustrates the way developers often ignore the old laws, and with consequences only later understood in the context of a dream:

> I recently went to Peren where they are cutting this new ground. I found that they had cut off a stream. And in Angami culture cutting off streams is a very big taboo. And that day I travelled there and saw them cutting off the stream and I went near the stream and I felt very uneasy – I had a very uneasy feeling. I am not sure what other people saw, but when I got home I felt very sick and when I finally fell asleep I only saw that place in my dreams, I prayed and only then I recovered.

In a further example, and reminding me of Hutton's bungalow experiment, Senyü described the re-appearance of a specific spirit haunting people's sleep in a specific place – in this case guests in his own home. He contextualises his account by describing the old layout of Kohima - once known as the 'land of seven lakes' – which included a large stream near the present-day Kohima War Cemetery:

> There is a river here in Kohima and there is supposedly a path

where spirits travel and it comes across my house like this. In this house it also can get disturbing. The people who stay here – they start seeing someone with very hairy arms or something else – sometimes they see these spirits. This doesn't necessarily have anything to do with war or whatnot but it is a traditional path.

As we see in Senyü's dream narratives, dreams can often index important cultural constructions of space. These often relate to the terrains of power that direct and restrict movement in waketime reality. Dreams can certainly open avenues for creative agency in negotiating constraints (Kempf and Hermann 2003), but dream narratives can also draw attention to the choices and indeed liberties one might take that might not be easily reproduced in waketime reality. Given Kohima's war-torn landscape, reminding its inhabitants daily of being surrounded by unpredictable forces they have little power to effect, it is not surprising that context is often foregrounded in the dream narratives of my informants. As Senyü's experiences attest, these are not always in obvious ways. But capacities for action, or indeed 'agency' to effect or negotiate exogenous forces – whether deemed evil or good – is also a process that may be socially distributed, and in the following section I discuss how this is done in relation to dream sharing.

THE SOCIAL LIFE OF DREAMS

Like Senyü's dream accounts and his own observations, many of my Angami informants articulated the notion of an ancestral, supernatural, or even divine agency in dreams – a kind of power that dreamers sometimes can consciously negotiate or even resist in the context of the dream. With the strong influence of Christianity, this supernatural agency increasingly appears as either coming from God or Satan, and occasionally angels or saints.[5] But what is consistent is the belief that the supernatural forces perceived in dreams have the potential to influence or 'bleed' into waketime reality. The process of dream narration among close kin, elders, a church counsellor, or neighbours, is understood to be a continuation of this process of acting on or negotiating this power, which, depending on its source, may inflict harm or bring blessing upon the dreamer. The physical effects the Baimho spirit had on Hutton and his 'victims' – causing him to sweat profusely, and frightening another so greatly as to force him to vacate the bungalow

[5]Indeed, the influence of Christianity on the interpretation or meanings of Naga dreams and dreaming is a topic that is of great significance, and merits at least a full paper of its own. Alas, this is beyond the scope of this present discussion regarding Hutton's 'science of dreams'.

immediately; or the way Senyü fell ill while trying to deal with demands of the spirit of his drowned friend in his dream; are illustrative of how this 'influence' can cross over from the dream into waking reality. In all the cases where Hutton identifies dreaming in divination, particularly among professional practitioners, he recognises that, beyond a simply cognitive exchange, in the sense of translating symbols and sharing 'information', there is a power transference; a power that is understood to originate with the supernatural, that may be also apprehended, negotiated, plumped for, or defused, in the narrating process. Indeed, in this paper, I use 'influence' deliberately, as it describes this permeation, of portentous knowledge and supernatural agency, between social others in dreamtime and social others in waketime experience. We might say that there is an ongoing productive social dialectic in the act of waking from imagined into wakeful, enacted sociality, or as Minna Opas (2016) states, 'dreams occupy an important place in the joint production and re-production of lifeworlds' (Ibid., p. 247). Analogous to the Naga context, in her work among the Yine of Amazonian Peru, Opas states, that 'In sharing their dreams with each other, the Yine attempted to ensure that the influence of the social others encountered in dreams would not leak uncontrollably into the sphere of normal daily existence, and so possibly have unwanted effects' (p. 247). The 'leakage' could be controlled through the intervention of the dreamer in the act of narrating the dream. Indeed, as she states: 'Telling others about one's dreams was a way to control and protect one's own human bodily condition and that of those around one. Nevertheless, these others were not merely passive bystanders but were also actively involved in these processes. This was apparent in Yine evangelicals' dreaming and their experiences of God's influence in their lives and bodies' (pp. 247-248). Interestingly, Opas describes a belief among the Yine resembling Naga beliefs in the dangers of venturing to close to forests where powerful spirits can entrap human souls – particularly the weaker souls of small children, namely 'Yine avoidance of entering the forest alone: they always went with a companion because it was thought that alone the risk of being influenced by the consubstantialising practices of other non-human beings was too great' (Opas 2016, 247).

CONCLUDING REMARKS

The privileged knowledge of premonitory dreaming is a subject of considerable interest to the Angamis and the Nagas more generally, and dreams are the most common mode through which revelatory knowledge is obtained – very often filtering through to dreamers with no special insight, although believed to be of consequence to the dreamer and his or her community. In this paper, I have described how ordinary dreams are interpreted based on community memory of symbolic meanings of dreams interpreted in the past. Based on this index of meanings, they judge the level of severity of the revelation, and communicate this knowledge to close kin, and if necessary to the clan. Unremarkable dreams are often quickly forgotten, or perhaps shared light-heartedly in conversation during morning chores. However, particularly cryptic, puzzling our troubling dreams are prayed on, or brought to a more experienced dreamer for interpretive consultation. The process of narrating a dream alone is seen as a kind of 'interference' that can 'plump for' a desired blessing, on the one hand, and on the other, lessen or defuse the harmful effects of an undesirable dream. There are also individuals like Senyü that are considered particularly gifted – *mhaphruo* – who interpret with greater facility, and in a sense are able to consciously act and communicate in the midst of their dream experiences. As with Senyü, *mhaphruo* dreamers may receive knowledge directly from the spirits of dead relatives and other non-human entities with whom they interact, and sustain a deeper personal linkage with their dream experiences, as compared with the first category. Although we cannot observe the totality of a dream 'system', we can infer that these two modes of experience are part of one integrated whole. Indeed, it is the person's own capacities that limit or accentuate their experiences in dreaming.

With the advent of Christianity and particularly its numerous charismatic variants, the cultivated practice of communicating dream-mediated knowledge has entered new ritual modalities and form new meanings. It also shows important continuities into the present of pre-Christian practices, likely preserved in the domestic practices not immediately scrutinised by the puritanical exigencies of the early American Baptist missionaries. In addition, Naga political and nationalist leaders have drawn on dream-mediated knowledge as they have sought to shape their political platforms, and nationalist agendas. In some instances, the knowledge obtained from dreams has informed daily strategies. One veteran combatant once shared with me that every company of Naga soldiers had at least one person that was a gifted dreamer. These would often wake from sleep with warnings not to proceed along a planned forest march to avoid possible ambush. Anecdotes like this are shared often during family meals, and the wonderment that surrounds dream-mediated knowledge, and especially knowledge about the future, sustains Naga popular fascination with dreams and dreaming today.

Finally, the aim of this article was to combine recent ethnographic material and archival material in substantiating Hutton's claim with regards to an 'Angami science of dreams'. I introduced several informants whose experiences serve as ideal-types – mhoté dreamers or dream experiences and *mhaphruo* dreamers and dream experiences – and thus indicate the breadth of dream experience in contemporary Angami society. In my research these two categories were helpful in mapping out the kinds of dream experiences most of my informants shared, and it became clear that personal circumstance, interest and the intensity of engagement with dreaming and communicating dreams translated into varying levels of expertise, or insight – regardless of any 'gift' they might have. These categories, placed as ideal-types along a continuum of experience form ontological dispositions from which one can explore the nexus between dream inspiration and experience on the one hand and revelatory diffusion in socio-cultural process on the other (Tonkinson 2003, 88).

■ ■■ ■■

REFERENCES

Abrams, R. 2013. When parents die: learning to live with the loss of a parent (3rd Edition). London: Routledge.

Achumi, G. 2011. The essence of Sumi ethnic traditional and modern attire. Kohima: published by the author.

Alemchiba, M. 1970. A Brief historical account of Nagaland. Kohima: Naga Institute of Culture.

Alia, V. 2009. Outlaws and citizens: indigenous people and the new media nation. International Journal of Media and Cultural Politics 5, 39–54.

Allen, B. C. 1905. Naga Hills and Manipur: socio-economic history. Delhi: Gian Publications.

Anand, V. K. 1980. Conflict in Nagaland. a study of insurgency and counter-insurgency. Delhi: Chanakya Publications.

Anand, V.K. 1967. Nagaland in Transition. Delhi: Associate Publishing House.

Anderson, B.I. 1978. A brief historical sketch of the American Baptist mission work in the Sema Naga tribe, Nagaland. In Sema Baptist Diamond Jubilee Souvenir 1904-1978. Aizuto, Nagaland: no publisher information.

Andrews, M. F. 2005. How (not) to find God in all things: Derrida, Levinas and St. Ignatius of Loyola on learning to pray for the impossible. In The Phenomenology of Prayer (eds) B. E. Benset, & N. Wirzba, 195-208. New York: Fordham University Press.

Angelova, I. 2015. Something like wind, unusual things came: the great evangelical revivals of the 1950s and 1970s in the memories of Sumi Naga. In: Passing things on: ancestors and genealogies in Northeast India, edited by M. Heneise. Dimapur: Heritage Publishing House.

Angelova, I. forthcoming. Identity change and the construction of difference: colonial and post-colonial conversions among the Sumi Naga of Nagaland, Northeast India. In Modalities of conversion in India (eds) P. Berger and S. Sahoo.

Anonymous, 2013. Finally, a no to extortion. In Tehelka. Available at: http://search.proquest.com.wwwproxy1.library.unsw.edu.au/docview/1459433930?accountid=12763, accessed 1 May 2017.

Ao, A.B. 2002. History of Christianity in Nagaland: the Ao Naga tribal Christian mission enterprise 1872-1972. Mokokchung: Shalom Ministry Publication.

Ao, L. 2002. From Phizo to Muivah: the Naga national question in Northeast India. New Delhi: Mittal Publications.

Ao, M. A. 1992. The art of the Nagas. In: The Nagas (eds) Somare, G., and Vigorelli, L Italy: Gallerial Lorenzelli.

Ao, T. 1957. Naga customary laws. Mokokchung: published by the author.

Ao, T. 1958. A history of Anglo-Naga affairs. Mokokchung: published by the author.

Ao, T. 2006. Identity and globalization: a Naga perspective. Indian Folklore, A Quarterly News Letter from National Folklore Support Centre 22, 6-7.

Ao, T. 2012. The Ao-Naga oral tradition, (2nd edition). Dimapur: The Heritage Publishing House.

Ao, T. 2014. On being a Naga: essays. Dimapur: Heritage Publishing House.

Aosenba. 2001. The Naga resistance movement: prospect of peace and armed conflict. New Delhi: Regency Publications.

Aphun K. 2008. The Kabui Nagas of Manipur: A study of identity and identity-crisis. The Shodhganga@INFLIBNET Centre. (Accessed August 5, 2017).

Archer, W.G. 1947. Typescript tour diary, 12/01/1947, Sema attitudes to young men's houses (Apuki) and the effect of Christianity'. Record R65545 in The Naga Database http://himalaya.socanth.cam.ac.uk/collections/naga/record/r65545.html. (Accessed on 16 July 2013).

Arnold-de Simine, S. 2013. Mediating memory in the museum: empathy, trauma, nostalgia. New York Palgrave Macmillan.

Arya, A. & V. Joshi. 2004. The Land of the Nagas. Ahmedabad: Mapin Publishing.

Asad, T. 1973. Anthropology and the colonial encounter. New York: Humanity Books.

Ashcroft, B. 2001. On post-colonial futures: transformations of colonial culture. London: Continuum.

Assam Baptist missionary conference 1936. Minutes. 3-6 February 1936, Jorhat (Assam). Archive of the Council of Baptist Churches of Northeast India, Guwahati. (Accessed on 5 October 2011).

Assumi, Z. 2009. The Sumi Ahuna. Dimapur: Heritage Publishing House.

Aye, K. 2005. The impact of Christian education (100 years of Christianity in Sumi Baptist churches, 1903-2003). Dimapur: Christian Education Ministry.

Balwally, D. 2003. Growth of totalitarianism in Arunachal Pradesh, Mizoram and Nagaland. Guwahati: Spectrum Publications.

Baptist Missionary Magazine (1873-1909), Jun 1901, 81 (6). American periodicals series online. Accessed via the Oxford Library e-Journals system.

Barclay, B. 1990. Our own image. New Zealand: Pearson Education.

Barooah, J. 2002. Property and women's inheritance rights in the tribal areas of the North East. In Changing Women's Status in India: Focus on the Northeast (eds) W. Fernandes & S. Barbora, 99-113. Guwahati: North Eastern Social Research Centre.

Barrett, J. 2011. Museums and the public sphere. Chichester, UK: Wiley-Blackwell.

Barrington, L. W. 1997. Nation and nationalism: the misuse of key concepts in political science. Political Science and Politics 30, 712-716.

Baruah, S. 1999. India against itself: Assam and the politics of nationality. Philadelphia: University of Pennsylvania Press.

Baruah, S. 2003. Confronting constructionism: ending India's Naga war. Journal of Peace Research 40, 321-338.

Baruah, S. 2007. Durable disorder: understanding the politics of Northeast India. Delhi: Oxford University Press.

Basso, E. B. 1997. The implications of a progressive theory of dreaming. In Dreaming: anthropological and psychological interpretations (ed) B. Tedlock, 86-104. New York: Cambridge University Press.

Basu, M. 2014. Exam-oriented learning hurts students' abilities. The Indian Express (available on-line: http://indianexpress.com/article/cities/mumbai/exam-oriented-learning-hurts-students-abilities, accessed 2 January 2017).

Bennet, T. 2004. Pasts beyond memory: evolution, museums, colonialism. London: Routledge.

Bensent, B. E. & N Wirzba. 2005. The phenomenology of prayer. New york: Fordham University Press.

Berliner, D. and R. Sarró. 2007. On learning religion: an introduction. In Learning religion: anthropological approaches (eds.) D. Berliner and R. Sarró. Oxford: Berghahn Books.

Bhuria 1985. Tribal education in India. Cultural Survival Quarterly (available on-line: https://www.culturalsurvival.org/publications/cultural-survival-quarterly/tribal-education-india, accessed 18 December 2016).

Bilu, Y. 2000. Dreams and the wishes of the saint. In Judaism viewed from within and from without: anthropological exploration in the comparative study of Jewish culture (ed) H. E. Goldberg, 285-314. New York: State University of New York Press.

Bird-David, N. 1999. Animism revisited: personhood, environment, and relational epistemology. Current Anthropology 40, S67-S91.

Boas, F. 1921 Ethnology of the Kwakiutl. Thirty-Fifth Annual Report, Bureau of American Ethnology.

Bonanno, G. A. 2008. Loss, trauma and human resilience: have we underestimated the human capacity to thrive after extremely aversive events? Psychological Trauma: Theory, Research, Practice and Policy S1, 101-113.

Bourdieu, P. 1977. Outline of a theory of practice. Cambridge: Cambridge University Press.

Bourdieu, P. 1984. Distinction: a social critique of the judgement of taste. London: Routledge.

Bower, U.G. 1950. Naga path. London: John Murray.

Brackney, W. 1990. American Baptist churches in the USA. In Dictionary of Christianity in America (ed.) D. Reid. Downers Grove (Illinois): Intervarsity Press.

Brahmaputra Tours, Nagaland. Available at: http://www.brahmaputra-tours.com, accessed 14 July 2015.

Brison, K.J. 1996. Becoming Savage: Western Representations and Cultural Identity in a Sepik Society. In Anthropology and Humanism 21, 5-18.

Bulkeley, K. 2016. Big dreams: the science of dreaming and the origins of religion. Oxford: Oxford University Press.

Burling, R. 2007. Language, ethnicity and migration in Northeast India. university of Michigan. (available on-line: http://wwwpersonal.umich.edu/~rburling/Language%20and%20Ethnicity.pdf, accessed on 06 February 2017.

Butalia, U. 1998. The other side of silence: voices from the partition of India. New Delhi: Penguin Books.

Butler, J. 1855. Travels and adventures in the province of Assam during a residence of fourteen years. London.

Butler, J. 1875. Rough Notes on the Angami Nagas and Their Language. In Journal of the Asiatic Society 4, 307–346.

Canetto, S.S. & Cleary, A. 2012. Men, Masculinities and Suicidal Behaviour. In Social Science and Medicine 74, 461–465.

Cannell, F. 2006. Introduction: the anthropology of Christianity. In The anthropology of Christianity (ed.) F. Cannell. Durham: Duke University Press.

Cartmell, D. & I. Whelehan. 2010. Screen adaptation: impure cinema. Basingstoke: Palgrave Macmillan.

Census 2011. Nagaland population census. (available on-line: http://www.census2011.co.in/census/state/nagaland.html, accessed 28 December 2016).

Channa, S. M. 1992. Nagaland, A Contemporary Ethnography. Delhi: South Asia Books.

Chasie, C. 1999. The Naga imbroglio: a personal perspective. Kohima: City Press.

Chidester, D. 2009. Darwin's dogs: animals, animism, and the problem of religion. Soundings: An Interdisciplinary Journal 92, 51-75.

Chishi Swu, I. 2004. Ashu Kushe (2004 Sumi Christian centenary, In memory of Kushe Chishilimi). Dimapur, Nagaland: Kushe Humanity Foundation.

Chishi, V. 2003. A strategy for the unification of the Sumi Baptist church through understanding the revival movement and its application (a history of the Sumi Baptist Church beginning from 1904). Dimapur: Revd Inaho Kinnimi Memorial Trust.

Chophy, G.K. (2015) An incongruent inheritance: the anthropology of J.H. Hutton and the Sema Nagas. Eastern Anthropologist 68 (2-3): 327-340.

Cole, J. & Durham, D. 2008. Introduction: Globalization and the Temporality of Children and Youth. In Figuring the Future: Globalization and the Temporalities of Children and Youth. Santa Fe: NML School for Advanced Research Press.

Conklin, B. A. 1997. Body paint, feathers and VCRs: aesthetics and authenticity in Amazonian activism. American Ethnologist 24, 711-737.

Convention, M. B. 1997. The first one hundred years of Christianity in Manipur. Imphal: The MBC Literature Committee.

Cottingham, J. 2002. On the meaning of life: thinking in action. London: Routledge.

Dalton, E. T. 1969. Nagas west of the Doyang River. In The Nagas in the nineteenth century (ed) V. Elwin, 440-2. London: Oxford University Press.

Das, B. 2014. India's northeast speaks out against racism. Al Jazeera (available on-line: http://www.aljazeera.com/indepth/features/2014/02/voices-from-india-northeast-201421811314600858.html, accessed 1 May 2017).

Das, G. 2013. Insurgencies in North-East India: moving towards resolution. New Delhi: Pentagon Press.

Das. N.K. 1980. Social system and territorial adaptation among the Naga tribes. In Development without destruction: proceedings of a symposium. Shillong: Government of Meghalaya.

Das. N.K. 1982a The Naga movement. In Tribal movements in India Vol 1 (ed) K. S. Singh. New Delhi: Manohar Publications.

Das, N.K. 1982b. Agrarian structure and change in Nagaland. In Economies of the tribes and their transformation (ed) K. S. Singh. Concept Publishing Company.

Das, N.K. 1984. Land management, dual inheritance and re-distribution among the Zounuo-Keyhonuo Naga. In Agrarian situation in India Vol 1 (eds) S. B. Chakraborty, B. R. Ghosh, and A. K. Danda. Calcutta Anthropological Survey of India.

Das, N.K. 1989a. Ethnic Identity, Ethnicity and Social Stratification in North East India. New Delhi: Inter-India Publications.

Das, N.K. 1989b. The segmentary lineage system of the Zounuo-Keyhonuo Naga. In Human Science 38, 210-214

Das, N.K. 1992. Kinship, Politics, and Law in Naga Society. Calcutta: Anthropological Survey of India.

Das, N. K. 1994. The Khiamngan Naga. In Nagaland (people of India, general editor K. S. Singh) (eds) N. K. Das & C. L. Imchen. Calcutta: Anthropological Survey of India.

Das, T. C. 1963. Aspects of tribal culture under modern impact in Eastern India. In anthropology on the march: recent studies of Indian beliefs, attitudes and social institutions (ed) B. Ratnam. Madras: The Book Centre.

Das, V. 2007. Life and words: violence and descent into the ordinary. Berkeley: University of California Press.

Davis, A. W. 1969. Neighbours of the Aos. In The Nagas in the nineteenth century (ed) V. Elwin, 398-399. London: Oxford University Press.

Davis, A.W. 1891. Report on the tribal population of the province of Assam. In Census of India 1891, Assam, 1.

De Beauvoir, S. 1949. The second sex. New York: Random House.

Dena, L. 2007. The Kuki-Naga conflict: juxtaposed in the colonial context. In Dynamics of identity and inter-group relations in North-East India (ed) K. S. Aggarwal, 182-187. Shimla: Indian Institute of Advanced Study.

Dena, L. 2010. AMCO's peace efforts during the Kuki-Naga conflict, 1992-1994. Kuki International Forum.

Descola, P. 1989. Head-shrinkers versus shrinks: Jivaroan analysis of dreams. Man, The Journal of the Royal Anthropological Institute 24, 439-450.

Dev, S.C. 1988. Nagaland, the Untold Story. Delhi: Dev Publishers.

Devi, L. 1968. Ahom-tribal relations: a political study. Gauhati: Cotton College.

Disney, A.E. & G. Recticker. 2008. Pray the devil back to hell. New York: Abigail Disney

Dittman, A. T. & H. C. Moore. 1957. Disturbance in dreams as related to peyotism among the Navaho. American Anthropologist 59, 642-9.

Douglas, T. 2015. Tales of the tribes: animation as a tool for indigenous representation (PhD thesis Bournemouth University).

Downs, F. S. 1992. History of Christianity in India, 5 (North-east India in the nineteenth and twentieth centuries), part 5. Bangalore: The Church History Association of India.

Downs, F. S. 1993. Essays on Christianity in North-East India. New Delhi: Uppal Publishing House.

Dudley, A. 1984. Concepts in film theory. Oxford UK: Oxford University Press.

Eaton, R. 1984. Conversion to Christianity among the Nagas, 1876-1971. In Indian Economic and Social History Review 21, 1-44.

Eggan, D. 1952. The manifest content of dreams: a challenge to social science. American Anthropologist 54, 469-485.

Elliott, M. 2014. Searching for ancestors: recognising Marguerite Milward's Naga portraits. In Passing things on: ancestors and genealogies in Northeast India (ed) M. Heneise. Dimapur, Nagaland: Heritage Publication House.

Elwin, V. 1957. A Philosophy for NEFA. Shillong: North-East Frontier Agency.

Elwin, V. 1959. India's north-east frontier in the nineteenth century. Oxford: Oxford University Press.

Elwin, V. 1961. Nagaland. Shillong: The Research Department Secretariat.

Elwin, V. (1964) 1998. The Tribal world of verrier Elwin: an autobiography. India: Oxford University Press.

Elwin, V. 1969. The Nagas in the Nineteenth Century. London: Oxford University Press.

Engelke, M. 2004. Discontinuity and the discourse of conversion. In Journal of Religion in Africa 34, 82-109.

Epstein, A. L. 1998. Strange encounters: dreams and nightmares of high school students in Papua New Guinea. Oceania 68, 200-12.

Evans-Pritchard, E.E. 1940. The Nuer of the southern Sudan. In African political systems (eds) M. Fortes & E. E. Evans-Pritchard. London: Oxford University Press.

Ewing, K. P. 1994. Dreams from a saint: anthropological atheism and the temptation to believe. American Anthropologist 96, 571-84.

Ewing, K.P. 2003. Diasporic dreaming, identity, and self-constitution. In Dreaming and the self: new perspectives on subjectivity, identity, and emotion (ed) J. M. Mageo, 43-60. Albany, NY: State University of New York Press.

Ezung, T. 2012. Corruption and its impact on development: a case study of Nagaland. International Journal of Rural Studies 19(1): 1-7.

Fabian, J., 1999. Remembering the other: knowledge and recognition in the exploration of central Africa. Critical Inquiry 26, 49-69.

Fanon, F. (1961) 2007. The wretched of the earth USA: Grove/Atlantic.

Firth, R. 1934. The meaning of dreams in Tikopia. In Essays presented to C.G. Seligman (eds): Kegan Paul.

Freud, S. 1900. The interpretation of dreams (trans. A. A. Brill). New York: MacMillan.

Fuller, C.F. & J. Spencer 1990. South Asian anthropology in the 1980s. In South Asia research 10, 85-105.

Fürer-Haimendorf, C. von. 1939. The naked Nagas. London: Methuen & Co.

Fürer-Haimendorf, C. Von. 1969. The Konyak Nagas: An Indian frontier tribe. New York: Holt McDougal.

Fürer-Haimendorf, C. von. 1973. Social and cultural change among the Konyak Naga. Highlander 1, 3-12.

Fürer-Haimendorf, C. von. 1982. Tribes of India: the struggle for survival. Berkeley: University of California Press.

Fürer-Haimendorf, C. von 2005. The men who hunted heads - the Nagas of Assam [Video file]. http://www.dspace.cam.ac.uk/handle/1810/34585

Galtung, J. 2000. Leaving the twentieth century, entering the twenty-first: some basic conflict formation. In Searching for peace: The road to transcend (eds) J. Galtung & C. G. Jacobsen, 51-65. London: Pluto Press.

Ganguli, M. 1984. A Pilgrimage to the Nagas. New Delhi: Oxford & IBH Publishing Co.

Glancey, J. 2011. Nagaland: a journey to India's forgotten frontier. UK: Faber and Faber.

Goodman, J. H. 2004. Coping with trauma and hardship among unaccompanied refugee youths from Sudan. In Qualitative Health Research 14, 1177-1196.

Goswami, R. 2010. Socio-economic realities in Nagaland: the case of Khonoma. The Peripheral Centre (ed) P. Gill. New Delhi: Zubaan.

Goulet, J.-G. 1994. Dreams and visions in other lifeworlds. In Bing changed by cross-cultural encounters: the anthropology of extraordinary experience (eds) J.-G. Goulet & D. E. Young, 16-38. Peterborough, Ontario: Broadview Press.

Graburn, N. 1996. Ethnic and tourist arts, cultural expressions from the fourth world. Berkeley: University of California Press.

Graham, B. and P. Howard. 2008. Introduction: heritage and identity. In The Ashgate research companion to heritage and identity (eds.) B. Graham and P. Howard. Aldershot: Ashgate Publishing.

Graham, L. R. 1995. Performing dreams: discourses of immortality among the Xavante of central Brazil. Austin: University of Texas Press.

Gregor, T. 1981. A content analysis of Mehinaku dreams. Ethos, 9, 258-275.

Griffith, R. M., O. Miyagi & A. Tago. 1958. The universality of typical dreams: Japanese versus Americans. American Anthropologist 60, 1173-8.

Guha, R. 1999. Savaging the civilized: Verrier Elwin, his tribals, and India. Chicago:

University of Chicago Press.

Guite, J., 2013. Colonialism and its unruly? The colonial state and Kuki Raids in nineteenth century Northeast India. In Modern Asian Studies 48, 1188-1232.

Gundevia, Y.D. 1975. War and peace in Nagaland. New Delhi: Palit & Palit Publishers.

Gupta, D. 2005. Wither the Indian village. Economic and Political Weekly 40, 751-758.

Gurye, G. S. 1943. The aboriginals so-called and their future. Poona: Gokhale Institute of Politics.

Hall, C. S. 1951. What people dream about. Scientific American, 184, 60-3.

Hall, C. S. & R. L. Van de Castle. 1966. The content analysis of dreams. New York: Appleton-Century-Crofts).

Hall, C. S. & V. J. Nordby. 1972. The individual and his dreams. New York: New American Library.

Handique, M. 2015. Nagaland: post accord, a revolt rises east of the sun. In The Qaint (available on-line: https://www.thequint.com/opinion/2015/09/21/nagaland-post-accord-a-revolt-rises-east-of-the-sun, accessed 30 December 2016).

Hazarika, S. 2011 [1994]. Strangers of the mist: tales of war and peace from India's Northeast. New Delhi: Penguin.

Hearne, J. 2008. Indigenous animation: educational programming, narrative interventions and children's cultures. In Indigenous media: cultures, poetics, and politics (eds) P. Wilson, and M. Stewart. London: Duke University.

Hechter, M. 2004. Containing nationalism. New York: Oxford University Press.

Hefner, R. 1993. Introduction: world building and the rationality of conversion. In Conversion to Christianity (historical and anthropological perspectives on a great transformation) (ed.) R. Hefner. Berkeley: University of California Press.

Heijnen, A. 2005. Dreams, darkness and hidden spheres: exploring the anthropology of the night in Icelandic society. Paideuma: Mitteilungen zur Kulturkunde 51, 193-207.

Heneise, M. 2013. The Konyak Nagas: a socio-cultural profile by Ashim Roy. Reviewed in The South Asianist 2(2), 137-139.

Heneise, M. & E. Moon-Little. 2015. Introduction. In Passing things on: ancestors and genealogies in Northeast India (ed) M. Heneise. Dimapur, Nagaland: Heritage Publication House.

Heneise, M. 2016. The Naga Tiger-man and the modern assemblage of a myth. In Anthropology and Cryptozoology (ed) S. Hurn. London: Routledge.

Henningsen, B. 2007. The church's contribution for unity and welfare in Nagaland. Kohima: Council of Naga Baptist Churches.

Herdt, G. 1997. Selfhood and discourse in Sambia dream sharing. In Dreaming: anthropological and psychological interpretations (ed) B. Tedlock. New York: Cambridge University Press.

Herr, B. 1981. The expressive character of Fijian dream and nightmare experiences.

Ethos 9, 331-352.

Hobsbawm, E. & T. Ranger 2000 [1983]. The invention of tradition. Cambridge: Cambridge University Press.

Hodson, T.C. 1911. The Naga tribes of Manipur. London: Macmillan.

Hodson, T.C. 1975 [1908]. The meitheis. Michigan: University of Michigan.

Hollan, D. 1995. To the afterworld and back: mourning and dreams of the dead among the Toraja. Ethos 23, 424-436.

Horam, M. 1977. Social and cultural life of Nagas (The Tangkhul Nagas). Delhi: B. R. Publishing Corporation.

Horam, M. 1988. The Naga Insurgency: the last thirty years. Delhi: Cosmo Publications.

Horam, M. 1990. Nagas Old Ways and New Trends. New Delhi: Cosmo Publications.

Horam, M. 1992 [1975]. Naga polity. Delhi: D. K. Fine Art Press.

Hudson, T.C. 1991. The Naga tribes of Manipur. Delhi: B.R. Publishing.

Hutton, J. H. 1921a. The Angami Nagas: with some notes on neighbouring tribes. London: Macmillan & Co.

Hutton, J.H. 1921b. The Sema Nagas. London: Macmillan.

Hutton, J.H. 1923. Type dreams: a request. Folklore 34, 376-8.

Hutton, J.H. 1929. Diaries of two tours in the unadministered area East of the Naga Hills. Calcutta: Asiatic Society of Bengal.

Hutton J.H. 1965. The mixed culture of the Naga tribes. In Journal of the Royal Anthropological Institute of Great Britain and Ireland 95, 16-43.

Hutton, J. H. 1986. Report on Naga Hills. London: Oxford University Press. Hutton, Ms. Box 3, 26. Pitt rivers museum archive, oxford, and available online at http://himalaya.socanth.cam.ac.uk/collections/naga/record/r73000.html, accessed 30/05/2014.

Hutton, J.H. 1987. Chang language, grammar, and vocabulary of the language of the change Naga tribe. New Delhi: Gian Publishing House.

Iralu, E. 2009. Naga folktales retold. Norway: Barkweaver.

Iralu, K. 1999. Nagaland and India: the blood and the tears. Kohima: published by the author.

Iralu, K. 2000. Nagaland and India: the blood and the tears. Nagaland: Privately published.

Iralu, K. 2009. The Naga saga: a historical account of the 62 years of Indo-Naga war and the story of those who were never allowed to tell it. Kohima: published by the author.

Iralu, K. D. 2005. The fifty-four year Indo-Naga conflict. In Coming out of violence: essays on ethnicity, conflict resolution and peace processes in North-East India (ed) M. Hussain, 170-196. New Delhi: Regency Publications.

Jacobs, J. with A. Macfarlane, S. Harrison, & A. Herle. 1998. The Nagas: hill peoples of Northeast India: society, culture, and the colonial encounter. Bangkok: River Books.

Jedrej, M. C. & R. Shaw. 1992b. Dreaming, religion, and society in Africa. Leiden: E. J. Brill.

Jimo, L. 2008. Marriage prestations and "Ame" bridewealth in the Sumi Naga society. Indian Anthropologist 38, 43-60.

Johnstone, J. (1896). My experiences in Manipur and the Naga hills. London: Sampson Low, Marston and Company.

Joshi, V. 2001. Nagaland: Past and Present. New Delhi: Akansha Publishing House.

Joshi, V. 2007. 'The birth of Christian enthusiasm among the Angami of Nagaland'. Journal of South Asian Studies 30(3): 541-557.

Joshi, V. 2008. The Naga: An Introduction. In Naga: A Forgotten Mountain Region Rediscovered (eds) R. Kunz & V. Joshi. Museum der Kulturen Basel, Christoph Merian Verlag: 37-49.

Joshi, V. 2012. A matter of belief: Christian conversion and healing in North-East India. New York: Berghahn Books.

Kabui, G. 1994. The Naga-Kuki ethnic conflict. In Economic News and Views, July 16-31, 17.

Kamei, G. 2004. A history of the Zeliangrong Nagas: From Makhel to Rani Gaidinliu. Guwahati: Spectrum.

Karlsson, B. G. 2002. Entering into the Christian Dharma: contemporary tribal conversions in India. In Christians, iultural Interactions and India's religious traditions (eds) J. M. Brown & R. E. Frykenberg. London: William B. Eerdsman Publishing Company.

Keane, W. 2007. Christian moderns: freedom and fetish in the mission encounter. Berkeley: University of California Press.

Khamrang, L. 2015. Geography of insurgency – contextualization of ethno-nationalism in Northeast India. Open Journal of Social Sciences 3(6): 103-113.

Khiamnuingan, T.L. 2014. Inequality in Nagaland: a case study of "advanced" and "backward tribes'. International Journal of Sustainable Development 7(2): 71-78.

Kiho, T. 2004. The impact of Christianity on the Sumi tribe (with special reference to Sumi Aphuyemi Baptist Church Association). Dimapur: published by the author.

Kikon, D. 2002. Political mobilisation of women in Nagaland: a sociological background. In Changing women's status in India: focus on the Northeast (eds) W. Fernandes & S. Barbora. Guwahati: North Eastern Social Research Centre, 174-182.

Kikon, D. 2004. Experiences of Naga women in armed conflict: narratives from a militarised society. New Delhi: WISCOMP.

Kikon, D. 2005. Engaging Naga nationalism: can democracy function in militarised societies? Economic and Political Weekly 40, 2833-2837.

Kikon, D. 2005. Operation hornbill festival 2004. In Gateway to the east: a symposium on Northeast India and the look east policy. Seminar # 550, June 2005.

Kikon, D. 2008. Cultural construction of nationalism: myths, legends and memories. In Naga identities: changing local cultures in the Northeast of India (eds) M. Oppitz, T. Kaiser, A. Von Stockhausen & M. Wettstein, 97-106. Ghent: Snoeck.

Kikon, D. 2009. The predicament of justice: 50 years of armed forces special powers Act. In Contemporary South Asia Journal 17(3): 271-82.

Kikon, D. 2015. Making pickles during a ceasefire: livelihood, sustainability, and development in Nagaland. Economic and Political Weekly 50(9): 74-78.

Kilborne, B. 1981. Pattern, structure, and style in anthropological studies of dreams. Ethos 9, 165-185.

Kire, E. 2011. Forest song. Kohima: Barkweaver Publications

Kire, E. 2013. When the river sleeps. New Delhi: Zubaan.

Kohn, T. 1995. She came out of the field and into my home: reflections, dreams, and a search for consciousness in anthropological method. In Questions of consciousness (eds) A. P. Cohen & N. Rapport, 33, 41-59. London: Routledge.

Konnikova, M. 2015. You have no idea what happened. The New Yorker.

Kracke, W. 1979. Dreaming in Kagwahiv: dream beliefs and their psychic uses in an Amazonian Indian culture. Psychoanalytic Study of Society 8, 119-171.

Kracke, W. 1981. Kagwahiv mourning dreams of a bereaved father. Ethos 9, 258-275.

Kracke, W. 1999. A language of dreaming: dreams of an Amazonian insomniac. The International Journal of Psychoanalysis 80, 257-271.

Kracke, W. 2003. Afterward, Beyond the Mythologies: A Shape of Dreaming. In Dream Travelers: Sleep experiences and culture in the Western Pacific (ed) R. Lohmann. New York: Palgrave Macmillan.

Kreidie, L. H. & K. R. Monroe. 2002. Psychological boundaries and ethnic conflict: how identity constrained choice and worked to turn out ordinary people into perpetrators of ethnic violence during the Lebanese civil war. International Journal of Politics, Culture and Society 16, 5-36.

Kristensen, P., L. Weisaeth & T. Heir. 2012. Bereavement and mental health after sudden and violent loss: a review. Psychiatry, Interpersonal & Biological Processes 75, 76-97.

Kunz, R. & V. Joshi. 2008. Naga: a forgotten mountain region rediscovered. Basel: Museum der Kulturen Basel.

Kuotsu, N. 2013. Architectures of pirate film cultures: encounters with the Korean wave in 'Northeast' India. In Inter-Asia Cultural Studies 14, 579-99.

L. Ao, 1993. Rural Development in Nagaland. New Delhi: Harand Publishers.

LaCapra, D. 1999. Trauma, absence and loss. Critical Inquiry 25, 696-727.

Lanunungsang, A. & N. T. Jamir. 2005. Naga Society and Culture. Mokokchung: Nagaland University Tribal Research Centre.

Larson, C. C. 2009. As we forgive: stories of reconciliation from Rwanda. Grand Rapids: Zondervan.

Lasuh, W. & V. K. Nuh. 2002. The Naga chronicle. New Delhi: Regency Publications.

Latham, R.G. 1969. Ethnology of India. In The Nagas in the nineteenth century (ed) V. Elwin, 96-102. London: Oxford University Press.

Lattas, A. 1993. Sorcery and colonialism: illness, dreams and death as political languages in West New Britain. Man (New Series) 28, 51-77.

Lederach, J. P. & A.J. Lederach. 2010. When blood and bones cry out: journeys through the soundscape of healing and reconciliation. New York: Oxford University Press.

LeVine, S. 1981. Dreams of the informant about the researcher: some difficulties inherent in the research relationships. Ethos 23, 276-293.

Lhousa, Z. 2016. Nagaland for the Nagas. Nagaland: Private publication.

Linyu, K. 2004. Christian movements in Nagaland. Kohima: Published by the author.

Lohmann, R. I. 2003d. Dream travelers: sleep experiences and culture in the Western Pacific. New York: Palgrave MacMillan.

Lohmann, R.I. 2000. The role of dreams in religious enculturation among the Asabano of Papua New Guinea. Ethos 28, 75-102.

Longchar, W. 2000. The tribal religious traditions in northeast India: an introduction. Jorhat: Eastern Theological College.

Longkumer, Arkotong 2008. Circling the altar stone: Bhuban cave and the symbolism of religious traditions. In Changing Local Cultures in the Northeast of India. Gent: Snoeck Publishers, pp. 403-417.

Longkumer, A. 2010. Reform, identity and narratives of belonging: The Heraka movement in Northeast India. London: Continuum International Publishing Group.

Longkumer, A. 2013. 'Who sings for the Hornbill? the performance and politics of culture in Nagaland, Northeast India. The South Asianist, 2(2), 87-96.

Longkumer, A. 2013. The power of persuasion: Hindutva, Christianity, and the discourse of religion and culture in Northeast India. Unpublished paper presented in 2013 conference far from the nation: close to the state: hazy Sovereignty and anxious citizenship in India's Northeast, Stanford University.

Longkumer, A. 2015. As our ancestors once lived: representation, performance, and constructing a national culture amongst the Nagas of India. Himalaya, the Journal of the Association for Nepal and Himalayan Studies 35, 51-64.

Longkumer, A. 2016a. Lines that speak: the Gaidinliu notebooks as language, prophecy and textuality. Hau: Journal of Ethnographic Theory 6(2): 123-47.

Longkumer, A. 2016b. Rice-beer, purification and debates over religion and culture in Northeast India. Journal of South Asian Studies 39(2): 444-461.

Longvah, S. 2001. Nagawui Kharing-Kharak (the life style of the Nagas). Imphal: Goodwill Press.

Longvah, S. 2015. Peace process in Nagaland and the role of Naga People's front (PhD thesis, North Eastern Hill University).

Lorin, P. S. & E. R. Spees. 1990. Religion: backbone on Naga nationalism. International Journal of Intercultural Relations 14, 355-363.

Lotha, A. 2007. History of Naga anthropology, 1832-1947. Dimapur: Chumpo Museum.

Lotha, A. 2013 The raging mithun: challenges of Naga nationalism. Kohima: Barkweaver Publications.

Lotha, A. 2016. The hornbill spirit: Nagas living their nationalism. Dimapur: Heritage Publishing House.

Luhrmann, T. 2012. When god talks back: understanding the American evangelical relationship with God. New York: Alfred A. Knopf.

Luikham, R. (ed.) 2002. Phungyo Baptist church history 1901-2001. Ukhrul: Phungyo Baptist Church.

Luikham, R. 2009. Tangkhul land use system and related custom. Ukhrul: Ukhrul District Community Resources Management Society (UDCRMS).

Luikham, T. 1961. Wung (Tangkhul) Naga Okthot Mayonza. Imphal: Tarun Printing Work.

Luithui, L. & N. Haksar. 1984. Nagaland file: a question of human rights. New Delhi: Lancer International.

Lunghar, M. K. 1986. Hao Mi-un Ngashan kala Tangkhul Khararchan (History of Tangkhul). Imphal: Goodwill Press.

Macfarlane, A and M. Turin 2008. The digitization of Naga collections in the west and the return of culture. In Naga identities: changing local cultures in the Northeast of India (eds) M. Oppitz, T. Kaiser, A. Von Stockhausen and M. Wettstein, 367-78. Ghent: Snoeck.

Mackenzie, A. 1884. History of the relations of the government with the hill tribes of the North-East frontier of Bengal. Calcutta: no publisher information.

Mageo, J. M. 2003. Dreaming and the self: new perspectives on subjectivity, identity, and emotion. Albany, New York State University of New York Press.

Mamdani, M. 2001. When victims become killers: colonialism, nativism, and the genocide in Rwanda. New Jersey: Princeton University Press.

Mancini, A., & G.A. Bonanno. 2006. Resilience in the face of potential trauma: clinical practices and illustrations. Journal of Clinical Psychology 62, 971-985.

Mao, X. P. 2013. Nagas: past, present and future. The Morung Express (Nagaland). 31 June. (available on-line: https://www.facebook.com/permalink.php?story_fbid=1459323160970885&id=1411098625793339, accessed on 19 April 2017.

Mao., X. P. 2009. The origin of tiger, spirit and humankind: a Mao Naga myth. Indian Folklife, (33). North East Hill University.

Mar, I, 2011. God-land-people, an ethnic Naga identity. Nagaland: Heritage Publishing House.

Markusen, A. Rendon M. and Martinez, A., 2008. Native American artists, gatekeepers and markets:a reflection on regional trajectories [online]

USA: University of Minnesota (available on-line: http://www.hhh.umn. edu/projects/prie/pdf/275NativeAmRegionalTrajectories.pdf, accessed 3 November 2013).

Mauss, M. 1979. Body techniques. In Sociology and psychology: essays by Marcel Mauss (trans. B. Brewster). London: Routledge and Kegan Paul.

Mawon, S. & S. Longvah. 2014. The struggle for power: church leaders in the Naga political movement. Asian Journal of Research in Social Sciences and Humanities 4, 336-343.

Mawon, S. 2014. Understanding the origin of the terms 'Wung', 'Hao', and 'Tangkhul'. International Research Journal of Social Sciences 3(5), 36-40.

Mawon, S. 2015. Traditional Tangkhul Naga festivals: a study of the use of music and musical instruments (PhD thesis, North-Eastern Hill University).

Mawon, S. 2016. Reading continuities and change in vernacular architecture among the Hao Naga. In The South Asianist 4, 182-94.

Maxwell, N. 1980. India, the Nagas and the Northeast. London: Minority Rights Group.

McDuie-Ra, 2015. 'Is India racist?': murder, migration and Mary Kom. Journal of South Asian Studies Vol 38, 304-319.

McFarlane B. 1996. Novel to film: an introduction to the theory of adaptation. Oxford: Clarendon Press.

Michell, J. F. 1883. The North–East frontier of India. Calcutta: The Superintendent of Government Printing.

Miley, L. 2006.White writing black, issues of authorship and authenticity in non-indigenous representations of Australian aboriginal fictional characters. Thesis (MA), Australia, Queensland University of Technology.

Miller, D. 2003. Why some things matter. In Material cultures: why some things matter (ed.) D. Miller. London: Routledge.

Mills, J.P. 1922. The Lhota Nagas. London: Macmillan & Co.

Mills, J.P. 1926. The Ao Nagas. London: Macmillan.

Mills, J.P. 1935. The Naga headhunters of Assam. Journal of the Royal Central Asian Society 22, 418-28.

Mills, J.P. 1937. The Rengma Nagas. London: Macmillan & Co.

Mines, D. & N. Yazgi. 2010. Introduction: Do villages matter?. In Village matters: relocating villages in the contemporary anthropology of India (eds) D. Mines & N. Yazgi. Delhi: Oxford University Press.

Misra, P.K. 2012. J.H. Hutton and colonial ethnography of North-East India. In North-East India: a handbook of anthropology (ed) T.B. Subba, 57-78. Noida: Orient Blackswan.

Misra, U. 2000. The periphery strikes back: challenges to the nation-state in Assam and Nagaland. Shimla: Indian Institute for Advanced Studies.

Mittermeier, A. 2010. Dreams that matter: Egyptian landscapes of the imagination. Berkeley: University of California Press.

Mofatt-Mills, A.J. 1854. Report on the province of Assam. In Nagas in the nineteenth century (ed) V. Elwin (1969). Bombay: Oxford University Press.

Mohan, S. 2016. Creation of social space through prayers among Dalits in Kerala, India. Journal of Religious and Political Practice. 2, 40-57.

Morung Express 2016. 'ENNG' formed for governance of Myanmar eastern Nagaland (available on-line: http://morungexpress.com/enng-formed-for-governance-of-myanmar-eastern-nagaland, accessed 30 December 2016).

Mosse, D. 1999. Responding to subordination: identity and change among south Indian untouchable castes. In Identity and affect: experiences of identity in a globalising world (eds.) J. Campbell and A. Rew. London: Pluto Press.

Mukherjee, A. 2012. Our education system is only focused on exam: knowledge is not a priority. Outlook (available on-line: http://www.outlookindia.com/magazine/story/our-education-system-is-only-focused-on-exams-knowledge-is-not-a-priority/281312, accessed 2 December 2017).

Murtagh, F., A. Ganz, & S. McKie. 2008. The structure of narrative: the case of film scripts. (available on-line: https://arxiv.org/pdf/0805.3799v1.pdf, accessed 1 January 2017).

Nag, S. 1999. Nationalism, separatism and secessionism. New Delhi: Rawat Publications.

Nakhro, M. 2017. The two missing ingredients in Naga politics. The Morung Express (Nagaland). 22 February (available on-line: http://morungexpress.com/two-missing-ingredients-naga-politics/, accessed on 2 April 2017.

NBCC Platinum Jubilee Souvenir. 2012. One new humanity in Christ: Nagaland Baptist Church Council celebrates Platinum Jubilee 1937-2012. Kohima: NBCC.

NCRC Souvenir. 2012. Nagaland Christian revival church, souvenir revival: golden jubilee (1962-2012). No publication details.

Ngully, M. 2015. Stories in a curiosity box: John Henry Hutton administrator-collector in the Naga Hills. In Passing things on: ancestors and genealogies in Northeast India (ed) M. Heneise. Dimapur, Nagaland: Heritage Publishing House.

Ngullie, A. 2016. Nagaland media & the need to reinvent the colonial dross. Eastern Mirror (available on-line: http://www.easternmirrornagaland.com/nagaland-media-need-reinvent-colonial-dross [Accessed 16 December 2016).

Nibedon, N. 1978. North-East India: the ethnic explosion. New Delhi: Lancers Publishing.

NKJV 1988. The holy bible. Nashville: Broadman & Holman Publishers.

Nshgo, A. 2009. Traditional Naga village and its transformation. New Delhi: Anshah Publishing House.

Nshgo, A. 2009. Traditional Naga village system and its transformation. New Delhi: Anshah Publishing House.

Nuh, V.K. 1986. Nagaland church and politics. Kohima: published by the author.

Nuh, V. K. 2002. My native country: the land of the Nagas. Guwahati: Spectrum Publications.

Nuh, V. K. 2006. 165 years history of Naga Baptist churches. Kohima: Naga Baptist Church Council.

O'Nell, C. W. 1965. A cross-cultural study of hunger and thirst motivation manifested in dreams. Human Development 8, 181-93.

Odyuo I. 2013. The various aspects of Naga art. Journal of Humanities and Social Science 9(4) (available on-line: http://www.iosrjournals.org/iosr-jhss/papers/Vol9-issue4/C0941322.pdf, accessed 18 December 2016)

Opas, M. 2016. Dreaming faith into being: indigenous evangelicals and co-acted experiences of the divine. Temenos 52, 239-26.

Oppitz, M, T. Kaiser, A. Von Stockhausen & M. Wettstein (eds.) 2008. Naga identities: changing local cultures in the Northeast of India. Ghent: Snoeck.

Ovung, A. 2012. Social stratification in Naga society. Delhi: Mittal Publication.

Owen, J. 1844. Notes on the Naga tribes in communication with Assam, Calcutta: W.H. Carey and Co., Cossitollah.

Padel, F. 1995. The sacrifice of human being (British rule and the Konds of Orissa). Oxford: Oxford University Press.

Pandey, R.S. 2010. Communitisation: third way of governance. New Delhi: Concept Publishing Company.

Patnaik, S.M. 2014. Consuming culture: the refiguration of aesthetics in Nagaland cultural tourism in India's North East. In Arts and aesthetics in a globalizing world (eds.) R. Kaur and P. D. Mukherji. London: Bloomsbury Academic.

Peal, S.E. 1874. The Nagas and neighbouring tribes. In Journal of the Anthropological Institute of Great Britain and Ireland 3, 476-481.

Petersen, R. D. 2002. Understanding ethnic violence: fear, hatred and resentment in twentieth-century eastern Europe. Cambridge: Cambridge University Press.

Pheirei, P. 2010. Tangkhul Wung Hao customary law. Imphal: Goodwill Press.

Poddar, P. K., & T. B. Subba. 1991. Demystifying some ethnographic texts on the Himalayas. In Social Scientist 19, 78-84.

Poirier, S. 2003. This is good country: we are good dreamers. In Dream travelers: sleep experiences and culture in the Western Pacific (ed) R. Lohmann. New York: Palgrave Macmillan.

Pongener, M. 2011. Morung speaks: cultural values and elements for the enrichment of Naga Christian community. Jorhat: TDCC Publications.

Propp, V. (1928) 2009. Morphology of the folktale. Austin: University of Texas.

Report 1936. Assam Baptist missionary conference, 1-6 December 1936, Gauhati (Assam). Archive of the Council of Baptist Churches of Northeast India, Guwahati. (Accessed on 5 October 2011).

Rizvi, B.R. 2012. J.P. Mills and India's Northeast. In North-East India: a handbook of anthropology (ed) T. B. Subba. Noida: Orient Blackswan.

Robbins, J. 2004. Becoming sinners: Christianity and moral torment in a Papua New Guinea society. Berkeley: University of California Press.

Robinson, A. 1969. Stratagum and Ambuscate. In The Nagas in the nineteenth century (ed) V. Elwin, 530-540. London: Oxford University Press

Robinson, W. 1841. A descriptive account of Assam: with a sketch of the local geography and a concise history of the tea-plant of Assam, to which is added a short account of the neighbouring tribes, exhibiting their history, manners, and customs. Delhi: Sanskaran Prakashak (a reprint of the 1841 edition, Ostell and Lepage, Calcutta).

Ross, E. K. 1969. On death and dying. New York: The Macmillan Company.

Rowney, H.B. 1969. The wild tribes of India. The Nagas in the nineteenth century (ed) V. Elwin, 167-75. London: Oxford University Press.

Roy, Ashim. 2004. The Konyak Nagas: a socio-cultural profile. Leicestershire: Upfront Publishing.

Ruivah, K. 1993. Social change among the Nagas (Tangkhul). New Delhi: Cosmo Publications.

Rustomji. N.K. 1969. Foreword. In Nagas in the nineteenth century (ed) V. Elwin, v-vi. Bombay: Oxford University Press.

Säid, E. 1978. Orientalism. New York: Pantheon Books.

Sakha, T. 2015. History of Naga nationalism from the religious perspective. Eastern Mirror (Nagaland). 17 November (available on-line: http://www.easternmirrornagaland.com/history-of-naga-nationalism-from-the-religious-persppective/, accessed 2 April 2017).

Samson, K. 2012. The Zeliangrong Movement in North-East India: An exegetical study. Sociological Bulletin 61(2): 320-334.

Sanders, J. 2006. Adaptation and appropriation. London: Routledge.

Sangma, M. S. 1987. History of American Baptist mission in North-East India (1836-1950), Volume I. Delhi: Mittal Publications.

Sangtam, S. 2016. Naga nationalism and the death of God: a reflection. The Morung Express (Nagaland). 13 December. (available on-line: http://morungexpress.com/naga-nationalism-death-god-reflection/, accessed on 2 April 2017.

Sashinungla, 2013. Nagaland insurgency and factional intransigence (Available on-line: http://www.satp.org/satporgtp/publication/faultlines/volume16/Article%204.pdf, accessed 30 December 2016).

Schulte-Nordholt, H. 2005. Decentralisation in Indonesia: less state, more democracy?. In Politicizing democracy: the new local politics of democratization (eds) Harris, J., K. Stokke, and O. Törnquis, 29-47. New York: Palgrave.

Sears, W. E. 1948. The Navaho and Yir-Yoront, their primitive dreams. BA thesis: Harvard University

Seligman, C. G. 1921. Notes on dreams. Sudan Notes and Records 4, 156.

Seligman, C. G. 1924. Anthropology and psychology: a study of some points of contact. Journal of the Royal Anthropological Institute of Great Britain and Ireland 54, 13–46.

Sema, H. 1986. Emergence of Nagaland. New Delhi: Vikas Publishing House.

Sema, H. J. 2013. Traditional and modern political institutions of the Nagas. New Delhi: Mittal Publications.

Sema, P. 1992. British policy and administration in Nagaland 1881-1947. New Delhi: Scholar Publishing House.

Sema, P. 1992. British Policy and Administration in Nagaland 1881 -1947. New Delhi: Scholar.

Sen, S. 1987. Tribes of Nagaland. Delhi: Mittal Publications.

Shikhu, I. Y. 2007. A re-discovery and re-building of Naga cultural values. New Delhi: Regency Publications.

Shimray, A. S. A. 2005. Let freedom ring: the story of Naga nationalism. New Delhi: Promilla and Co. Publishers.

Shimray, A.S. 2005. Let freedom ring: story of Naga nationalism. Delhi: Promilla.

Shimray, A.S.W. 2001. History of the Tangkhul Nagas. New Delhi: Akansha Publishing House.

Shimray, R.R. 1985. Origin and culture of Nagas. New Delhi: Pamleiphi Shimray.

Shimray, R.R. 1986. Origin and Culture of Nagas. Delhi: Samsok Publishers.

Shimray, S.W.A. 2000. The Tangkhuls. Imphal: Goodwill Press.

Shyamacharan D. 1993. Dialogue on tribal and folk culture. Dialogue on tribal and folk culture: articles from Parishad's publication 'Chaumasa' (ed) Pratyaya. Madhya Pradesh: Adivasi Lok Kala Parishad.

Singh Y. 2000. Globalization and local cultures issues and perspectives in India. New Delhi: Rawat.

Singh, A. K. 2008. Ethnicity and inter-community conflicts: a case of the Kuki-Naga in Manipur. New Delhi: Akansha Publications.

Singh, C. 2004. Naga politics: a critical account. New Delhi: Mittal Publications.

Singh, C. 2008. The Naga Society. New Delhi: Manas Publications.

Singh, D. K. 1996. The early days of William Pettigrew among the Tangkhul. In A Pioneer Missionary of Manipur (eds) Rev. William Pettigrew. P. C. Committee, 70-78. Imphal: Fraternal Green Cross, VVD.

Singh, P. 1977. Nagaland. In Naga culture. New Delhi: National Book Trust.

Sitton, D. 1998. The basics of animism: spiritual warfare in tribal contexts. International Journal of Frontier Missions 15, 69-74.

Smith, A. D. 2001. The Origins of nations. Nations and Identities: Classic readings (ed.) V. P. Pecora, 333-353. Massachusetts: Blackwell Publishers Ltd.

Smith, L. 2006. Uses of heritage. London: Routledge.

Smith, L. T. 1999. Decolonizing methodologies, research and indigenous peoples. London: Zed Books.

Smith, W. 1925. The Ao Naga tribe of Assam: a study in ethnology and sociology. London: MacMillan and Co. Ltd.

Solo, J. M. & K. Mahangthei. 2006. Forty-years mission in Manipur: mission reports of Rev. William Pettigrew. Imphal: Christian Literature Centre.

Spivak, G. C. 1988. Can the subaltern speak?. Marxism and the Interpretation of Culture (eds.) C. Nelson & L. Grossberg. Urbana: University of Illinois.

Sproul. R. C. 2014. The place of prayer in the Christian life. In Ligonier ministries: the teaching fellowship of R.C. sproul. Online source www.ligonier.org/blog/

place-prayer-christian-life/ Accessed on January 11, 2017.

Stephen M. 1979. Dreams of change: the innovative role of altered states of consciousness in traditional Melanesian religion. Oceania 50, 3-22.

Stephen, M. 1982. 'Dreaming is another power': The social significance of dreams among the Mekeo of Papua New Guinea. Oceania 53, 106-22.

Stephen, M. 1996. Dreams and self-knowledge among the Mekeo of Papua New Guinea. Ethos 24, 465-490.

Stewart, C. 1997. Fields in dreams: anxiety, experience, and the limits of social constructionism in modern Greek dream narratives. American Ethnologist 24, 877-894.

Stewart, C. 2003. Dreams of treasure: Temporality, historicization and the unconscious. Anthropological Theory 3, 481-500.

Stewart, C. 2004. Special Issue: Anthropological approaches to dreaming. Dreaming 14, 2-3.

Stirn, A. & P. van Ham. 2000. The Seven sisters of India: tribal worlds between Tibet and Burma. Munich: Prestel.

Stirn, A. & P. van Ham. 2003. The hidden world of the Naga: living traditions in Northeast India and Burma. Munich: Prestel

Stockhausen, A. von and M. Wettstein. 2008. Cultural extravagance and the search for identity in present-day Nagaland. In Naga: a forgotten mountain region rediscovered (ed.) R. Kunz and V. Joshi. Basel: Museum der Kulturen Basel.

Stockhausen, A. von. 2013. lmag(in)ing the Nagas: the pictorial ethnography of Hans-Eberhard Kauffmann and Christoph von Furer-Haimendorf. Stuttgart: Arnoldsche.

Strathern, A. 1989. Melpa dream interpretation and the concept of hidden truth. Ethonology 28, 301-315.

Subba, T.B. & S. Som. 2005. Introduction. In Between ethnography and fiction: Verrier Elwin and the tribal question in India (eds) T.B. Subba & S. Som, 1-8. New Delhi: Orient Longman.

Subba, T.B. and J.J.P. Wouters 2013. North-East India: ethnography and politics of identity. In The modern anthropology of India: ethnography, themes and theory (eds) P. Berger and F. Heidemann 193-207. London: Routledge.

Sutter, R. 2008. Shadows and tigers: concepts of soul and tiger-men. Naga identities: changing local cultures in the Northeast of India (eds) M. Oppitz, T. Kaiser, A. Von Stockhausen & M. Wettstein. Ghent: Snoeck.

Tariq, S. 2011. Problem in Northeast India: a case study of Nagaland. Journal of the Institute of Regional Studies 29, 78-97 (available on-line: http://www.irs.org.pk/indiapakistan/spjan11.pdf0, accessed 30 December 2016).

Taylor, E.B. 1871. Primitive culture: researches into the development of mythology, philosophy, religion, language, art and custom. London: John Murray.

Taylor, E.B. 1960 [1881]. Anthropology. Ann Arbor: University of Michigan Press.

Tedlock, B. 1987. Dreaming and dream research. In Dreaming: anthropological and psychological interpretations (ed) B. Tedlock, 1-30. Cambridge UK:

Cambridge University Press.

Tedlock, B. 1987. Dreaming: anthropological and psychological interpretations. New York: Cambridge University Press.

Telo, A. R. 2013. Participatory film production as media practice. International Journal of Communication 7, 2312-2332.

Temjensonong. 2013. Self-Governing Institutions of Nagas. Delhi: Akansha Publishing House.

Theidon, K. 2006. The mask and the mirror: facing up to the past in post war Peru. In Anthropologica, Canadian Anthropology Society 48, 87-100.

Thiranagama, S. 2013. In my mother's house: civil war in Sri Lanka. Philadelphia: University of Pennsylvania Press.

Thomas, J. 2016. Evangelising the nation: religion and the formation of Naga political identity. New Delhi: Routledge.

Thomas, N. 1991. Entangled objects: exchange, material culture, and colonialism in the Pacific. Cambridge: Harvard University Press

Thompsom, M. & P. Vardaman. 1997. The role of religion in coping with the loss of a family member to homicide. Journal for the Scientific Study of Religion 36, 44-51.

Thong, J. 2012. Headhunting culture of the Nagas: historic culture of Nagas. New Delhi: Mittal Publications.

Thong, T. 2012. Civilized colonizers and barbaric colonized: reclaiming Naga identity by demythologizing colonial portraits. History and Anthropology 23, 375-397.

Thong, T. 2012. To raise the savage to a higher level : the westernization of Nagas and their culture. In Modern Asian Studies 46(4): 893-918.

Thorat, S.P.P. 1986. From reveille to retreat. New Delhi: Allied Publishers

Tohring, S. 2010. Violence and identity in North-East India: Naga-Kuki conflict. New Delhi: Mittal Publications.

Tonkinson, R. 1997. Ambrymese dreams and the Mardu dreaming. In Dreaming: anthropological and psychological interpretations (ed) B. Tedlock. New York: Cambridge University Press.

Tumminia, D. G. 2002. In the dreamtime of the saucer people: sense-making and interpretive boundaries in a Contactee group. Journal of Contemporary Ethnography 31, 675-705.

Tunbridge, J. and G. Ashworth. 1996. Dissonant heritage: the management of the past as a resource in conflict. Chichester: Wiley.

Tunyi, Z. and J.J.P. Wouters 2016. India's Northeast as an internal borderland: Domestic borders, regimes of taxation, and legal landscapes. In The NEHU Journal 14, 1-17.

Tutu, D. M. 1999. No future without forgiveness. New York: Doubleday

Tylor, E. B. 1870. Researches into the early history of mankind and the development of civilization. London: John Murray.

Upreti, B. C. 2006. Nationalism in South Asia: trends and interpretations. The

Indian Journal of Political Science 67, 535-544.

Van Ham, P. and J. Saul. 2008. Expedition Naga: diaries from the hills in Northeast India 1921-1937-2002-2006. Antique Collectors' Club Ltd: Woodbridge.

Vashum, R. 2000. Nagas' right to self-determination: an anthropological – historical perspective. New Delhi: Mittal Publications.

Veerbhadranaika, P., R. S. Kumaran, S. Tukdeo & A. R. Vasavi. 2012. 'The education question' from the perspective of Adivasis: conditions, policies and structure. Bangalore: National Institute of Advanced Studies.

Venuh, N. 2005. British colonization and restructuring of Naga polity. New Delhi: Mittal Publications.

Vetch 1969. A soldier observes. In The Nagas in the nineteenth century (ed) V. Elwin, 92-6. London: Oxford University Press.

Viveiros de Castro, E. 1998. Cosmological deixis and Amerindian perspectivism. Journal of the Royal Anthropological Institute 4, 469-88.

Weiner, J. 1986. Men, ghosts and dreams among the Foi: literal and figurative modes of interpretation. Oceania 57, 114-127.

Wells, P. 2013. Thou art translated: analysing animated adaptations. Adaptations: From Text to Screen, Screen to Text (eds) D. Cartmell & I. Whelehan. New York: Routledge.

West, A. 1999. The Most Dangerous Legacy: the development of identity, power and marginality in the British transfer to India and the Nagas. Hull: The University of Hull, Centre for South-East Asian Studies.

West, A. 2011. Museums, colonialism, and identity: a history of Naga collections in Britain. London: Horniman Museum and Gardens.

Wettstein, M. & A. von Stockhausen. 2012: connecting to the past. In Hill Peoples of Northeast India: the Nagas society, culture and the colonial encounter (eds) Jacobs, J., A. Macfarlane, S. Harrison and A. Herle 1990. The Nagas: hill peoples in North-East India. London: Thames and Hudson.

Wettstein, M. 2014. Naga textiles: design, technique, meaning and effect of a local craft tradition in Northeast India. Stuttgart: Arnoldsche Art Publishers.

WGBH Educational Foundation, 2011. Adaptation: From Novel to Film (available on-line:

Wontong, T. 1992. Outline of a culture in transformation. The Nagas (eds) G. Somare & L. Vigorelli. Rome: Gallerial Lorenzelli.

Woodthorpe, R.G. 1882. Notes on the wild tribes inhabiting the so-called Naga hills, on our North-East Frontier of India, part II. In Journal of the Anthropological Institute of Great Britain and Ireland 11, 196-214.

Woodthorpe, R.G. 1969. Notes on the wild tribes inhabiting the so-called Naga Hills, on our North-East Frontier of India. In The Nagas in the nineteenth century (ed) V. Elwin, 63-83. London: Oxford University Press.

Wouters, J.J.P. 2011. Keeping the hill tribes at bay: a critique from India's Northeast of James C. Scott's paradigm of state evasion. In European Bulletin of Himalayan Research 39, 41-65.

Wouters, J.J.P. 2012. Reconfiguring colonial ethnography: the British gaze over India's Northeast. In: North-East India: a handbook of anthropology (ed) T.B. Subba 99-124. Noida: Orient Blackswan

Wouters, J.J.P. & T. B. Subba. 2013. The Indian face: India's Northeast and 'The Idea of India'. In Asian Anthropology 12, 126-140.

Wouters, J.J.P. 2014. Performing democracy in Nagaland: past polities and present politics. Economic and Political Weekly 49, 59-66.

Wouters, J. J. P. 2015a. Feasts of merit, election feasts, or no feasts? on the politics of wining and dining in Nagaland, Northeast India. The South Asianist 3(2), 5-23.

Wouters, J.J.P. 2015b. Polythetic democracy: tribal elections, bogus votes, and the political imagination in the Naga uplands of Northeast India. HAU: Journal of Ethnographic Theory 5, 121-151.

Wouters, J.J.P. 2015c. The battle of Kikrüma: how a single Naga village took on the British empire. Himal South-Asian. Online: http://himalmag.com/the-battle-of-kikruma/

Wouters, J. J. P. 2016. Sovereignty, integration or bifurcation? troubled histories, contentious territories and the political horizons of the long lingering Naga movement. Studies in History 32, 97-116.

Wouters, J.J.P. 2017. The making of tribes: the Chang and Chakhesang Nagas in India's Northeast. Contributions to Indian Sociology 51, 79-104.

Wright, S. 1998. The politicization of culture'. Anthropology today. 14 (1), 7-15.

Yeptho, H. 2011. Lycanthropy revisited. Published by Philemon Quinker, Sub-divisional officer, Tuensang, Nagaland.

Yeptho, N. 1991. Sumi chine eno apine jeliqo (Sumi rites and prohibitions). Jorhat: Assam Printing Works Ltd.

Yimchunger, N. C. 2009. Folk Tales of Yimchungrü Nagas. Shamator: Author.

Yonuo, A. 1974. The rising Nagas: a historical and political study. New Delhi: Vivek Publishing House.

Zehol, L. & K. K. Zehol. 2009. The legendary Naga village: a reader (Khezakeno). Dimapur: Heritage Publication House

Zeliang, E. 2005. A history of the Manipur Baptist convention. Jorhat: Manipur Baptist Convention.

Zhimomi, H. 2012. Pioneer Sumi and mission. Pughoboto: Yeppo Educational Trust.

Zhimomi, K. K. 2004. Politics and militancy in Nagaland. New Delhi: Deep and Deep Publishers.

Zhimomi, V.H. 1985. Sumi kughuko eno aqo-aho kuxu (Sumi genealogy and socio-customary life). Kohima: Modern Press.

.

INDEX